# INTRODUCING RELIGION:
# FROM INSIDE AND OUTSIDE

H. Armstrong/Philadelphia

# INTRODUCING RELIGION
# FROM INSIDE
# AND OUTSIDE

Robert S. Ellwood, Jr.

University of Southern California

Prentice-Hall, Inc., Englewood Cliffs, New Jersey 07632

*Library of Congress Cataloging in Publication Data*

ELLWOOD, ROBERT S.     (date)
  Introducing religion.

  Bibliography: p.
  Includes index.
  1. Religion.  I. Title.
BL48.E43     200.1     77–13837
ISBN  0–13–477505–8

Printed in the United States of America

10     9     8     7     6     5     4     3

PRENTICE-HALL INTERNATIONAL, INC., *London*
PRENTICE-HALL OF AUSTRALIA PTY. LIMITED, *Sydney*
PRENTICE-HALL OF CANADA, LTD., *Toronto*
PRENTICE-HALL OF INDIA PRIVATE LIMITED, *New Delhi*
PRENTICE-HALL OF JAPAN, INC., *Tokyo*
PRENTICE-HALL OF SOUTHEAST ASIA PTE. LTD., *Singapore*
WHITEHALL BOOKS LIMITED, *Wellington, New Zealand*

*My feet were set upon a narrow pathway*
*Crossing worlds of worlds to find Love's Center;*
*I shall not return as I.*

G.F.E.

For Fay Elanor Ellwood
*May she find that path.*

# CONTENTS

# FOREWORD

This book is intended to provide the reader with openings into the study of human religion in all its diversity. Its concern is essentially with description and understanding. We will look at what all religion seems to have in common, at the overall history of religion, and at some of the ways religion works in human thinking and culture. In the process, we will examine some specific religious ideas and practices and the points of view of some important students of human religion.

This may be the first contact of many readers with a book that surveys religion in this manner, rather than from the perspective of a particular tradition. This approach may seem novel and possibly irritating and disturbing. At first glance this study may seem to look at religion in human life in the style of an entomologist looking at insect colonies. It may seem irreverent, relativistic, falsely superior, and coldly analytic. Why should one presume to study in this way something that for many involves deep and sacred beliefs and commitments? Why not leave religion to its believers and its traditional authorities, like the Bible?

Of course, no one *has* to study religion in any way except the way he or she wants, but I think that a study of religion that includes examination of its history, psychology, and sociology is not inconsistent with profound appreciation of religion and deep commitment to one's own. Indeed, it can enrich one's appreciation and commitment. True, enrichment may come only after strenuous rethinking of what it is in religion that is to be most appreciated and what the nature of one's commitment is to be, or it may be simply a deepening of previously held convictions. In any case, understanding is not the enemy of enrichment but its ally.

When we talk about historical, sociological, or psychological interpretations of religion, we are not saying that religion is to be wholly *explained* on these grounds, or that a religious belief or experience is *nothing but* a product of history, psychology, or sociology and has no being outside its realm. Some may believe that to be the case, but their opinion—like that of the religionist—would ultimately rest on philosophical grounds outside the historical, psychological, or sociological description itself. A minute description of the germination, growth, structure, and vital dynamics of an apple tree does not finally tell us why the tree is there, why people enjoy seeing apple blossoms and eating apples, or why there is any world with apple trees and people at all. The description, however, may help some people who like to know about things to understand and appreciate the apple tree better or even to grow better apples for themselves.

In the same way, the study of religion does not explain away religion or provide cheap answers to the deep questions religion raises. Religion, the questions it asks, the various answers it offers, and the commitments it invites are still there, for all persons to deal with in their own ways.

The study of religion is a process of translation back and forth on the same plane between religion and other disciplines. It may translate a religious experience from the original religious language into the language of psychology or the life of a church from its theological rationale into the language of sociology. This is not to say the latter language is better or truer to the ultimate reality of the experience or church; it is just different and gives us the enrichment of more than one way of viewing the same thing. The value of the alternative language is that it enables us to relate the religious phenomenon to the worlds of the other discipline and so to other ranges of human experience.

In this book, then, we shall look at religion with the aid of several disciplines. An attempt has been made to utilize representative authorities and perspectives in each and to present them fairly. At the same time, this book is not a handbook or catalog of these disciplines respecting religion but has a perspective of its own and seeks to develop certain themes.

I freely acknowledge that my own philosophical and methodological preferences are evident in much of this book. They have influenced my choice of authorities with which to work, and indeed some passages are more than anything else original constructions of positions on some point or another. On some things I may be wrong; on others my perspective may be highly debatable. It seemed better, as well as more satisfying, however, to put together a book of this sort with a set of sustained themes and perspectives than to pretend a dry objectivity that in a field like this is likely to be deceptive. Whether through agreement or disagreement, it is hoped this book will stimulate its readers to reflection, argument, and above all further investigation of the fascinating field of religious studies.

First Communion in the Roman Catholic Church is one of many religious rites that, in the context of various traditions, seek to actualize who one really is in the face of ultimate reality.

## CHAPTER ONE

# SCENARIOS
# FOR THE REAL SELF

## PICTURES OF RELIGION

What is religion? Nearly everyone has some idea, perhaps some mental picture, to go with the word. If one tries to turn that idea or picture into a clear, comprehensive definition, however, the task may be surprisingly difficult. Time and again, one may feel he or she has pushed and pulled his or her words until they neatly package the picture and wrap up what in mankind's experience ought to be labeled religion. But wait! Here is an odd corner still sticking out; there something has slipped and a whole side is bare to the sun. The definer has failed to deal with the tribal rain dance, which surely looks like religion but seemingly has nothing to do with ultimate salvation, or with the Buddhist sutra-chanting of robed monks in incense-laden temples, which also looks like religion but seemingly has nothing to do with God, at least as God was known amid the mountains of Sinai.

In the pages that follow, we will pursue some lines of thought that, if they do not settle the definition of religion once and for all, may at least lead to some fresh perceptions of what religion is and how it works. They may also lay the groundwork for further study of human religion past, present, and future.

Our basic idea will be that religious thought and activity represents one's acting out, or actualizing, who one thinks he or she really is deep within. It simultaneously includes the corresponding relationship to our

1

ultimate environment, infinite reality itself. (Of course, who one thinks one really is may not coincide with reality, for there are various kinds of self-deception that can be practiced in these matters. Moreover, not everyone would make the assumption that his or her inner nature has a relation to ultimate and infinite reality. Religion must assume, however, that one can come to know his or her true nature and that it is meaningful and dwells within a universe of meaning with which it can have a relationship.)

First let us look at some of the phenomena that suggest both the diversity and unity of the entity called religion.

Picture the great shrine at Ise in Japan on the eve of the Harvest Festival. Ise is the preeminent place of worship of Shinto, the religion of the ancient gods of the island nation. Here at Ise are worshipped Amaterasu, the solar goddess said to be ancestress of the imperial family, and Toyouke, goddess of food and bestower of plenty. Each of these high goddesses has her own shrine, the two nearly identical fanes being about five miles apart. Each shrine is a simple, rustic house of unpainted but gold-tipped wood set in a rectangular field spread with white gravel. The field, which holds three or four auxiliary buildings, is surrounded by four wooden palisades. Every twenty years, the entire shrine complex is rebuilt with new wood in exact imitation of the old on an adjacent alternative site, also spread with white gravel.

On the night of the Harvest Festival, torches flare in the crisp October air as a procession of white-robed priests bearing boxes of food offerings, their black wooden shoes crackling like snare drums on the white gravel, approaches the shrine. The priests enter behind the fences and are lost to the observer's view as they carefully spread the plates of rice, water, salt, rice wine, vegetables, and seafood before the encased mirror that represents the presence of Amaterasu. One can, however, hear the shrill, mysterious music of the reed flutes, so suggestive of uncanny divine activity. A prayer is read, and then the offerings are slowly and solemnly removed. The priests next proceed to a smaller shrine on higher ground above the principal temple. This is a shrine to the *aramitama*, the "rough spirit" or aggressive side of the divine Amaterasu. Here offerings are also presented. Later, in early morning while it is still dark, the whole ritual is repeated. The following night it is repeated—again, twice—at the shrine of Toyouke. Why it is done twice and why it is done at night are matters lost in centuries of tradition at the Ise shrines (if there ever existed an explicit reason). The very sense of mystery evoked by the feeling of something lingering from a half-forgotten past and the atmosphere of mystic wonder in which actions seem weighted with meanings the human mind does not quite grasp give Shinto rites their particular kind of religious aura.

The Grand Shrine of Ise in Japan, a simple but lovely place of worship amid ancient trees, is dedicated to the solar goddess Amaterasu and the goddess of food Toyouke.

Now turn to another scene. It suggests not only one kind of self-finding religious experience but also one major type of religious personality, the founder of a great religious movement lasting many centuries. Although based on real experiences, the following retelling is a stylized and idealized account of a self-transformative religious experience in a Christian context. It is not presented as being representative of all Christian experience. It offers, however, a subjective counterpart to the preceding religious expression in rite, and subjective experiences vary, to some extent, from individual to individual. The account shows three common characteristics of such experiences: the rise to a high pitch of feeling followed by joyful calm, the pivotal role of key symbols such as scripture and the internalized image of the founder or savior, and the tendency of such transformation experiences to fall into stylized, paradigmatic patterns as they are remembered or retold. Here is the scene:

An American girl was in her room reading the New Testament and praying. As she read, a vivid image came before her mind's eye. The land rose somewhat, becoming a small hill. He was near the top of the hill, and a crowd was around him. The hill was crawling with them—short, sick, hungry human bodies, bundled in patches of rough handwoven material. She saw Jesus on that hill with all those short, tremulous bodies in homespun around him. He stood out because he was taller, was dressed in something a bit fuller and whiter, and was on higher ground. Above all, he had an air of power and calm amidst the suffering, and his hands were raised in healing. His face had in it a simple majesty, and his eyes made you want to keep looking at them. Then he seemed to step out of the gospel scene to look directly at her. He beckoned.

She prayed on, and deep and warm feelings about the image sang through her, rising and falling like cresting surfs of molten light. She saw other scenes from the story—the manger, the cross with the bleeding flesh on it, and the garden where the ecstatic women saw the figure in calm white outside the empty tomb. These tableaux grew brighter and brighter. In contrast, her life, as it came into view beside the mind-painted images, was gray, lacking all sparkle or color. Indeed, much in it was worse than gray, things she wished could be washed out or made to belong to another life. She thought of people she liked and even envied who talked of accepting Christ and of being forgiven or being saved. She saw the beckoning hand wanting to make her a part of his story.

She felt herself entering the vision and prayed still more deeply. She then sensed clear and distinct words being spoken in her, almost as though by a new person coming into being within her mind and body, words of accepting Jesus Christ as the center of her personal faith. She arose, tingling, feeling full of light, and almost floating, with a queer but beautiful sort of quiet deep-seated joy. She sat down, with little sense of time or place, just bathing in the new marvelous experience.

## ANOTHER REALITY

You have just read two very different vignettes that have one thing in common. Both would be accepted by most people as expressions of human religion. Primarily this would be because they are thoughts, feelings, or actions that do not meet ordinary, practical needs in ordinary, practical ways. They do not directly spin cloth or pick grain. Even if they were directed toward a practical end, such as a better harvest, they do not go about it through a practical course of planting and cultivating. They add to what is practical by implying another point of reference and another level of activity. Even if a religious act is a dance or prayer for rain, it does not set about meeting the practical need using ordinary deduction about cause-and-effect (and contrary to what some have believed, primitive peoples are nearly as aware as moderns of the distinction between the practical and the nonpractical). Certainly modern Shinto priests at a Harvest Festival are as aware of the facts of meteorology and agricultural science as are Americans expressing gratitude to God on Thanksgiving Day.

Religion, however, adds other dimensions full of color, stylized acts, and symbols that outsiders sometimes see as bizarre and totally nonsensical. In this they are akin to such human practices as wearing clothes even in hot weather, writing poetry, or flying to the moon. These are also impractical things that, like religion, must be profoundly human, for they are only dimly foreshadowed in the behavior of our animal kin. Something in these gestures must be making a statement about a side of being human that is not just concerned with doing practical things. They must, in fact be trying to tell us—emphatically—that there is another side to being human. Apart from speech and fire, in fact, what most obviously separates even very primitive human societies from animals are things such as haunting masks, paintings on rocks of spirit ancestors, and the magic rocks or tufts of grass of sorcerers. They tell us across great gulfs of cultural development that here were creatures who did not just deal in practicalities, but who feared pictures in the mind, thought about who they were and where they came from, told stories, sensed the working of indirect invisible currents of force in the cosmos as well as the obvious, and doubtless knew wonder, humor, joy, and dread.

Even more puzzling, if the only point of life were to know in a practical way how to eat, drink, reproduce, and fend off death as long as possible, is that side of religion that does not relate to practical means or ends. It is hard to see any practical point to experiences of salvation or mystical rapture or any practical value to such means toward them as are usually urged—reading scriptures, praying, accepting a saving doctrine or figure (as did the girl caught up in the New Testament), chanting, yogic postures, and so forth. Yet such things are far from uncommon. Indeed, it can be observed that often those people whose lives seem to be focused primarily on meeting practical needs and solving practical problems are the ones most likely to keep some counterbalancing area of life secure for its opposite. They are careful to hold sacred one day a week, to read the scriptures a bit after a hard day's labor in the fields, or to put an offering at the household shrine before going out to work.

Religion is gestures that make no sense at all if ordinary practical reality is all there is, if the universe is only matter and space, if humans are only organisms that feed, mate, and die. If the latter were the case, religion might still be explained as a widespread psychological quirk, but it would not have grounding in any reality, inner or outer. Religion always presupposes a reality other than the visible. This other reality can hardly be weighed or measured and is usually seen and heard only with the eyes and ears of the soul. Yet, religion affirms, it is the true undergirding of the visible and tangible universe and is somehow also submerged in the depths of consciousness. Religion declares that, compared to that reality, what we think about most of the time is like sound and foam on the surface of a deep lake or the hopping about of grasshoppers beneath the infinite sky.

## TRANSCENDENCE

The added dimension implied by religion is often called *transcendence*, which means "climbing across" or "going beyond." Students of religion have often made the existence of transcendence a central point in any definition of religion. Thomas Luckmann, for example, has argued that the essence of religion lies in the ability of humans to transcend or go beyond their biological nature by means of the cultural construction of universes of meaning—music in place of noise, art in place of the haphazard coloration of nature, societies and political systems in place of herd instincts. These cultural constructions are objective, and condition moral and social behavior and even one's inner, subjective experience.[1] Supernaturalism—concepts of God or gods—expresses transcendence in the language of a society. By this definition, social and political structures and scientific world views that construct universes of meaning in which human life is lived as more than strictly biological would be included along with symbol systems involving gods. Thus everything really human is religious.

Peter Berger, while accepting the basic type of argument pursued by Luckmann, feels that his understanding of religion is so broad as to lose usefulness. Berger argues that it is necessary to distinguish between, for example, a scientific and a strictly religious view of the cosmos even though there is value also in showing that the two can function in parallel ways. Berger would say that the term *religion* should be used only for systems that establish a *sacred* cosmos.[2]

The term *sacred*, as it has been used by such historians of religion as Rudolf Otto and Mircea Eliade (to be discussed in chapter two), indicates a reality not only transcendent over biology but also transcendent over the ordinary human in a way that implies another order of reality. Indeed, as Otto would have said, it suggests something "wholly other."[3] It creates in humans a special kind of reaction not induced by mere scientific or social transcendences—a sense we are dealing with reality

[1]Thomas Luckmann, *The Invisible Religion* (New York: The Macmillan Company, 1967).

[2]Peter L. Berger, *The Sacred Canopy* (Garden City, N.Y.: Doubleday & Company, Inc., 1969). For the discussion of Luckmann, see especially pp. 176–77. See also their joint work, Berger and Luckmann, *The Social Construction of Reality* (Garden City, N.Y.: Doubleday & Company, Inc., 1966).

[3]See Rudolf Otto, *The Idea of the Holy* (London: Oxford University Press, 1950).

that is in some way alive, tremendously alive, that outcrops in our world in specific times and places (temples, festivals, visions), and to which we can relate.

The sacred is not only conceptual but is also a power and presence with definite demarcations—within one's mind and probably outwardly by such signs as the gates of a shrine or the doors of a church and the special, different atmosphere behind them. Otto spoke of the sacred as the "numinous," as "mysterium tremendens et fascinans," a tremendous yet fascinating mystery, which evokes in those brought near it deep responses that combine wonder, fear, awe, attraction, dread, and love.

The sacred, according to Otto, can seem uncanny, weird, even terrible. It is always a breaking through of "otherness," yet people, despite a wholesome timidity, are drawn toward it, for it possesses a fullness of reality beside which all else is gray and empty. It has the feel of the Ise shrine on the night of the Harvest Festival or of Jesus amidst the sick or in the believer's heart. Religion, Berger claims, is the enterprise by which a "sacred cosmos" is established—a universe of meaning that ratifies the social order and moral values and above all gives individuals what sense of meaning and relation to the cosmos they have. It is centered on some form of the power and presence of the numinous, sacred realities that are transcendent above the human order as the human order is above the biological.[4] It is a three-story universe instead of a two-story structure.

Robert Bellah has emphasized this point by speaking of religion as "transcendent experience"—as a level of consciousness, rather than as a particular kind of concept that transcends both the biological and the human.[5] He also stresses, however, that this level of consciousness and experience is necessarily expressed in symbols, verbal, visual, or whatever. "The experience must be symbolized in order to be completed as experience."[6] Yet the particular symbol used, although of great meaning within the context of a culture and an individual life, is ultimately less important than the articulation of a symbol that successfully establishes the existence of transcendent experience and enables others to move into its orbit, as did the symbol of Jesus for the girl living nearly two thousand years after him.

The philosopher Alfred North Whitehead has spoken of symbolism

[4]Berger, *The Sacred Canopy*, p. 25.

[5]Robert Bellah, "Transcendence in Contemporary Piety," in *The Religious Situation*, ed. D. Cutler (Boston: Beacon Press, 1969).

[6]Personal communication by Robert Bellah to Morris Augustine and Richard Kalish. Cited in Morris J. Augustine and Richard A. Kalish, "Religion, Transcendence, and Appropriate Death," *The Journal of Transpersonal Psychology*, 7, 1 (1975), 7.

in this way: "The human mind is functioning symbolically when some components of its experience elicit consciousness, beliefs, emotions, and usages, respecting other components of its experience. The former set of components are the 'symbols,' and the latter set constitute the 'meaning' of the symbols."[7] Symbols, in other words, are like bridges. They enable us to link, to relate, to cross between one experience and another. They show how one experience has meaning for another and can even form the ordering nucleus of others. A symbol can be polyvalent—it can have different, but related, meanings in different contexts.

The cross in itself is a symbol of the death of Jesus Christ. The cross in a church builds a bridge between that event and today by indicating that one can today find self-transcending meaning in that event and that an important institution can be built around the meaning. The cross on the crown of a European king shows that the event and its meaning can also legitimate the general social order that gives people their place in communities and repels chaos.

Conceptualizations of what the sacred reality *is* are like symbols of the sacred within the mind. (They may, of course, correspond to what the sacred really is.) These conceptualizations are our ideas of the divine. As we shall see later, they may take the form of a personal God, an impersonal absolute; of a universe of many gods; of human figures like buddhas; or of spirits and ancestors. These conceptualizations function as sacred symbols *within* the mind, building bridges from one area of its experience to another, just as do crosses or Muslim minarets *outside* the self in the fabric of man-made culture or those sacred trees and mountains where religion has seemed to break through in the midst of nature.

## BRIDGES FROM THERE TO HERE

Returning to Bellah's thought, we note that for him symbols are essential just because there is a need for bridges since two points of reference are involved—transcendent experience and human experience.[8] Symbols complete the experience itself because only they can bring these two together; even the one having the experience is human and needs symbols to relate the experience to himself or herself and to communicate it to others or enable others to participate in a similar experience. We need symbols, as Whitehead's definition shows, even to relate different parts of our own minds.

[7]Alfred North Whitehead, *Symbolism: Its Meaning and Effect* (New York: Capricorn Books, 1959), pp. 7–8.

[8]Robert Bellah, *Beyond Belief* (New York: Harper & Row, Publishers, Inc., 1970).

This member of the Black Jews of Harlem wears the symbol of the Star of David to express his religious identity, which he must feel in turn to express his real self.

Words are such symbols, and it could be argued that their function in enabling us to think things through to ourselves is even more important than their function in communicating to others. (Try thinking through a fairly complicated idea totally without employing words, without "talking to yourself.") Certain gestures, mental pictures, feelings, and acts by which we signify to ourselves the relating of one experience to another are also symbols we use to talk to ourselves—to relate one part of our experience meaningfully to another.

Symbols are necessary to complete the transcendent experience that underlies religion because religion, above all other human affairs, implies two realms that need to be bridged and related. (The chief priest of the ancient Romans, like the modern pope, was called *pontifex*, which means "bridge-builder.") The other, invisible reality implied by religion can only be communicated to others or even to oneself by symbols having their being in this side, the visible and audible side, of reality. Yet symbols must point toward and participate in the other side in such a special way as to make them stand out amidst all else on this side that is visible or audible. That is what affords them, from our perspective, those qualities of numinousness, uncanniness, mystery, and fascination that entitle them to be called sacred.

Such religious symbols are much the same as what the historian of religion Joachim Wach has called "forms of religious expression."[9] Religious symbols are not only such discrete artifacts as crosses or images of a Buddha but are also religious concepts, persons, services, groups, institutions, or practices—whatever is like a bridge, signpost, sentence, activity set up between the religious reality and this side. The forms of expression really comprise together the whole of what can be called the phenomena of religion—the things that appear around numinous or transcendent experience, from art to ethics. According to Wach, there are three basic forms of religious expression: the *theoretical*, which covers what is thought and said, the stories, rhetoric, doctrines, and ideologies of religion; the *practical*, which includes what is done, the rites, worship, spiritual techniques, and customary practices; and the *sociological*, referring to the types of groups, leadership, and interpersonal relations that appear. All of these are best understood if they are seen as ways in which one component of experience—the transcendent experience—is eliciting a response in the form of consciousness, belief, gesture, action, or interpersonal interaction in another and so becomes an interpretative bridge between the two. (Later in this book, we look in more detail at these three forms. Chapter four deals in large part with the practical form of rite and related practices. Chapter five treats the sociological side of religion, showing how a religious group or institution is in itself a symbol of transcendent reality. Chapter six discusses the theoretical

[9]Joachim Wach, *Sociology of Religion* (Chicago, Ill.: University of Chicago Press, 1944), pp. 17–34.

form of religious expression and endeavors to demonstrate how religious words, sentences, stories, and concepts are symbols in several different ways at the same time.)

Think again of the notion of an inner reality, an invisible but more real reality than the outer, concealed like bones beneath the flesh, which religious expression presupposes. Religion wants both to perceive it and to call it into perceivable and participatory reality. Religion is both an x-ray and a drum calling dancers to the floor. On its contemplative side, religion wants to see and know what the inner reality is, to perceive it with awe and wonder and even love. On its active side, it wants to create rituals, dances, words, books, and moods in which the inner comes to life. In the Ise Harvest Festival, as in any church service or even in looking at a piece of sacred art, one *sees* and, if he or she fully participates, enters the other side. That is why in religious rites people may wear garments, say words, play music, and even walk and gesture in ways different from someone on the street, in ways that make no sense on any other grounds than religious reality. It is as though one had crossed an invisible boundary to a very different country, as Dorothy crossed the Great Sandy Desert from Kansas to Oz.

Nevertheless, the other worlds of religion—the world of the Harvest Festival when mankind becomes coworkers and exchangers of gifts with the fecundating deities, the fresh new inner world of becoming a new person in Christ, the world of spiritual reality evoked by Mass, Yom Kippur, or dancing before Krishna—are not just fantasy alternative worlds like Oz. For the religionist, they are *more real* than the outer universe. To call them into being is *to see things as they really are* or *to act in accordance with the way things really are*, regardless of appearances.

People may differ about which proffered religious reality is the way things really are and may think that others than their own are no more real than Oz. It is, however, important to realize that to every real believer, at the moment of transcendent experience, the religious world is the real world—a reality greater, more profound, and older than the deepest sea or the oldest mountain on this side.

This brings us to perhaps the profoundest thing about religion's self-understanding that can be put into words: in religion one is his or her real self. (We mean, of course, that this is how a believer experiences himself or herself in religious participation.) In religion one acts out who he or she really is; the real self is the one who participates in transcendent experience and through it enters the other side. Religion may be called scenarios for the real self. Its theme is "I am a somebody," and in it, if not in the outer world, one becomes that somebody. In the outer world one may be just another face on the street, another hand in a factory or field, or another presence bobbing up and down in the circle of family and friends, sometimes in and sometimes out in the lotteries of kinship and love. When one's religious world takes form around one, in rite or prayer or meditation, one becomes what one really and always is, a beloved child of God, a flame of the eternal fire, or a member of the great dance of gods and wheeling seasons.

## BECOMING A SOMEBODY

What is the difference between a somebody and a nobody? First, a somebody has a sense of place. He or she belongs—to family, to community, to the universe. Second, a somebody has an inner place—an inner identity he or she can really accept—and even if one does not always exemplify it or even recall it consciously, somehow on a deeper level one knows it is there. A nobody, on the other hand, feels like a wallflower in the dance of life and like wastepaper instead of an identity card inside. Religion old and new has tried to meet these two needs for place in manifold and often dramatic ways. In rites like the Shinto Harvest Festival, in sanctifying family life, or in making church or temple a center of community life, it has made the biological and social units to which one belongs important enough—and closely enough related to the transcendent level—to afford one a sense of absolute place in them.

Religion draws maps of the invisible world—the real, bones-of-the-universe world—in the architecture and location of temples and shrines and in their art and symbols. When one is around them one can feel near the way things are, which is the same as being near place and home. The realities so represented step out of the shrine for the believer to be interiorized as guarantees of his or her own inner place.

Religion may even offer a place to ostensible outsiders, such as holy men, monks, wanderers, widows, orphans, and the insane, who are often given residences and special places to pray and accept alms in or around temples and churches. Religion often suggests that though people like these seem at disjuncture with ordinary society, they are actually closer to God or the religious reality than the ordinary, and so require special veneration as living signs on the map of the invisible world.

Whatever the identity, however, the devout religious participant feels that his religious identity is the real one; in religion he or she is an actor in a play that is true and not just made up. The true identity can be thought of as the quality that comes through in those snapshots of friends and loved ones that cause us to say, "This is *really* so-and-so."

Sometimes a picture catches a particular smile or crinkling of the eyes that provokes that reaction. Even if it is a look the person pictured has only once a week or so, in some unfathomable way it shows who that person really is. Similarly, there are times when we *feel* as though we are now being who we really are, even if it is only on rare occasions. Ideally, religion facilitates those occasions.

Not all religious experience, of course, provides this for everyone. A lot of religious participation is not right in that sense for many participants. For some, religion indeed seems more like acting out a false and made-up role than almost anything else they do. Some people have experiences that give them a sense of who they really are mostly outside of formal religion—in exploring nature, in sports, in love, even in their work. Our purpose now, however, is to understand religion, and the first realization to be grasped in the quest for this understanding is that what is implicitly *intended* in the acts and attitudes of religion is to make one who he or she really is in the largest frame of reference.

Religions may have any number of practices, teachings, and names that assure one that the real self afforded by the faith is oneself as seen from the highest perspective, from a mountaintop where the view is unlimited. This is the one thing all religion does and is what separates it from that which meets only biological or limited psychological needs. In studying religion, one must realize that in any significant religion many people have found that sort of identity, and for some that is doubtless the most important fact in life.

Who one *thinks* one really is and who one really is may be two different things. A self is a bewildering and complex thing whose riddle is not necessarily solved just by one religious adjustment. The theologian Paul Tillich has spoken of "pseudo," "crypto," and "quasi" religion, and no doubt there are many religious conceptions, as well as nonreligious conceptions, of the self that are partial or evasive ways of dealing with the problem of who one is rather than actually helping toward becoming one's real self. To understand the meaning and power of religion, we must understand its intention and the fact that it does work as a real self identity for many, many people. While to be a real self may be an ideal, it is striving after such ideals that leaves cultures and societies in the wake; the forms of religious expression are the waves and surf above the underlying current toward the real self. Despite qualifications, then, it seems that to think of religion as scenarios for the real self, as ways of acting out and so becoming who one really is, provides an understanding of religion that is most conducive to an inner empathy with what it means to religionists themselves.

The distinction between one's real self—the clear, genuine, authentic identity—and a false, empty self without place is a manifestation (perhaps the most fundamental manifestation) of something very basic to human thought, making distinctions. For religion, though, this distinction is not only within oneself but is also reflected or observed in the outer world as well. Some outer times, places, people, or modes of behavior are most compatible with the real self and others with the false self.

Scholars of religion in the tradition of Emile Durkheim and Mircea Eliade (to be discussed in the next chapter) have talked about this distinction as a distinction religion makes between the *sacred* and the *profane*. Eliade rightly tells us that for religious persons, the world is "nonhomogeneous."[10] Certain times and places have a special quality about them. The sacred is touched by the numinous; it inspires awe, wonder, and dread because it has a feel of a transcendent presence, of pristine power, and of being itself unmatched by the circles of the profane. The profane is not cursing but just plain, drab, ordinary reality as we live it in the context of empty and meaningless workaday lives. The nonhomogeneous quality of religious life, though, indicates that some times and places have for the religious person more of a sense of the sacred about them than do others. They are times and places when one can best act out a scenario for the real self. It may be that an ordinary, secularized, modern individual feels nothing different in a cathedral or temple from in a factory or city park. That would be far from the case for one for whom the cathedral or temple actualizes the real self and provides access to the farther ranges of his or her infinite environment. It is in this perspective that *sacred space* and *sacred time* must be appreciated.

Sacred space is the precincts of temples or churches, holy shrines, or sacred hills—any place that has a special, different, awesome feel about it as a spot where the transcendent power breaks through. When you are in a church or temple, even if nothing is going on, you may feel something special that makes you want to walk quietly and talk in hushed tones. It is a different aura from walking down the street or going to school or the store. You may, however, get a similar feeling in the midst of a lovely grove or on a mountaintop—and these places have also been made sacred down through the ages. The difference is that a real

[10]Mircea Eliade, *The Sacred and the Profane* (New York: Harcourt Brace Jovanovich, Inc., 1959).

sacred space has probably been believed to be a place where gods descended to earth, visions (as at Fatima in Portugal in this century) were experienced, the creation of the world began, the central pillar of the earth stands, or access to the transcendent world above is particularly easy (as at Mecca for Muslims or Mount Zion in Palestine for medieval Christians).

Sacred time is the different time of festivals, rites, reciting sacred stories, or holidays—any block of time in which the flow of ordinary, one-thing-after-another time stops and the transcendent, where time goes at a different rate or ceases altogether, takes over. The time of Mardi Gras or Carnival in Latin countries is an example. At Carnival, one can wander through the streets, seeing brilliant costumes, hearing lively music, dancing, laughing, without thought of past or future, just being there full of joy. This is close to the way a real self feels, and the festive atmosphere makes it possible. Sacred time can also be a solemn rite, such as the Roman Catholic High Mass, the Greek Orthodox Liturgy, or a formal Buddhist rite with offerings and chanting of scriptures accompanied by drums and bells. In a different way, these can lift one into a place where ordinary time stops and one feels united to what really is, beyond all change or dimension.

Sacred space and time are felt by the religious to be sources of power and especially of rejuvenation or renewal. Eliade tells us that is because they are felt to be like continuing islands of the beginning, the time when the gods were strong or God was vigorously active, and the world was made. Ordinary time and space seem to run down, becoming thin and gray, but in sacred time and space it is as though the clock were wound back up, the first sunrise had ventured back to the east again, and what had become unraveled were reknitted. To participate in sacred space and time is to bathe again in the power of the beginning or its restitution. To the Shintoist, to worship in the sacred space of Ise at the sacred time of the Harvest Festival is to return to the primal "Divine Age." For the Christian, receiving baptism or holy communion, probably in the setting of a sacred place full of signs and symbols of faith, is a trip back to the New Testament power and presence of Jesus Christ.

- Religion, then, ideally can be summed up by saying that it presupposes a twofold cosmos of experience, in which pairs come down not only to nourishing versus nonnourishing or ordered versus chaotic but also good versus bad or right versus wrong. The nourishing, ordered, good, and right are all part of a single integrated set that ties together the good end of every polarity through sacred space and sacred time into the infinite, unconditioned source of all value and being. It makes one most a real self when he or she is aligned to the good side of choices, even if only by being in a society on that side. Like a network, this religious set expresses itself in many dimensions: as ideas, as art and symbols, as social groups, as sacred space and time, as ethical actions. Being part of a polarity pattern, the existence of the network implies there are those persons and ideas within it and those outside of it. This is indicated by its setting up such pairs as the converted versus the unconverted, the ethical versus the unethical, orthodox versus heretical teaching, and those in the rite versus those out of the rite.

## SPREADING A NETWORK

As in all human affairs, ambivalences arise. We find differing emphases in practice. Some people respond to Christian art but little to Christian theology, while some are interested in theology but not at all in art. Some people are deeply attracted to worship services but are not notably ethical, while some are extremely virtuous but never attend services. Ideally, though, all these aspects should reinforce each other and show that a religion is a network operating in all areas of life. It is not just a philosophy or a ritual or a social unit.

What really makes a pattern of experience a religion is that it is also a pattern of meaning that derives directly from the transcendent and so makes anyone participating in it a real self. It is this, and not any particular subject matter such as gods, spirits, or God, that makes a pattern religious. For example, Buddhism and the cultic side of Confucianism certainly look like religion with their temples, sacrificial rites, altars, and chanting ministers and have played a role in their societies comparable to Western religion, but one would be hard put to find in them an idea exactly like that of the Western monotheist God. However, as we have seen, in practice virtually every religion uses concepts and symbols that represent transcendent sentient beings—gods, spirits, buddhas, or immortals in unconditioned states of consciousness—to indicate that its network is in line with the sacred pattern that radiates from the absolute source.

Here is an illustration that may indicate how, following the categories of Berger and Eliade, a religious pattern of meaning might differ from other options. I once visited the home of a family firmly convinced that their house was haunted. They said that strange markings on the earth could be detected by a flashlight swept across the crawl space under the house, that household objects sometimes mysteriously flew through the air or appeared and disappeared, and that high rapid voices were heard in the rooms. It seemed to me that the family could take one of four attitudes toward this phenomena. They could have considered the forces behind these uncanny appearances good, as envoys of another plane of reality or even of ultimate transcendence. They would then have doubtless regarded them with awe and reverence and sought to communicate with them in an attitude of worship. Second, they could have considered the forces evil, demonic influences and sought to exorcise them. Third, they could have regarded the matter as simply a subject for examination and sought to study the phenomena scientifically. Fourth, they could have just tried to ignore it, having no heightened attitude toward it one way or the other, endeavoring insofar as possible just to live their ordinary lives despite the occurrences.

The first response clearly would have been religious; interaction with the mysterious forces would have been a way for the family members to bring out a fresh aspect of their real selves through a new and special alignment with the deep realities behind the universe. As we have seen, real self and transcendent experience or alignment go together in religion; that is the crux of religion. In a sense the second response would have been religious too. It would have implied the existence of the religious network and of religious reality, since it would have been based on a presupposition that the forces were excluded from such a network (therefore being called evil or demonic). Supernatural evil usually implies supernatural good. The third response suggests the creation of a universe of meaning that parallels the religious but has other values. It presupposes a universal, scientific law and the view of what constitutes the cosmos that goes with it. The concurrent attitude of study, examination, and analysis, however, suggests an attitude of mind different from that of awe, wonder, and worship; it does not indicate a feeling that the transcendent and numinous are behind the phenomena. The fourth response, though, is most clearly not religious, since it does not relate any universe of meaning at all to the phenomena.

## WORKING AND DANCING

The diverse aspects of religion that validate one as a real self may seem, both in one's own experience and in reflection on religion in general, to fall into two parts that are hard to reconcile. On one hand, religion offers meaningful subjective realizations: the joy of renewal in sacred space and time, the fulfillment of being a real self through conversion experience and through rapport with the absolute. Even appreciation of religious ritual, music, and art just on an aesthetic or feeling level falls on this side. On the other side are the strictures of religion: the ethical maxims, the models for behavior, the taboos to be observed and conditions to be met before one participates in the more sacred usages. It is likely the conditions uphold the normative values of society and support its ways of doing things, affirming they are also sacred and that society's values derive their authority from the sacred source and are part of the sacred network.

These two sides fit together, at least in theory, although the roughness of the fit provides one of the major dynamics for change in the history of religion. The principle is evident in the response members of the Uitoto tribe of Indians in South America gave an anthropologist who asked what they did. "We work and we dance," they said, "but we work

*Fujihira/Monkmeyer Press Photo Service*

Igorot mountain people in the Philippines performing a war dance.

in order that we may dance." Among them, as in many primitive societies, it was usual to follow a cycle of hunting and gathering until enough food was stockpiled to last for several weeks, then to shift the mood to dancing and feasting until it was time to start work again and repeat the cycle. Inevitably in such societies, feasting and dancing were definitely religious things—done in the name of the gods and with a sense of mystically participating in their deep and rich lives. Dancing time was sacred time, and perhaps done in a sacred place, the tribesmen becoming who they really were in the widest cosmic context.

Indeed, the feeling we have for the difference between working and dancing suggests something basic about human life that can help us to understand the difference between a false or alienated self and a real self and between sacred and profane time and space and even to understand the ideal meaning of religion itself. To a visitor from another planet it might seem incomprehensible that humans would labor just to free themselves to do another activity that expends as much if not more energy and yet is nonproductive.

*We* as humans know from within that dancing *feels* different from working, possessing as it does a dimension of ecstasy and completeness that makes it a goal for which working is the means. Even more oddly, the dances of many primitive societies are simply stylized pantomimes of work activities—hunting, planting, harvesting, cooking. Yet to *imitate* doing them in dance seems to be joyous, a celebration of life, and festive fulfillment, while the actual doing of these chores is work, the profane drudgery done in anticipation of dance (although actual labor is often done to music or song and made into as much of a dance as possible). What is the explanation of this odd state of affairs, which can also be noted in such ritual, token communal meals as the Christian holy communion and the Jewish seder? Perhaps religion and the festive spirit implicitly see all practical human deeds as shadows cast by a more transcendent meaning to being human, in whose light all characteristic human activities can be raised to "dancing." Still work and dancing have an inseparable connection—the work is given point and purpose by dance, and the dance fulfills and completes human life just because the working side gives it something to complete.

The inner experience side of religion—festive joy, devotional rapture, being a *felt* real self—is the result and reward of doing the work necessary to human society. Religion both gives inward joy and enforces the normative standards for work and behavior of a society. The two must go together; that is what the structural role of religious institutions is about. Religion cannot just give out sheer inward joy for everyone all the time. If it did, people would be so absorbed in ecstasy that no one would do the work—hunting or hoeing, raising families, and guarding the boundaries. Nevertheless, religion cannot offer only moral codes and prohibitions with no inward joy. Ideally, these two sides must be in balance, so that one has compensatory joy in dancing after the crops have been harvested, the enemy defeated, and the moral law kept even at the cost of repressing strong desires. Christian holy communion is for the devout a richly meaningful experience, at times even rapturous. Tradition, however, has it given only to those who have confessed and repented of their sins and are members in good standing of the church. There are many examples of religious reward in this life and the next that are offered as compensation for doing the work and observing the rules necessary to make society function.

A precise balance between constraints and rewards is very hard to attain or preserve. With generational changes, with changes in the economies and external circumstances of a society, the constraints that are needed and rewards that are persuasive can shift. For this reason a society's religion, however powerful and stable it may appear on the surface, has a built-in destabilizing factor that keeps it changing. Religion—that is, what in practice makes people feel like real selves—is always changing, sometimes at a fast rate and sometimes very slowly, and disequilibrium between religious constraints and rewards is one of the basic dynamics for motivating change.

If religion becomes too oriented toward reward and if its pleasant experiences of festive fellowship and aesthetic or spiritual joy are too easily accessible, voices will arise to say that the necessary standards of moral and ethical behavior are slipping, that the work of society is not getting done, and even that its foundations are crumbling. Then a work of reconstruction appears, either from within the old religion or through a new one that comes in as (at first) a welcome wind of harsh but clean vigor. People may chafe sometimes at the new constraints, but they also sense as even more disturbing the chaos and accompanying loss of being a real self that would ensue should sanctioned standards fall away. Examples of this reconstruction are Christianity in the later Roman Empire, early Islam, Puritanism, and (on a smaller scale) numerous strict sectarianisms, ancient and modern.

On the other hand, when the religion seems over-heavy on constraints, and the dollops of ecstasy given out seem too small, perfunctory, or perhaps outdated in form, new venues of ecstasy are likely to arise as compensation. Perhaps there will be a new movement of the pietistic or charismatic sort within the religion that will emphasize feeling, conversion, or consciousness-changing mystical experience. Perhaps a new religion of the mystical sort will develop, or even ostensibly nonreligious experience-givers such as psychedelic drugs or political fanaticisms will arise to fill the void. Examples might be Tantrism in Hinduism and Buddhism, Sufi mysticism within Islam, the Quaker reaction to Puritanism, the Romantic reaction to the religion-without-mystery of the eighteenth-century Enlightenment, and the various mystical responses of the American counterculture in the 1960s to the oversuburbanized American churches of the 1950s. In any case, religion continually shifts, molding itself to changing circumstances but always keeping the goal constant.

## A SIMPLE AWARENESS
## AND A COMPLEX HISTORY

In the first chapter of this book, we have centered an understanding of religion around the idea of being a real self—that is, one who has a full sense of unity within him or herself and with all that is and so feels what we call meaning and fulfillment. It is perhaps a very simple awareness, so simple that its essence has to be either intuited from the yearning for it within oneself or inferred from the more elaborate manifestations of its presence or the desire for its presence in human life. It can hardly be described except in symbols such as the words *real self*.

We have just finished examining some of these manifestations and symbols: the real self as requiring more than just practical means and ends; the something more indicated by a sense of what we call transcendence; the transcendent that is concretized in particular sacred symbols, places, acts, and ideas that are different just because they put people in mind of, or in the midst of, the other side. They reassure us there is more to us, and to human life, than just the practical. They reinforce the comforting concept that a real self is other than the ordinary empty self we so often feel ourselves to be. These symbols and forms of the transcendent then spread like a network through human society, taking remarkably elaborate forms so that they have some relation to nearly everything, either positive or negative, and interact with the rest of life in a rhythm such as that between work and play.

How did this simple real self awareness come to have such a complicated grip on human life and such an elaborate set of ways of working itself out? At least part of the answer, as one might suspect, lies in an equally complex history. Tracing its outline is the task of the next chapter. First, a preliminary word or two about that chapter. Its narrative, perhaps unexpectedly, starts very far back with the physical formation of our globe. It then indulges in some remarks on the development of life and animal behavior. The continuity of human and animal ways of thinking and doing, especially in societies, has been a significant theme of recent thought, and it is both interesting and important to put religion into this context. Some of the complexity of religion—its involvement with rite, feeling, social order, symbol, place, and time—becomes a little clearer in light of the complex heritage humankind has brought over from the prehuman earth. Also, religion often most fundamentally illumines what is distinctive about humans. Because it is the pivotal point relative to a general study of religion, the matter of the emergence of human religion at the dawn of human history (speculative as it is) is given preeminent attention. The major periods of religious history, each of which has responded to new experiences of what it means to be a real self and has shown that response through new symbols and new networks throughout the world, are outlined in very cursory form.

We pause a bit longer, though, at the end of the next chapter to take up some nineteenth- and twentieth-century interpreters of religion as an aspect of human life. They are introduced here because one of the most significant of all events in religious history has been the profound change in the way people view themselves and their society that has come with modernization in these last two centuries and especially with the appearance of such disciplines as social science and psychology. What it has meant is that, at least as an ideal, one views something human not just in terms of one's own involvement but from a larger perspective and with categories that could be used to describe and interpret several such phenomena. (Of course, there were classical writers and philosophers who did this before the last century, but it has only been in modern times that cross-cultural human studies and interpretations of human activities have approached extensive systematization and, more importantly, become cultural forces of immense power in their own right.)

The revolutionary meaning of this new attitude for religion was self-evident. We now had tools of thought for reflecting on religion in other than just the theological terms a religion itself used; this eliminated the necessity of pitting one's own religion as true against others as false. While the ultimate importance of the question of religious truth has not diminished, one also had tools—such as those employed in this chapter—for looking at religion as a human experience crossing many cultures. Not accidentally, it was also only in the nineteenth century that accurate information about all religions began to be circulated worldwide and that people began, often painfully, to reflect in a modern way on the fact that we live in a pluralistic world. The hermetically sealed circle of culture and faith in which most premodern people lived, and the abysmal ignorance of others that went with it, is (even though it sometimes still exists) not easy for educated modern people to comprehend fully. That change is, in itself, one of the most important events in religious history.

We shall then conclude the history of religion with a notice of some of the thinkers who have been articulators of that change. (The change itself, of course, was grounded not only in modern intellectual currents but also in modern technology and Western expansion.) Some of these interpreters of religion have been describers, and others have sought to interpret religion in terms of other perspectives, such as psychology, economics, historical forces. It is important to know about them; it is equally important to know what they collectively represent in the history of religion. They mark a new discovery about what it means to be a real self. Let us turn from the real self to the story of discoveries about it and the way it has manifested itself through the language of the sacred.

This volcanic eruption in Hawaii in 1959 is suggestive of the violent primordial forces that shaped the face of the earth over countless geological ages.

# CHAPTER TWO

# HISTORY OF RELIGION
# ON PLANET EARTH

## THE ROOTS OF A WORLD

Some five billion years ago, the planet took form as molten and gaseous globs of material wheeling around a sun coalesced and spun into a roughly spherical shape. That earth of billions of years ago would have seemed a different and far more hellish world from the one known to its present inhabitants, who could not have survived unaided on it for more than a few minutes. The atmosphere contained no free oxygen. The cooling crust was fractured continually by immense volcanic eruptions and lava flows. It was repeatedly hit by asteroids as big as those that made the gigantic craters still visible on the moon, Mars, and Mercury; the impact of each such giant rocked the world with mountain-shattering shock waves and seas high enough to inundate continents.

There were seas on the planet as soon as it had cooled enough for the great primal rains that made the first oceans. It was here in the oceans, not on the scarred and barren land, that things began to happen. More and more complex molecules, gathered around amino acids, enriched the "soup" of tidal basins and quiet coves. Little by little, over thousands and millions of years, the molecules crossed the diffuse boundary between inorganic and organic matter; they "ate" and "evacuated" by adding or releasing atoms while continuing discrete existences as ongoing units, and they could program detached segments of their systems to reproduce the original. Eventually, an even greater step was taken. Multitudes of complex molecules united to form one-celled organisms. They floated or propelled themselves in the water, absorbing food and reproducing by dividing.

Can we talk of religion in this primordial protoplasmic sea, amid the countless one-celled plants and animals that animated it during the many millions of years when earth knew no higher life than theirs? It is impossible to think of religion apart from consciousness, even though there may be parallels between inorganic and even subatomic phenomena and religious phenomena, and doubtless everything in the universe is interrelated. (Is it too fanciful to think metaphorically that there is something like meditation in the agelong vigil of a rock high on a mountainside, or something like a ritual in the endless circling of electrons around a nucleus or planets around a sun?) We do not know if conscious awareness comparable to that of humans, even if far dimmer, is characteristic of all life or only of some. We cannot prove there is consciousness in anything other than humans, though few today would deny (as Descartes did) that it is present at least in the higher mammals such as chimpanzees, horses, and dogs.

On the other hand, it is hard to explain consciousness even in humans, for the human or animal brain could, from a naturalistic point of view, function as a vastly complex computer without the added fillip of conscious awareness. With no more consciousness than that of a windup doll, it could make the organism go through the motions necessary to live and reproduce, though to what point would be hard to say. Indeed, to many it has seemed that consciousness is so different from the material side of biology as to be a separate sort of reality that has somehow gotten embedded in certain biological systems and to require a separate explanation. Some very important religious and philosophical ideologies have been built on such reflections.

But back to the world of the one-celled. For these creatures, birth and death as we know it did not exist in principle; they were virtually deathless bits of protoplasm that divided over and over again and absorbed others of their kind over and over. Each was a drop in a nearly immortal sea of life that continually changed in its internal configuration. If they had had a religion, it might with considerable justice have been similar to that of those mystics who see all reality as but manifestation in many forms of one immortal spirit and who say that death is only a transition from one form to another.

In time this primal mystical paradise, if so it was, gave place to something else for some of life. (Of course, the way of the one-celled continues around and in us as the vast majority of our fellow creatures on this planet, the protozoa and bacteria and viruses, invisibly swarm through air, land, sea, and our own bodies.) Some cells linked themselves in combinations far more efficient in swimming and eating than single cells. With this advance, however, came death as we understand it: what is made up of many parts can be broken down to its parts, and then neither it nor the parts function any longer as life. True, the organic matter within the complex organism may continue in its eaters, large or small, because little of life is not sooner or later recycled through the chain of living beings. That sort of immortality, however, is not a reality for the complex organism. Its primary concern is to fend off potential decomplexification of itself; life not only wants to continue to exist but also to continue to exist on the highest level of complexity it has attained. On the complex union of cells, and not the separable parts, is fixated whatever of consciousness and self-awareness there is. In animals it coordinates searching for food and escaping from enemies to preserve the life of the integrated complex; it would seem that consciousness chooses to identify itself only with the whole, not the parts, even at the cost of living with death (identified with dissolution) as a dreaded and constant threat.

The coming of death sharpens acuteness of consciousness. Brains, the organ of consciousness as we know it, are fragile but immensely complex, consisting of millions of cells. Among animals, strategems for eating, defense, and reproduction became more complicated and required more flexible behavior as the organisms evolved further from their single-cell beginnings. Down the ages these complexities multiplied. Worms and mollusks gave place to fish, and fish came onto the land and learned to breathe air. On land there bred a mighty swarm of life, from tiny gnats dancing in the air to gigantic reptiles shearing at each other with teeth like daggers. Finally, small hairy creatures appeared—they may have been unprepossessing at first, but they more than made up for that with flexibility and intelligence. They were the mammals that in time dominated the earth.

The vast epochs when earth belonged to animals, plants, and geology, so inconceivably long compared to the short span of human history, are now on the other side of a door that has been firmly shut behind us. We can study them from fossil records and reconstruct them in imagination, but we cannot fully recapture the nonhuman rhythms of time in those ages. In this prehuman past there would usually have been a sort of stillness outside the experience of most moderns. Behind the calm was the endless fear, wariness, hungry search, occasional satiety, explosive sexual outburst, or merciless violence of the wild, all repeating itself as the sun rose and set over countless millennia.

Yet down through those millions of years, long before the first human word was spoken, phenomena occurred paralleling what in human societies has been given religious sanctions and been enveloped in the aura of the sacred. Far from being chaotic and governed by irrational impulse, as one might think, the animal world is in fact a world highly routinized and structured, like an immense ritual.

## SPACE AND TIME, LOVE AND DEATH IN THE WILD

Observers of the world of animals do not see anything suggestive of human institutional or conceptual religion. Yet one can notice striking parallels to religious behavior, though motivated by inherited instinct rather than culture or subjectivity. Above all, one sees parallels to the patterns of society and individual development that among humans are so often sanctified by religion. There are colorful and remarkable behaviors, dances, and rituals that cannot be wholly explained on practical grounds.

Animal societies (herds, packs, schools, colonies) are not chaotic but have a definite structure that is sometimes quite elaborate. Most groups have an explicit order of dominance among the members. In chickens the pecking order puts each bird somewhere in a hierarchy, pushing some around and being pushed around by others. Among mammals such as elk and sealions, dominant males defend their rights to the females by fighting; younger males challenge the older until they displace them. Often the social hierarchy is indicated by ritualistic gestures such as harmless but symbolically aggressive behavior toward inferiors or deferential slouching around or standing aside for superiors. These gestures are acted out over and over again by the young in play until thoroughly learned.

All this is hardly unfamiliar to humans and reminds us that the side of religion that reinforces the social order may well be deeply interwoven with patterns such as these. Generally religion teaches veneration of age, seniority, parents, and the conventions of marriage (whatever they may be). Instead of relying on instinct, however, we may call the rules of human society morality taught by deity and consider the dominant leaders appointed by God or at least endowed with a special mystique of supernatural power that makes acts of deference to them similar to acts of worship.

A related matter is territoriality. Some animals, individually or in groups, establish a definite territory as terrain for hunting or grazing. All rivals are excluded from this territory. Often the territory is established and defended in symbolic ways. If you have ever taken a cat or dog with you to a new house, you may have noticed that one of the first things the animal does is to run around the new territory systematically marking its boundaries. If an intruder approaches, the animal will hiss or growl in a manner that symbolizes to other members of that species that it will defend the territory to those marked limits.[1]

This reminds us of two things in religious life. One is the traditional tendency to believe that one's own land is sacred. It is a place of order in the midst of chaos because it is patterned on the will of the gods or was made and given by the gods to its people. Its boundaries may be ritually established and sanctioned. When Columbus first landed in the New World, he knelt in prayer as he planted the flag of Spain. Traditional Japanese thought of their land as the "land of the gods," uniquely ruled over by a descendent of the solar goddess. Animal territoriality also reminds us that mankind establishes smaller sacred spaces—miniaturizations or intensifications of the sacredness of a larger space—in the areas of shrines and temples and churches. These too are demarcated in highly symbolic ways, with gates, crosses, curtains, and expectations of special behavior in the sacred place. People demonstrate the sacredness by taking off their shoes or speaking in a low voice.

Still another aspect of animal behavior relevant to the understanding of human religion is ritualization. By ritualization is meant the establishment of behavior that repeats, although often in a curtailed manner, an act that was once extremely significant. Because the behavior is condensed—only a token gesture in the direction of what it once was—it can be called symbolic; it satisfies the feelings that once adhered in the original act but does not need to go all the way in repeating it. Konrad Lorenz, a distinguished student of animal behavior, tells us about the duck, Martina, he raised in his home. When he first brought Martina into the house she was understandably frightened and, as frightened birds do, made for the light, in this case a large window, before following Lorenz up the stairs. Ever after, she walked a little out of her way toward the window, although no longer really frightened, before going upstairs with him in the evening. She continued to gesture toward the window, a behavior started when she was only six days old, although it became no more than a slight turning of the head when she waddled past that spot.[2] Owners of horses know that it is virtually impossible to take an animal past a place where it has long regularly stopped without making at least a token gesture of pausing before riding on.

Ritualization like this can be compared with the ongoing desire we have to pause out of reverence at places or in situations where we once had rich spiritual experience and to repeat their circumstances ritually by

[1]See Robert Ardrey, *The Social Contract* (New York: Atheneum Publishers, 1970), pp. 108–9.

[2]Konrad Lorenz, *On Aggression* (New York: Harcourt Brace Jovanovich, Inc., 1969), chapter 5.

reading or hearing words or hymns associated with them, whether or not the complete experience is repeated. At the same time, the repeated circumstances may help to recreate the experience. Even if it does not there is something very satisfying about the ritualized expression. Much of religious rites, prayer, and worship, both private and public, can be seen in this light, although of course there is much more to human religion than Martina's level of ritualization.

The elaborate dances some animals enact, particularly in connection with mating, come to mind also. They are instinctual rather than repetitions of a particular experience, and so are not really the same as Martina's ritualization. The Nile crocodile, for instance, raises its head and tail in the water before the female, sinks in this position causing a stream of bubbles to rise out of his mouth to the surface, splashes and thrashes with his jaws and tail, and finally sends up a high vertical spray or jet of water by forcing air through its slightly submerged nostrils. Perhaps the author of the Book of Job had this in mind when he said, "Out of his nostrils goeth smoke, as out of a seething pot or caldron."[3] The colorful performances of birds like the kite, who lock talons with their mates and ecstatically fall hundreds of feet through the air, and the display dances of ostriches and flamingos are well known. So are the magnificent mating flights of the queens of the social insects, bees, wasps, ants, and termites. The lowly and unloved scorpion (whose ancestors had the honor of being among the very first of the animal kingdom to move onto the land many hundreds of millions of years ago) performs a remarkable square dance with its mate, vigorous and interesting even though it may end with the female eating the male after copulation.

These rites may be no more religious than social dancing or honeymoons among humans, but sex and religion are closely interwoven in much of human life and ritual. Wedding ceremonies have both sexual and religious overtones, and so do countless traditional dances and other rites to encourage fertility or to celebrate the harvest or the turning of the new year.

In any case, animal dances share with festive performances among humans the fact that there is more to them than meeting material ends on a minimalistic basis. They are ritualization and symbolization in that they incite the partner by symbolic action suggestive of sexuality. In many instances the symbolization goes to extremes that would seem to be unnecessary from a purely functional point of view, especially since other species are content with a more direct and immediate approach.

[3]Hugh B. Cott, *Looking at Animals* (New York: Charles Scribner's Sons., 1975), pp. 142–44.

Why do crocodiles and scorpions have a much more elaborate courtship performance than dogs or cats? All this suggests that in nonhuman lives as well as human there run capacities for action aimed more at ecstasy than function and toward quite elaborate degrees of symbolic rather than direct expression and fulfillment. Both capacities are familiar to students of human religion.

While parallels are evident between some animal behavior and human religion, the differences should be equally recognized. Among animals it is precisely those patterns, such as territoriality and courtship displays, seeming most to mimic religion that are instinctual. Among humans, however, religious behavior is distinctively cultural and tradi- tional, passed on deliberately through communication and imitation generation after generation. There *is* tradition among animal colonies, in the sense of learned information about water and feeding areas and so forth passed on to the young through example, but there is no instance of the learning and passing on of social or ritual behavior. It must be kept in mind, then, that while some human customs may be rooted in in- stinctual needs like those for territoriality and the celebration of mating, our *religions* are passed on more in the way an animal shows its young how to hunt or where the waterhole is. In contrast to animals with instinctive rites, a human brought up outside of society would know nothing about the rituals or beliefs of the species.

A second difference is that animal rituals are not really separate value-giving areas of life like human religion. An animal's territory really is crucial as its source of food and safety; inciting a partner to mate is crucial to the species. Human religious exercises are *believed* to be cru- cially important because they make us feel like real selves. They are likely to be things apart from, yet related to, the practical world, symbolically or paradigmatically replicating it to give meaning to the real act, like the relation of the wedding ring and sexual union or of religious conversion and change in one's manner of life. The wedding ring and holy commun- ion do not incite us to mate or eat, rather they give social and spiritual meaning and validation to those acts. They are parts of dramas in which we act out who we really are in terms of our ultimate environment. This is a dimension that animal ritualization does not seem to have, any more than animals have the ability to think in such abstract terms.

This is a respect in which human religion may be less related to animal ritualization than to animal play. Among humans, there is a significant parallel between religion and play. Roger Caillois has written that play and games have the following characteristics: (1) free, not obligatory; (2) separated in time and space from ordinary life; (3) un- certain in outcome; (4) unproductive of goods and wealth (though there may be exchanges, as in gambling); (5) governed by rules; (6) fictive, imaginary, make believe. Types of play, he says, are (1) competition, (2) chance, (3) simulation (mimicry, pretending), and (4) those that aim at creation of vertigo, dizziness, and disorder.[4] Religious activities clearly share most of these characteristics, and while competition and chance have been parts of various religious events, most include simulation and many suggest vertigo, if we see the latter as a play parallel to ecstatic and mystical states. The main point is that in both play and religion a particular time, and perhaps space, is set apart in which different and stylized behavior and rules are observed; this is often indicated by particular dress, like football uniforms or church vestments. The game and the religious activity are like miniature worlds detached from the ordinary world, though bearing a meaningful relation to it. Both can well be dramas that act out the scenario of the real self, heighten consciousness, and do in a right or orderly and successful way, albeit symbolically, what is chaotic in the outer world. They create paradigms or value-giving models of the outer world; we say, then, that life ought to be played like a game, just as we say we ought to take religion out of church and into everyday life.

Animals, too, have play, particularly the young of mammals. They run, slide, and tussle with each other, partly because the activity is physically pleasant in itself and partly for other reasons. Much of play is training in skills useful in hunting or escape or in the fighting or deference behavior that is necessary when the animal finds its place in the dominance order. Part of the play is simply learning to follow rules, like the play of human children—how to play at fighting without really hurting the other or how to run with a group. Animal and human children alike really *want* rules—far from craving to be free of all rules, they make for themselves more rules than adults actually impose, striving to make all they do as close to the stylized world of games and rituals as possible. Anything is more fun to the young *with* rules to control the limits of a situation, especially when one's situation is precarious in this hard world.

Religion is like a perpetuation into human life and adult life of this aspect of animal play and childhood play. Religion creates a place, a state of mind, and a view of what the world is *really* like (as God's world underneath its seeming lawless chaos) in which everything is done right and one is right—a real self. It maintains rules as does play, even if only in a small place or for oneself; it is a symbol and paradigm of meaning and order.

[4]Roger Caillois, *Man, Play and Games* (New York: The Free Press, 1961). See also Johan Huizinga, *Homo Ludens: A Study of the Play Element in Culture* (Boston, Mass.: Beacon Press, 1955), and Ardrey, *The Social Contract*, pp. 152–53.

Monkmeyer Press Photo Service

A troop of monkeys in Chile.

Still another side of the animal background of human religiosity should be mentioned. This side pertains to a very different aspect both of animal life and the human spirit from what we have dealt with thus far. That is the extent to which animals may share with us feelings of depth and specialness in the great moments of life—in times of accomplishment, of the birth of young, of attachment to offspring and kin, and of death.

Heightened feelings in relation to these occasions are closely connected to the subjective sources of human religion; these are the moments that on a natural level most define or threaten awareness of being a real self. It is hard to document such feelings among animals, and doubtless most animals feel some or all of them very little. Observations of chimpanzees, the animal physiologically and psychologically most like humankind, suggest that while there is no religion among them, they do have an incipient capacity for feelings of meaning and depth. Among members of a chimpanzee band, affection appears to be shown by mutual stroking and grooming. Mothers and children are closely attached to each other; orphaned young fall into depression and decline even if food is still available. Mothers whose children die pass through a period of apparent grief.[5] This last illustrates a sense of a difference between the way things are and the way things ought to be, which among humans is a fundamental dynamic of religion and is related to the sense of inauthentic versus real self. It does not, however, become religion because the chimpanzee does not attempt to handle the desolation by, say, acting out ritually an alternative world stronger and more real than this one in which the child is *not* dead; she only feels the loss and the poignancy.

Here is an even more impressive story. A young female chimp named Washoe was brought up entirely by humans and was taught to communicate in the sign language of the deaf. She learned it remarkably well, acquiring some 350 words. Once, when the chimpanzee was looking in a mirror, her human mentor asked her "Who is that?" She replied, "Me, Washoe," in sign. Here, one feels, was a beginning of that awareness of self that has led humans beyond instinctual ritualization to feelings and behavior that, though they may sometimes be ritual, are intended to establish in one the sense of being a real self.[6] The discovery of selfhood is not religion because it is not a drama in which one acts out who one really is, but it is a tremendous step toward it.

### HUMAN RELIGIOUS BEGINNINGS

How did religion begin? This question that perplexed scholars of an earlier generation has not been definitively answered and is probably unanswerable. It is, however, probably unanswerable because it is put the wrong way. The words *religion* and *begin* are misleading in this question. In regard to religion, it was a long time before those elements of human culture and mentation we now call religion could meaningfully be separated from the totality of such processes as acquiring speech, conceptual thought, social order, and awareness of selfhood. Myth, magic, ritual, sacred art, and spiritism were not just a chapter in the process of becoming human, but in a real sense they *were* the process because fundamentally they were not adventitious beliefs or cult but tools with which to think, talk, and know about self and world. They were (and are) a kind of language. This is not to say that other aspects of life, such as improved hunting, toolmaking, and fire, were not important for the emergence of the earliest humans. These advances were probably *inseparable* in their discovery and continuation from the parallel discovery and use of concept and memory, and the formation of human

[5]See Jane van Lawick-Goodall, *In the Shadow of Man* (Boston, Mass.: Houghton Mifflin Company, 1971).

[6]Ibid., p. 250.

thought was *inseparable* from the use of mythic "pictures in the head" and ritual gestures as pegs on which to put thoughts and memories. Thoughts about birth, feelings, and death arose also; these too needed symbolic pegs in thinking and doing.

The idea of a beginning of human religion is equally misleading. There certainly was no single dramatic moment when it all started. Instead, as we have seen, humankind brought over from the animal world the raw material with which to make human religion, including instinctive capacities for ritual, hierarchy, and social morality; for territoriality; for play as a means of setting apart separate time and space for learning and creating paradigmatic situations; and for sensing depth and meaning in certain events. It remained, as the human mind undertook that strange and unprecedented expansion that endowed it with capacity for concepts and choices, to get all of these things together in a way that would help humans to think about and handle their world and above all themselves, their own turbulent subjectivity, now alive with memories, moods, and awareness of birth and death.

Let us imagine a scene at the very beginning of our human heritage. This scene is only an illustration, a kind of myth. We have stated that religion had no single dramatic beginning. It is not likely that new realizations came as precipitously as on this fictive morning, but let us watch anyway.

A splendid vista was spread under a brightly shining sun. The water of the lake was blue and sparkling that morning. On the far side, snowy mountains reflected the azure, but below it was comfortably warm. The trees of the forest reached down to the fringes of the water, and all was still. Nowhere was there sign or hint of mankind, no human structure or artifact. Yet this morning any gods there be might have felt in the breathless calm something momentous building up. It was as though something were waiting and growing more and more impatient, something that once it came would make numbered the days of the forest that had seen the winters and summers of eons of quiet years.

A two-legged figure approached the lake, stooped to drink, and then jumped onto a rock and sat still, looking into the water. He had eaten and rested. He had nothing to do and no strong urges at the moment, so he simply sat and looked. He was human, or almost so, though he may have been somewhat more slouched and hairy than we are. As he looked into the water, he saw a form. He moved his hands; they moved too. He grimaced; the face grimaced. Suddenly, in few words but with clear perception, a new thought struck him: This is I. I am an I, a creature who looks like this, can move his hands and face as he wants to, and can think. He may have put it differently, in the language of story: The spirit in the water imitates my spirit as a child does his mother. Nevertheless, it would still mean the same.

It was an exciting moment. Something about thinking of himself as a self brought a flood of memories and associations—he knew not why, but it did not matter now. He thought of his mother, his childhood tumbling and playing with the other young of his troop, and his first mating. It was rich; he kept thinking these things over and over as he looked at the face in the lake. Then another thought struck him with equal force. He thought of other creatures like himself who lay on the ground, grew cold, and did not move again. He thought, I am like them; *that* will happen to me someday. A chill, as though the beginning of *that*, shook through him, and he became still and solemn.

He thought of how sometimes it was light, then dark, then light again. Some things, he mused, go around in circles. Then he thought of when he was a child. He had left that and could not imagine becoming small and a child again. Other things, he considered, change and do not change back. Beyond that, he did not know what to think. Again, he may have thought differently—of magic (that is, anything that makes you feel strange and solemn) making the creatures grow cold and not move, of the times when spirits left and came back after sleep and of the times when they did not, and of the daytime as a spirit that came back after night passed. The excitement of what he had seen and thought returned. He stood up on the rock and let out a great yell. The forest and mountains echoed. Then he began to dance. He had danced before, but just because that was what his people did, especially when they felt sexual. Now he was dancing as he had played as a child, simply feeling full of energy and wanting to. The energy, however, came from his mind, as though a very great life with a name had come into him. Although he could not think it out very clearly, he danced to show the wonder and to forestall the dread in what he had seen and because it was a way to be the self he had seen.

Later, he would bring his own young to the lake, show them the reflection, teach them the dance, and tell them the story. The story was that his own spirit had left him in order to appear in the lake and to talk to him, telling him all about his growing up and the important things in his life. When spirits left the body and did not come back they simply went to live in the lake and could come back out of the lake, as the sun does out of the night, to fill people with life and make them dance.

The most important, distinctively human inputs into emergent religion were the discovery of death and articulation of memory, both coeval with language. Both were reinforced by association with the sacred and the numinous, as at the lake. Most likely both were first thought out through stories, as were all other complex ideas; we first think in stories because we learn sequence of action from the memory making one's past a story.

Stories themselves are a kind of language. When the development of language along with a mind powerful enough to use it opened up past and future as well as present, people began to query where all things had come from and what their destiny was. At first the answers were in terms of stories, just as our own memories come out as stories that help to tell us who we are today. We had to put word-symbols in the face of birth, life, and death, talk and chatter about them, tell stories about them, feel their glory or horror in new and different ways, and sometimes forget about them in the fascination of a tale. These stories were (at least the most significant of them) what is called in religious studies *myth*. Myth does not here mean a story that is not true. Rather, myth means a story that presents in the form of a narrative the basic world view of the society. Whether it tells of the world being made by the gods from the body of a monster or emerging from a cosmic egg or of the first men and women rising out of the ground, it tells a great deal about how the society views itself and about the relation of people to the universe.

Memory is a rough instrument in humans. We do not remember everything that ever happened to us with equal clarity but remember only certain things, generally those that have a major symbolic or actual bearing on who we think we are today. They are what has gone into making you or me real selves. In the same way, myth and religion do not remember everything just as it was in the sacred past, but concentrate on moments from the past that, clothed in symbolic significance, illuminate the present. Not every primitive society has stories about the beginning of the world or even of mankind, and far fewer have any idea of the ultimate end of the world. Nearly all, however, have narratives about gods, animals, divine ancestors, or heroes that help to explain who the people of today are. Most have some concrete idea expressed in myth and burial cultus about what happens to a person after death—for all humans have confronted death, and few are prepared to accept it.

## THE RELIGION
## OF PRIMITIVE HUNTERS

The earliest humans were hunters and gatherers. The hunt was very important to them and was a ritual affair. It was typically undertaken after fasting, dancing, and magic. After an animal was taken his spirit might be propitiated, for the archaic hunter saw himself as part of a web of life through which all souls, animal and human, circulated.

Another characteristic feature of primitive religion is initiation.

American Indians in Arizona performing a buffalo dance.

Typically all young men, and often young women, experienced an initiation into adulthood that involved isolation and pain, in effect a symbolic death and rebirth. It was a way of acquiring the society's knowledge of memory and death. Indeed, initiation was really a way of learning the symbolic language of the society, for initiates would be taught the myths in the context of experiences to reinforce them.

The most striking representative of early religion is the *shaman*. That is the title, derived from Siberia, given to a figure common in primitive religion (though not universal) who foreshadowed much of what religion was to become. The shaman is much the same as the person more popularly called "witch doctor" or "medicine man." The shaman, through a process usually involving going into an altered state of consciousness, is able to contact spirits, find lost or strayed souls, heal, and

ascertain the will of the gods, all the while providing a dramatic performance that in itself is a religious experience for his public.

According to commentators like Mircea Eliade, the most important
fact about the shaman is the means by which he comes to his office.[7] His
is not an easy accession through heredity or professional schooling.
Rather, the shaman has felt himself called out by the gods or spirits and
has then acquired mastery over them through an intense initiatory
ordeal. He has, in the process, felt himself torn apart, nearly killed, by
invisible entities. He has then gone through an arduous training to
control them—perhaps by a senior shaman, perhaps in dreams or visions, perhaps alone deep in the woods or mountains. As one Eskimo
shaman put it, "All true wisdom is only found far from men, out in the
great solitude, and it can be acquired only through suffering. Privation
and sufferings are the only things that can open a man's mind to that
which is hidden from others."[8]

As a result, the shaman is reborn a new person who is able to use
the spirits as supernatural allies. He is subsequently able to divine and
heal; often he enacts dramatic scenarios in which, entranced by the beat
of his drum or the throb of his chanting, he flies invisibly to the lands of
the gods and the dead to intercede or seek out lost and stolen souls. The
Altaic shaman in Siberia, for example, sacrifices a horse and transfers its
spirit into a wooden mount. For his public performance, he seats himself
astride it and beats his drum as he enters a light trance. When fully in the
spirit, he moves to a tree trunk, representing the axis of the world, to
which platforms have been attached—each of these stands for one of the
nine heavens. He climbs them, calling down to the assembled tribesmen
his dialogue with the gods at each level. This shaman also has a scenario
in which he rides his wooden steed to the underworld, bearing messages
to and from the departed souls of his people.

The shaman is a key figure in human religion and culture because
he early made the transition from the parareligious behavior of animals
to that of beings for whom religion is a quest for the real self. His call and
trances are individual and are given in his ecstatic chants and mutterings
a verbalized or artistic meaning. In many archaic societies the shaman is
the principal custodian and creator, out of his visions, of what art and
poetry there is. His vocabulary is often much larger than that of ordinary
people, and he is said to speak the language of birds.

The shaman's vocation is perhaps the first example of division of

[7]Mircea Eliade, *Shamanism: Archaic Techniques of Ecstasy* (New York: Pantheon
Books, Inc., 1964).

[8]Andreas Lommel, *Shamanism: The Beginnings of Art* (New York: McGraw-Hill
Book Company, 1967), p. 151.

labor in which an individual is set apart, and supported by the rest, on the grounds of a subjective experience he has had and for the sake of his contribution to the spiritual, psychological, and cultural good of the whole. However bizarre the shaman's behavior may seem (though the psychotherapeutic value of much of what shamans do is being increasingly appreciated), the paleolithic shaman advanced human society far along the road toward becoming the kind of community it now is. He healed mind and body, saw visions, told the future, spoke to the gods, made costumes and artwork rich with symbols from out of his preternatural encounters, and chanted the lore of the gods and the tribe. In his craft lay the seeds of those cultural growths that would lead to the physician, the psychiatrist, the scientist, the priest, the mystic, the magus, the poet, the artist, and the spirit medium. These callings are now quite diverse and not always temperamentally sympathetic to each other, but they have in common a creative use of the human power both to sense the beauty and relationships of inner processes as they come and go and to lay creative patterns from this inner loom over the outer world, even bringing others into the same web for their healing, joy, or enchantment.

Perhaps more than anyone else in earliest times, shamans articulated the most distinctive and striking idea in religion: the existence of gods, supernatural beings, or a supreme God. There is some evidence that the last idea may have actually been the first. Shamans, in their vision flights, were not bound by ordinary perception but met and even married spirits and gods who transformed them, or they encountered a high God who had made the world.

For a million years or more, human societies subsisted by hunting and gathering. As is always the case, the forms of religious expression were deeply interwoven with the economic sources of life. The animal, the source of economic life, was a symbol of the ultimate sources. Beasts were bridges from here to there and there to here. As sacrifices they were messengers from one world to another; as totem of a tribe they represented its life.

When looking into the animal's shining eyes, early mankind saw an ambivalent spiritual power with which he had to establish a harmonious working relationship, learning the skills and magic that would enable sufficient animals to be taken and the propitiations that would satisfy the spirits of the killed animals and their divine protectors, thus allowing them to return and be taken again. Over the years, as good a spiritual balance as one could hope for in this uncertain world was achieved by the hunting society. Human population was sparse and could not grow beyond what could be supported by a fairly mobile life of following game. While certain species, such as the giant ground sloth of North

America, may have been driven to extinction by paleolithic hunting, archaic hunters learned their ecological niche in the world and generally took no more than was needed. Also, men and women, leaders and followers, were far more equal in the small bands and tribes of archaic hunters than they have been in the more complex, male-dominated societies of kings and slaves.

## ARCHAIC AGRICULTURE

The next development shattered forever this equilibrium. It set humankind off on a course of meteoric growth and change that was very sudden from the perspective of geological or biological timetables. Population grew phenomenally, as it still sometimes grows, when fertile areas were suddenly able to support many times the people they could from hunting. Towns and finally cities appeared where once there had been only wandering bands, and empires where before had dwelt only tribes. Mankind was off on its careening ride in history as we know it, with its incredible misery and splendor and above all the rapid rate of change in the world—a world in its horrors and glories alike so different from that of animals or even primeval hunters.

The catalyst of all this change was, of course, agriculture. Planting and harvesting crops and keeping domestic animals meant a change in the way most people spent most of their time and in the relationship between them and the earth on which they lived. All of which was enough to cause the dramas in which people enacted their real selves to be revised.

Agriculture emphasized the idea (although the thought was not new) that the earth was like a mother; in the religion of archaic agricultural societies appeared a new emphasis on the mother goddess. The turning of the seasons, and the sacredness of place, understandably became newly important, for agricultural people were sedentary and bound to the cycle of seeding and harvest, expressed in anxious planting and protective rites and joyful harvest festivals such as that of Ise.

At the same time a darker side of spiritual experience also appeared. This was the relationship of death to life, the experience that blood and death were necessary for life to flourish, analogous to the seed that seemed to die and be buried in the soil or the animal whose slaughtered body gave life to many. Archaic agriculture was the milieu in which animal and human sacrifice, cannibalism, and headhunting most prospered.

As indicated, however, archaic agriculture also made possible a great increase in population. A given amount of land, if fertile, could support far more farmers than hunters. Furthermore, farmers were bound to one place and often dependent on organized systems of trade, irrigation, and defense against raiders. For this reason agriculture led to the creation of larger political units, particularly along the banks of great rivers where commerce and massive hydraulic works were feasible—the Nile, the Two Rivers of Mesopotamia, the Ganges, the Yellow River in China.

## ANCIENT EMPIRES

Let us imagine one of those ancient riverside empires, so important as transitions between prehistoric and semimodern culture. In their bosoms appeared writing, philosophy, and the great religions that still flourish.

Here, along the banks of a vast watercourse, a procession of singing priests is moving with the slowness of ancient ritual. Behind them, surrounded by courtiers, comes the king resplendent in gold cloth and green jade. He is making progress toward the vast burnished temple of the young god who returns to these riverbanks every spring and then grows old with the year. The sacred king opens the planting time by ritually plowing three furrows in the temple courtyard, while incense burns and trumpets blare.

The ancient empires above all idealized order, both human and cosmic, and the two were thoroughly integrated. For them, a real self— usually symbolically personified for all in the king—dwelt as harmoniously as well-tempered ritual or music with the seasons and the gods. Order was far from consistently achieved, but it was the ideal toward which religion, politics, and philosophy strove. That was understandable, for order was the apotheosis of agrarianism; what the farmer even today desires above all else of the universe is security and reliable seasons. The ancient empires, profoundly attuned to agriculture, wished a universe as regular as planting and harvest in a good year. Generally they held a concept of a universal law or regulating principle: Maat in Egypt, Rita or Dharma in India, T'ien or Heaven in China. It embodied the order, and gods above, like kings below, were themselves servants of order, and its exemplars and upholders.

One common institution of the ancient empire was sacred kingship. The sovereign would ritually fight and defeat the forces of chaos to create anew the world every new year, as in ancient Babylon, or begin the new planting season by wearing colors appropriate to the force of growth and creativity and by plowing the first furrows, as in China. The ruler, like the pharaoh or the Chinese emperor, was no mere political figure. He was a part of the divine order. He represented heaven—the sacred law and primal power—to his people, even as he represented them to heaven. His ritual actions, which occupied a large part of his time, were deemed crucial to society because they mystically harmonized human life with the power of the turning of the seasons and the life-producing work of the gods. It was usually felt that if the king performed his ritual and moral obligations wrongly, nature itself would respond with flood or drought and society with war or revolution.

The ancient empires also represented the beginning of widespread religious networks, for priests or scholars allied with the court were the king's representatives in far-flung provinces and incorporated the common people (and their gods) into the religious system centering on the king. The religion of the ancient empires exhibited a rich polytheism. Primitives had, to be sure, accepted a plurality of gods and spirits, even as they also often venerated a high god who represented the steady, creative, and regulative force. The ancient empires brought together many tribes, each contributing its own deities to a common pool. Furthermore, the increasing complexity and variety of the new imperial and urban ways of life suggested divine functions unthought of before. The pantheon tended to become a heavenly court that was a celestial model of the earthly, as in China, or a set of options for spiritual experience to match the many temperaments and ways of life of mankind, as in Egypt or India.

Polytheism came to full flower in the ancient empires. It meant not only that there were a great quantity of gods but also that spiritual life had a special quality. For the polytheist, the universe was a rich spiritual complexity with every time, place, and occasion having its own sacred meaning, being in a deep but finite sense its own spiritual center. It was in every grove, mountain, and hearth and in every hour whether of war or love, dread or rapture.

The old heritage of the shaman was perpetuated too. Teachers brought client or disciple through private initiations into a new sacred conciousness. The gurus of India and the mystagogues of the ancient Mediterranean were popular within ancient imperial societies, as they have been before and since. The related mystery religions of the Greek and Roman world spoke of the same quest; they offered elaborate rites, such as those of Eleusis or the Egyptian goddess Isis, to give recipients an assurance of salvation in the life to come.

That increasingly individualized quest for salvation points up a basic religious problem affecting the ancient world; the cosmic and social order it so deeply craved never seemed quite attainable. Things kept changing and would not change back. Try as one would, the old gods would not meet the needs of new generations, and even sacred kings fell as warlords marched back and forth across the earth. Old rituals of familiar tribes and groves faded before a new individualism. In this situation, many a person felt that seeking for personal salvation in a better world and adhering only to a deity who could provide it was the best one could do; let society and nature crumble away if they must.

Fundamentally, of course, what was happening was that a new image of what it meant to be a real self was emerging as experience taught new meanings for life and time. A person was not just a part of nature or of a sacred order ruled over by a sacred king but an individual who had to find salvation amid change and even chaos in a hard world. This was not fully understood consciously by everyone, to be sure, but it was what seemed to be suggested by the next great religious development, and the new forms of religious expression it brought—new kinds of religious thought, worship, and sociology that often had foci other than harmonizing with nature, the seasons, and the organic society presided over by a sacred king—even though much of the old world was incorporated into the new forms. The next stage was the work of the great religious founders and the great religions started by them, which persist into the world of today.

## RELIGIOUS FOUNDERS AND THE GREAT RELIGIONS

We cannot here discuss in any detail the history and teachings of the major world religions, and other books are devoted wholly to that task.[9] What we shall do is to name and identify the most important faiths and to discuss briefly the significance of their appearance in history around the time of the ancient empires and the principal stages of their development.

Hinduism is perhaps the most difficult to encompass in a few words, for it includes the vast complex of ideas and practices associated with the culture of India, from yoga to village shrines. While it has no single founder, its main philosophical and devotional traditions first emerged in roughly the same period as the founding of the other major faiths. Especially on an intellectual level, its main emphasis is on knowing the divine in all things and oneself and realizing this divinity through meditation or devotion to the gods.

Buddhism started in India with the teaching of Gautama, called the Buddha or Enlightened One (563–483 B.C.), but is now established mostly outside of India in Southeast and East Asia. Centering around the *sangha*, or order of monks who are successors of the Buddha's disciples,

---

[9]See, for example, Robert S. Ellwood, Jr., *Many Peoples, Many Faiths* (Englewood Cliffs, N.J.: Prentice-Hall, Inc., 1976).

Children worship and learn about religion in a modern Hindu temple in India.

Buddhism teaches that one attains liberation through meditation and related methods that counteract attachment to partial realities.

Chinese religion should be considered as a whole, even though it is comprised of several strands. Confucianism is based on the teaching of Confucius (551–479 B.C.), which emphasizes the good society based on virtue, family loyalty, and a respect for tradition and ancestors affirmed by solemn rites. Taoism, according to tradition ascribed to an older contemporary of Confucius called Lao-tzu, inculcates a more romantic and mystical path aimed at oneness with the Tao, nature or the cosmos. Buddhism and folk religion were also very important in China. Most prerevolutionary Chinese had some relation to all of these faiths.

Japanese religion is a comparable matter. Here Buddhism and Shinto, the veneration in lovely shrines of the polytheistic gods of ancient Japan, both have a place in the worship of most people. Confucianism has been very influential too, and more recently a number of new religions have flourished.

In the West, three great monotheistic religions have dominated the spiritual scene for centuries. All three worship a single personal God, and all are rooted in the spiritual experience of Jews in ancient Israel.

The faith that most directly continues this heritage is Judaism, found in the state of Israel and as a minority around the world. Believing

45

that God has a special calling for them in world history, serious Jews have kept their identity intact by being faithful to the moral and ceremonial norms of the Law and the passion for righteousness of the prophets.

Christianity traces its origin to the ministry of Jesus, called the Christ or Anointed One (about 4 B.C.–30 A.D.). Traditional Christianity is based not only on following the moral teachings of Jesus but also on belief that in Jesus, God worked in a special way for the salvation of humankind. Christianity has taken many forms throughout history, but all have been seen as ways of identifying oneself with God's work in Jesus.

Islam (the name means "submission," submission to the will of God) derives fron the ministry of Muhammad (570–632 A.D.) in Arabia. Believing that the Koran, the Islamic scripture, is the final revelation of God given through Muhammad, Islam is concerned with applying the teachings of God in all areas of life, from the Muslim's devout life of prayer to the organization of society. Islam is a simple, deep faith with both legal and mystical aspects.

These great faiths and the five or six human beings who have been founders of major religions have influenced human history far more than countless kings and kingdoms. On the other hand, kings and kingdoms have been deeply intertwined with their histories. Faith has provided integration for large and complex cultures such as those of India, Japan, and medieval Europe. Religions sweeping across many diverse lands (such as Buddhism, Christianity, and Islam) have carried innumerable cultural gifts with them and have helped missionized lands awaken into the mainstream of history. Sometimes, as in Western Europe, the great religion arose to power only toward the end of the ancient empire stage. Sometimes the great religion aligned itself with an empire (Buddhism in India) or even helped create one (Islam and the Damascus-Baghdad caliphate). In retrospect, though, we can see religion as gestating in the world of the ancient empires but finally helping people to transcend their perspective of sacred king and agrarian/cosmic cycles and to facilitate a sense of internationalism and history. This was particularly true of the three most intercultural faiths, Buddhism, Christianity, and Islam, together with Judaism.

It is significant that all these great religions center on a set of sacred writings or scriptures. They also center on a symbolic pivotal person— the Buddha, Confucius, Jesus, Muhammad—or a pivotal period of history. Even if one quibbles about how important the founder and the scriptures actually were in relation to other factors in the development of the religion, the religious meaning of the emergence of these two new symbolic centers of the sacred was of immeasurably great significance.

If earlier religions found the sacred in the animal, the plant, or the shaman's scenario, as sources of communal life, or in kings and gods, as sources of order, the new great religions found the sacred in a person and in a product of a cultural development, writing. In a symbolic individual, a particular point in the stream of history, and permanently recorded words, the transcendent appeared to put a grid of meaning over the chaos of human life. This change of symbols clearly reflected changes in human life and society and finally in the intuited meaning of what a real self was. The person and the word now transcend nature, plants, ecstasy, and sociopolitical units. The new sacred person and words about him or her go beyond all that, even as did the figure of Jesus for the girl at the beginning of our last chapter.

This period of transition when the founders and great religions emerged has been called by philosopher Karl Jaspers the "axial age." It was a time of transition fron prehistoric and ancient empires. People were barely aware of the movement of history and thought (or hoped) either that things had always been and always would be about the same or that time moved in great cycles. Now some came to understand that time moved forward in an irreversible line (or else in cycles as immense as those of Hindu and Buddhist thought). This was expressed religiously in the idea of a teacher who appeared at one particular point, like Jesus or Muhammad, making time after him in history profoundly different from life before him.

The beginnings of the great religions all have that kind of meaning and impact. In this way they were different from those religions that seemingly had always been. This axial age when the great religions began, lasting roughly from 500 B.C. to A.D. 500 was really only a short period in the long history of humanity. Yet only in it (or as far back as 1000 B.C., counting Moses in the same category) did the major religious founders appear and great world religions originate. They have spread and changed on a large scale, but no new religions of comparable dimensions have arisen since the birth of Islam some fifteen centuries ago.

Let us now trace, roughly and in outline, the stages of development through which the great religions have passed. Each stage can best be understood as presenting a novel sort of drama that interprets the meaning of one's real self.

The first period may be called the apostolic. It is the first few generations after the founder in founder religions. It is a time of expansion within a culture ostensibly devoted to other values. There is tension and perhaps persecution. It is a time of rapid change in the new religion and of deep-seated personality conflicts and doctrinal debates. Indeed, the forms the religion take in all the forms of expression are in flux. For a religion that is to survive, enthusiasm is even greater than these difficulties and prevails.

The next period is one of doctrinal and institutional consolidation, of stylization, after a measure of success has been gained within the sociopolitical order. This is Buddhism in the empire of Ashoka, Confucianism in Han China, and Christianity in the Roman and Byzantine empires after Constantine. There emerge councils presenting dogmatic definitions, forms of worship meeting the needs of both peasants and converted intellectuals, and institutional structure appropriate to the dominant imperial faith that parallels the state. The doctrinal forms are probably made to tie in with existing wisdom traditions but are deepened by new symbols from the erstwhile underground faith. One thinks of Han Confucianism, Christianity, and Islam in this stage appropriating forms from Neoplatonism and of Buddhism relating to Vedanta philosophy. The theological emphasis is likely to be a reaction against the radical discovery of history implied by the life and work of the original founder, and movement toward putting his message in terms of eternal truths that are behind all changes in history and behind the existing forms of worship and structures of society adopted by his religion.

This religious structure is then likely to form the basis of a great civilization, perhaps of new empires but more likely of smaller kingdoms linked by a common international religion. Within them, however, grow the seeds and then the flower of the next religious form, what may be called devotionalism. It is characteristic of high medieval religion in the Christian, Jewish, Muslim, Hindu, and Buddhist spiritual worlds alike. In bhakti in India, Pure Land in Chinese and Japanese Buddhism, or the Franciscan style of devotion in medieval Europe, the emphasis is on the ability of even the simplest to achieve the highest liberation through devotional fervor, faith, and love for God, saints, or buddhas and bodhisattvas—a goal that might take the wise infinitely longer because of their insistence on proper technique or theological wisdom. In a subtle way, medieval devotion undercuts the hierarchical structure of the medieval type of society by saying it does not matter what class or caste a person is, or how wise, so long as the person loves the Lord in his or her heart.

In the next stage, reform, there is an intensification of the devotional mood within a major segment of the religion to the point of a radical break with the tradition, ostensibly in favor of return to its original or pure essence. This generally occurs after about fifteen hundred years of development. One thinks of Kamakura Buddhism in Japan and its Pure Land and Ch'an equivalents in China between A.D. 1000 and A.D. 1500; the kind of radical Hindu bhakti represented by Chaitanya, spiritual father of the modern Krishna Consciousness movement; and the Reformation of Luther and Calvin in Europe. Perhaps Islam, only some fifteen hundred years old now, is about ready for this stage in conjunction with modernization.

The last stage we shall here consider may be called the modern. Unlike the previous stages, it does not occur because of the internal dynamics of the history of the particular religion but is necessitated by developments in the world as a whole. For the last hundred and fifty years or so, all the world religions have had to adjust to the whole panoply of developments we call modernization: the industrial revolution, Western expansion (and then retreat), a rapid pace of change, new scientific ideas, population growth, educational growth, the worldwide spread of consumerism, nationalism, and Marxism. They have reacted to all this in many ways. Different parties in each religion have, in fact, taken diverse tacks: rigid conservatism, reformism, sanctifying nationalism, thorough-going adjustment to the new. None, however, are what they were before.

One event of especial interest to us in the last stage of the history of religion (to date) is the emergence of the *study* of religion. The academic study of the history and comparative forms of religion as a phenomenon within human life, in contrast to its study from the point of view of one religion or another, is (with a few ancient exceptions) a new departure and one that owes much to the modern mentality and the pluralism (experience of many religions and lifestyles coexisting side by side) it has facilitated. We shall close this chapter with a review of some of the persons whose ideas have affected the modern study of religion as a general human experience. These persons and positions may be taken as representative of ways of interpreting what has gone before in this chapter, as the last stage in a religious process beginning with the amoeba, or, if one prefers, the first human.

## MODERN INTERPRETERS OF RELIGION

Friedrich D. E. Schleiermacher (1768–1834), especially in his earlier writings, presented a view of religion that has been quite influential in the development of its general study. He saw religion as starting from a special feeling of wonder toward and dependence on the whole cosmos. This high feeling can become clouded by sensuous feelings, or it can be enhanced by communication of it through powerful symbols and through persons filled with it, such as Jesus Christ. The feeling itself does not necessarily have anything to do with morality, rational knowledge, or any particular concept of God. These may come later, as ways of symbolizing and passing on the experience. Schleiermacher's teaching provided a way of objectively understanding the great religions and their symbols while maintaining empathy. These religions, he thought, had grown up around figures who have preeminently radiated the religious feeling. As symbol systems, they retain the aura of the feeling and so serve as means to turn it on again.[10]

The German philosopher Georg W. F. Hegel (1770–1831) viewed religion as a way in which the spirit within man becomes aware of itself as *spirit*, that is, as a manifestation of the One. Hegel's spirit ( *Geist*) can also be rendered "mind." Consciousness, the searchlight of spirit or mind within mankind trying to know itself, cannot find a permanent object for its concentration outside itself and so finally must turn back upon itself and discover itself as the One. Until spirit finally achieves this, however, it creates images, forms, symbols, and ideas (in a word, religion) outside of itself as guideposts and reflections of this quest. History, for Hegel, is a process by which spirit drives on to reach the stage of absolute knowledge, "spirit knowing itself as spirit." When this comes, religion, as a reflexive mediator of spirit's self-knowledge, is no longer needed. Whether or not one accepted the full Hegelian system, the ideas that the origin of religion lay in the mind's trying to know itself and that the history of religion was a history of the evolution of consciousness had profound consequences for the development of the study of religion.[11]

Wilhelm Dilthey (1833–1911), in his work on the history of ideas, stressed that the metaphysical systems of each age are symbols of the way the world was experienced by that age, just as are its art and literature. One can see that this kind of approach induces a mood of relativism that defuses the intense, anguished confrontation with decision others would feel ought to be a part of our traffic with ultimate things. But it also makes possible a more or less open appreciation of ways of faith and culture in all times and places.[12]

Karl Marx (1818–83), seeing Hegel's evolution of spirit to be manifest in social and economic history, combined that insight with Ludwig Feuerbach's (1804–72) theory of religion as a projection of human nature. Marx viewed religion as a product of a stage in human development in which inner contradictions are not yet completely resolved. It is basically alienation between classes of society that produces those psychological

---

[10]See Friedrich D. E. Schleiermacher, *The Christian Faith*, 2nd ed., trans. Hugh Ross Mackintosh and J. S. Steward (Edinburgh: T. & T. Clark, 1928); and *On Religion: Speeches to Its Cultured Despisers*, trans. John Oman (New York: Harper & Row, Publishers, Inc., 1958).

[11]See Georg W. F. Hegel, *The Phenomenology of Mind*, trans. J.B. Baillie (London: George Allen & Unwin, 1931); and *The Philosophy of History*, trans. J. Sibree (New York: Dover Publications, Inc., 1956).

[12]See H. A. Hodges, *The Philosophy of Wilhelm Dilthey* (London: Routledge and Kegan Paul, 1952).

aberrations that result in religious projection. For the exploiting classes, religion is a means of controlling the masses and also of justifying their own role. For the exploited, ideas such as heaven and hell and God's love are desperately desired compensations for a hard lot. As in Hegel's final era of absolute spirit, however, when there are no more contradictions, no more exploitation, the need and desire for religion vanishes.[13]

Emile Durkheim (1858–1917) expounded the cultural basis of religion in another way. Holding that religion is essentially grounded in communal life, he taught that religious feelings stem from the *social effervescence* of primitive tribal societies—from the sense of timeless joy and coherence created by the festival. Religious objects, persons, and practices—the sacred—were ways of creating and perpetuating the community that realizes itself in festival. For Durkheim religion is essentially a social feeling that can be created in any number of external settings. Thus, there is no religion that is false.[14]

The German Protestant theologian Ernst Troeltsch (1865–1923) believed, following Kant, that a religious *a priori*, or absolute, exists that cannot simply be explained away by sociology or psychology. Its expression, however, takes many forms in different cultures and personalities, none of which are in themselves absolute. His work in describing types of religious groups has been of great importance in the study of religion.[15]

Several of these strands of the social and cultural approach have been brought together in the work of Mircea Eliade. The title of one of his books, *The Sacred and the Profane,* is a key to his thought. Like Troeltsch, Eliade accepted that there is a religious absolute that is *sui generis,* of its own type and not reducible to anything else. At its core is humankind's yearning for transcendence of the ordinary, profane world of space and time, to share in the mythic and absolute world of origins, the other time when the gods made the world or heroes walked the earth. Times of religious festival and rite are sacred times that try to recapture that strong time; temples, holy mountains, and sacred trees represent sacred space, places set apart as ways of access to the other world. Sacred space and time may also by interiorized, as by yogis and mystics; a charismatic individual may him or herself be a sacred object.[16]

[13]See Karl Marx and Friedrich Engels, *On Religion* (New York: Schocken Books, Inc., 1964); and John C. Bennett, *Christianity and Communism* (New York: Association Press, 1951).

[14]See Emile Durkheim, *The Elementary Forms of the Religious Life,* trans. Joseph Ward Swain (New York: Collier Books, 1961).

[15]See Ernst Troeltsch, *Social Teachings of the Christian Churches,* trans. Olive

[16]See Mircea Eliade, *The Sacred and the Profane* (New York: Harper & Row) Publishers, Inc., 1961); *Cosmos and History* (New York: Harper and Row, Publishers, Inc., 1959); and *Patterns in Comparative Religion* (New York: Sheed & Ward, Inc., 1958).

Another style of interpretation of religion that has been immensely influential in modern thought has been the psychological or psychoanalytic represented by such thinkers as William James, Sigmund Freud, and Carl Jung. It is discussed in the next chapter. One kind of interpretation that must be presented here, however, as a counterbalance to the social and cultural is the existential and orthodox (better, neo-orthodox), which starts not with religion as a cultural phenomenon but as an absolute reality impinging on the subjective consciousness of an individual and forcing him or her to react and choose.

Soren Kierkegaard (1813–55), a Danish theologian, vigorously opposed Hegel. He said that religion is a *choice*, not just the way a spirit knows itself through the process of a long historical unfolding in which the ordinary individual might seem to count for little. The point is emphasized by the title of one of his books, *Either/Or*. One cannot know what the plan of God in history is because one could not know the mind of God. Religious faith is simply choosing God when the arguments for or against God seem more or less equally likely. The alternatives to choosing God are a life of merely seeking aesthetic satisfaction or of fulfilling ethical duty; both options carry with them the seeds of inner despair. Kierkegaard made possible for the history of religions, as well as for philosophy, a new way of understanding religion, not according to its social, cultural, or symbolic expression but according to the nature of the personal subjectivity—the way one is inside—of the one who makes the *choice* it demands. Subjectivity, he and the existentialist thinkers who followed him said, is a world of its own and can never be reduced to rationalized categories.[17]

The German theologian and historian of religion Rudolf Otto (1869–1937) perceived religion as experience of the holy, or the numinous, that is always mysterious, strange, tremendous, and fascinating. It draws men by its uncanny power, yet also fills them with dread. It has a weird, intrusive feeling and may be grisly and uncomfortable, yet men run from it in vain. In a person like Martin Luther, and likewise in the temples and taboos of religious people through the ages, Otto saw the marks of this kind of encounter with divine Otherness. Religion was, for Otto, a kind of feeling, but difference from mere aesthetics or moral feeling was heavily stressed. One can study the manifestations of this feeling in psychology and symbol, and in myth and idea, but only if one first recognizes its unique, autonomous nature.[18]

For the Swiss Protestant theologian Karl Barth (1886–1968) and his

---

[17]See Robert Btretall, ed., *A Kierkegaard Anthology* (Princeton, N.J.: Princeton University Press, 1951).

[18]See Rudolf Otto, *The Idea of the Holy*, trans. John W. Harvey (London: Oxford University Press, 1950).

followers, the uniqueness of the vertical experience with God was the central spiritual event. Only God can initiate it by revelation. All religions of human origin, whether in the non-Christian world or in the Christian church when it is not founded solely on God's revelation, are attempts by humans to anticipate God and reveal only their alienation from God. Religion, then, is really mankind's attempt to fill the void left by the absence of God due to human rebellion. Religious phenomena, insofar as they are not based on direct revelation by the Holy One, are of a quite different and lesser nature, though they may serve as reminders of the possibility of true spirituality and of human need.[19]

These are a few figures representative of thought in the latest stages of the history of human religion. Many other thinkers are of equal, or almost equal, importance to those cited. Indeed, the day in the sun of some of them is already passing, but they are so monumental in recent history—and so important are their ideas beyond the passing fads and fashions of thought—that they must have a place in even the most haphazard history of religion. At the same time, let the reader, reflecting on this story and these ideas, begin to think out his or her own interpretation of the history of human religion.

[19]See Karl Barth, *Church Dogmatics,* trans. G. W. Bromily and T. F. Torrance, eds. (Edinburgh: T. & T. Clark, 1956), vol.I, part 2.

Religion can stimulate special and deep states of consciousness like that of this Zen Buddhist monk in meditation.

## CHAPTER THREE

# OASES OF THE MIND: THE PSYCHOLOGY OF RELIGION

## MENTAL SHIFTS

The discussion of psychology of religion centers around the concept of different states of consciousness. That means different ways in which one is aware of oneself and feels oneself, together with the resultant shifts in the way one perceives the world.

In ordinary life we pass through many transitions of consciousness every day. To pass from sleep to wakefulness, or from sleep without dreams to sleep with dreams, is to go from one state of consciousness to another. So is passing, as one nods over studies, from focused attention to diffuse reverie. The state of consciousness during a game, to refer back to the discussion of play in the preceding chapter, is quite different from that in war or from the deadly serious hunt of a famished man. Intense emotional states, such as fear or rage, bring about their own state of consciousness. Psychological researcher Stanley Krippner has listed twenty basic states of consciousness that range from dreaming, lethargy, hysteria, and rapture to trance, reverie, and the expanded states of consciousness often (though not necessarily) induced by psychedelic drugs.[1]

[1]Stanley Krippner, "Altered States of Consciousness," in *The Highest State of Consciousness*, ed. John White (Garden City, N.Y.: Doubleday & Company, Inc., 1972), pp. 1–5.

Think of spending a summer day at the beach. The day may seem wholly uneventful and pointless except for relaxation and fun. Even on a day like this, though, one moves through a number of states of mind, most of which in fact have religious parallels. Strenuous physical activity such as swimming or playing ball makes the mind alert and under a certain tension to perform, and it bathes the mind in a mild joy as performance is achieved. In times of quiet reading, the mind is passively receptive and the body is relaxed. A special concentration and excitement ripples through one's senses when talking animatedly with friends, playing out conversation full of warmth and humor. Parents and children together at the beach feel the special warmth of enjoying one another in a situation of considerable freedom and lack of pressure. Finally, there are those contemplative moods that the beach seems especially able to induce. One looks at the enjoyment of others and the sun sinking over the sparkling water in an almost godlike way, and begins to intuit some sort of unity behind it all.

Our streams of consciousness are comprised of unceasing series of shifts like these. One can think of the mind as a piano or organ and of these transitions as the ongoing music. Musical possibilities are virtually infinite, owing to the great number of possible combinations of a much smaller number of notes and tempos. In the same way, the almost infinite shadings of consciousness we experience are the product of combinations of a smaller number of basics, like Stanley Krippner's twenty, with each other and with circumstantial factors.

The psychologist Charles Tart has devoted considerable attention to the study of states of consciousness. His work could well become fundamental to modern discussion of the psychology of religion. For Tart, consciousness is a system composed of various subsystems or elements, such as emotion, memory, time sense, perception, and motor activity. These subsystems and elements are continually adjusting and readjusting in relation to each other. A state of consciousness is the particular structure or configuration of the total system that results from the particular level or mode of activity of the constituents at the moment. This model enables one to show how a state of consciousness is created by the meeting of such diverse factors as culture, personal life history, current circumstances, perceptions (which may induce such emotions as fear or desire), and physiological conditions such as fatigue or illness.[2]

---

[2]Charles T. Tart, *States of Consciousness* (New York: E. P. Dutton & Co., Inc., 1975). See also Charles T. Tart, "The Basic Nature of Altered States of Consciousness: A Systems Approach," *The Journal of Transpersonal Psychology*, 8, 1 (1976), 45–54. In summarizing Tart's position I have been helped by Arthur C. Hasting's clear and concise review of Tart's *States of Consciousness* in *The Journal of Transpersonal Psychology*, 8, 1 (1976), 66–67.

Tart emphasizes that we should speak of *discrete* states of consciousness rather than *altered* states, insofar as the latter term suggests that one state is normal and others are alterations of it that represent deviations from a norm. All states of consciousness, including those we commonly call normal or ordinary, are constructed equally of combinations of elements and subsystems. None is more ordinary or normal than any other in the sense that its functioning is less conditioned by culture, emotion, memory, time sense, or physical state. In fact, the states of consciousness considered ordinary or normal are preeminently conditioned by factors such as these; they are the ones least in tension with cultural environment and best suited for living in interaction with it.

To call the workaday consciousness normal is to make the workaday world the baseline. Tart argues that states of consciousness cannot be called higher or lower, normal or altered, except in relation to some purpose, value, or need extrinsic to consciousness itself. Tart states further that each state of consciousness has its own specific laws and perspectives for observing the world and ways of perceiving the self; we need to develop "state specific" sciences for understanding these states. The same outward experience, he adds (one might suggest participation in a religious rite), could be accompanied by very different states of consciousness in different people.

The idea that different states of consciousness have their own reality and that moving from one to another can both provide valid knowledge of ultimate reality and facilitate self-transformation, becoming a real self, is fundamental to religion. Equally fundamental is religion's assumption that some states of consciousness are better—more valuable to these ends—than others and its provision of extrinsic guidelines for evaluating them. These presuppositions underlie religion's emphasis on such states as those of meditation, conversion, worship, and philosophic or moral reflection and characteristic denigration of strongly sensual or negatively emotive states. Each of these is an altered or discrete state of consciousness in the senses of Krippner or Tart.

In the first chapter, we took note of Robert Bellah's concept of religion as transcendent experience. This implies that religion is ultimately a particular kind of consciousness, rather than a particular sort of belief or activity. Religion is not so much affirming specific ideas or behaving in certain ways as it is thinking or doing almost anything when these things are thought or done at a level of consciousness that gives them transcendent reference—in other words, makes them symbols of a meaning-giving pattern and a relation to the ultimate source.

To be sure, religion is associated with some of the most striking human behavior, and some actions may be so uniquely religious it would be hard to think of them as anything else. This is not surprising if religion were partly defined as ideas and acts inexplicable in terms of meeting ordinary practical or biological needs. The unusual, even bizarre, quality of much religion (at least to outsiders to the tradition) is, however, itself a symbol—a symbol that it pertains to a sphere that *is* different and not oriented toward the ordinary, practical means and ends of this world but those of another. Religious acts indicate another kind of consciousness, transcendent in implicit intent at least (suggested by the indifference to this world shown in many religious acts). Indeed, much of religion is like a form of one of Charles Tart's state specific sciences for exploring a state of consciousness. Any of the visible phenomena of religion—liturgies, asceticism, methods of prayer, joyful hymns, or whatever—are ways of exploring and then acting out what the transcendent experience is like. The unusual behavior, however, implies a corresponding state of consciousness, though for behavior that has become routinized or merely cultural it is perhaps not intensely distinguishable.

Yet entering into a religious situation always, at least on a symbolic level, implies entering a different discrete state of consciousness. As we have seen, each discrete state of consciousness brings with it its own reality—its own bearings, its own directions of orientation, its own meaning of objects and acts (different from what they would mean elsewhere), and above all its own way of perceiving reality shaped by these different bearings—and so its own way of thinking. A rock in a temple may be a locus of divinity; a rock outside may be just a rock. Standing or kneeling in church may be praising or praying to God; outside it may be just standing to look out the window or kneeling to work in the garden. In religion, we may think of the world as sharply divided between saints and sinners, or believers and nonbelievers; outside the distinction may blur a little.

If religion means moving into (and later out of) a different reality, the process of moving in and out is of great interest. We need to reflect on this process and these realities.

### SUBUNIVERSES

Any concept of different realities interplaned with different states of consciousness is reminiscent of the great nineteenth-century psychologist William James' concept of *subuniverses*. For James, reality in any sense meaningful to humans was what interacted with our emotional and active lives. When something stimulated one's interest and so came into relationship with that person, the combination created a special reality, a subuniverse of meaning.[3]

[3]William James, *The Principles of Psychology* (New York: H. Holt & Co., 1890), vol. II, ch. 21.

James' subuniverses have more recently been explored by Alfred Schutz.[4] He sees our experience as made up of countless "finite provinces of meaning." The paramount one is the world of everyday life, or working world. It is the mode of experiencing oneself and the universe that is the point of reference for all others. (This may be true insofar as it is probably the reality created by the culture whose world view one accepts, and so is in practice the norm for evaluating other perceptions, but Schutz does not concern himself with the sort of cautions about speaking of ordinary or normal consciousness presented by Tart.) Schutz tells us there are other worlds too—"the world of dreams, of imageries and phantasms, the world of scientific contemplation, the play world of the child, and the world of the insane."[5] These each have a "cognitive style," a way of knowing, unique to that world, and so each creates a realm of experience with inner consistency, even if different from the cognitive style of working, or everyday life.

A particularly important point in Schutz's discussion is transition from working reality to one of the others. The transition, he says, is accompanied by a sort of shock, such as falling asleep to enter the world of dreams or awakening to leave it. The transition may be marked by signs that indicate one is suspending one reality in favor of another while reading or hearing a story, playing a game, or starting a ritual. Anyone who has known the subtle but meaningful inward jolt or transition that marks entry into a meditation state or the outward thrill of response to the drums or organ music or processional panoply opening a splendid religious service knows the meaning of Schutz's words for understanding religious states of consciousness and their entry. More intense examples would be the jerking phenomena often observed as shamans or mediums go into trance or the strong psychoemotional effects, sometimes experienced as rhythmic waves of feeling, that can accompany intense spiritual conversion or rapture.

Religion fully and enthusiastically accepts the reality of different states of consciousness. If it did not, it would not be easy for it to postulate, as it must, transcendent patterns and the possibility that the real meaning of things can be better perceived if looked at in other than the ordinary way. Peter Berger has said that religion is man's audacious attempt to see the whole universe as humanly significant. That statement implies that ordinary perception does not render the universe humanly significant but that religion's task requires looking at things in a non-ordinary way. Entering the reality of other subuniverses and their corresponding states of consciousness (for it can be postulated that different realities and different states of consciousness come and go together), it

---

[4]Alfred Schutz, *Collected Papers*, ed. Maurice Natanson (The Hague: Martinus Nijhoff, 1973), vol. I, pp. 207–59.
[5]Ibid., p. 232.

sees, for example, the same deity behind sea and stars as behind human love.

What religion does is establish a scale of values among states of consciousness. It says that certain states are highly valuable for perception of transcendent reality and for acting out the dramas in which one is a real self, and others are counterproductive to this end. Therefore, religion provides techniques and situations to induce the desired states and sanctions to discourage the undesirable ones. Religion is a matter of the mind, and with its continuing music of ongoing states of consciousness, the mind is an instrument on which one can learn to play different scores. Thus, states of consciousness are the raw material with which religion works, as an artist works with oils or clay. With states of consciousness, religion makes a picture of a real self in tune with infinite reality.

This artistry can work because the psychology of religion has certain principles. It is extremely important to understand that states of consciousness do not remain the same. Not only do they change, but also we humans appear to have a need for them to change. It seems to be almost a natural law that a particular state of consciousness sooner or later wants to be supplanted by a contrasting state—a calm contemplative state with an active one, a highly emotional state with a clear tranquil one. When these changes do not occur, it is a sign of severe mental illness.

Religion, therefore, can speak of getting to more desirable states of consciousness because all of us do have the experience of going through at least a limited range of different states and through the realities that accompany them. Moreover, the principle of alteration in states of consciousness indicates that we have a need for states and realities that contrast with what we take to be ordinary consciousness and reality, since every state wants to be followed by a contrasting state. The more monochromatic a person's life is, doubtless the more intense is that need.

There are innumerable people around the world who generally live practical, commonsense lives close to the soil and to family and friends. They are concerned mostly with crops and prices, buying homes and planning parties—except in certain religious situations, when events long ago and far away but kept alive in stories and temples arise in vivid color in their minds and conversation. They may perceive miracles or real-life dramas that repeat the power of those times today. This other world is a part, a necessary contrasting part, of the lives of crops, houses, and families. Just as the people need the commonplaces of life, they also need the states of consciousness that open doors to an alternative reality of prophets, gods, and wonders. Tradition, temple, music, rites, preaching, and feeling open invisible doors to that other world, utterly remote though it may be in time and place, that can brighten the skies of this world more than a thousand sunrises. Indeed, that other world goes into this one like milk and love, giving point to the institutions that cement families and communities.

## DEVELOPMENT AND CHANGE

Another feature of human consciousness that supports religion is our capacity for development and permanent change. Alterations of consciousness do not need to go around and around a limited cycle. People can experience changes in the whole structure of the cycle, and very often religion is the major symbolic factor in this change. Something in nearly everybody wants to find a way of life in which he or she knows a more desirable, perhaps because it is more intense, state of consciousness a larger part of the time. For this some turn to adventure, romance, or drugs. Others, feeling that religion deals in states of consciousness and with the highest and widest ranges of being, turn to it.

Sometimes the permanently changing effect of religion is sudden. Consider a young man following a very ordinary life—getting up, getting dressed, going to work or school, worshipping perfunctorily in the way of his people, eating, sleeping. One fine day he has an experience. A tremendous power enters his life, in a vision or jarring psychological experience along the road or at the back of the barnyard, and he knows that from then on his life will be entirely different. Afterwards, he leaves home, wandering and possessing nothing, yet (in his mind) possessing all things. In ancient times, he might have become a disciple of the Buddha or Jesus, in the Middle Ages a Franciscan friar or itinerant yogi or dervish, nowadays a missionary or Zen monk. The religion-connected change was fast and deep; the new states of consciousness that now ring his mind make him feel more like a real self.

The change may also be gradual and, rather than wholly spontaneous, may well be deliberately sought through turning to religion. Indeed, it is a mistake to think the sudden, unexpected conversion is typical. Without going into the issue of what sort of unconscious psychological preparation there may be even for a change as dramatic as Paul's on the road to Damascus, it is safe to say that most people are first drawn to religion by a hope for change, sudden or gradual, and that many subsequently find it.

On the other hand, personality change is not necessary to the practice of religion as such; there is also the way of those ordinary believers for whom religion is a contrast within normal life rather than a radically new life. Even when extensive change occurs, it may be more a spiritual parallel to the radical enough changes nature itself gives than something of a wholly different order.

Quite apart from any effects of religion, everyone's life is a series of immense changes. We move from infant to child, from child to adult, and from student to sage, from maiden to mother. All these require giving up one pattern of thought and life and taking on another. The reprogramming of mind and feelings is never easy. It requires effort, some tension, and probably some symbolic reinforcement through such means as graduation and wedding ceremonies. New titles and status may go with the new role to uphold the individual's sense of identity and meaning during a difficult adjustment.

Everyone who survives infancy goes through changes like these. In the course of these transitions almost everyone experiences significant problems, moments of poignant regret for what he or she is leaving behind, and the excitement of attaining the new. The adult may wish to be a secure and happy child once more, the harried mother a glamorous maiden again.

Here, in conjunction with the ordinary transitions of life, religion provides assistance. It does so in three ways that may appear contradictory but that nevertheless seem to work well enough together.

One way is to offer times and places for symbolic returns to earlier stages, such as childhood, under controlled conditions. It can hardly be denied that much of religion does suggest, in contrast to the ambiguous adult world, a return to the subuniverse of the child's perception of things. Morality may become simple rules, like those of the nursery. Practices such as kneeling, chanting, and singing simple songs symbolically hint at returning to the child's height and modes of expression. Pentecostalists often talk of their tongues as "babbling like babes," which shows the speakers are reborn "babes in Christ." For many people, temporary returns to the world of childlike values, actions, and perceptions is doubtless of great benefit in maintaining psychological equilibrium.

Yet religion also works to support adult life and to reinforce the idea that one can and must transit from earlier to later stages. It marks these transitions with rites like confirmation and marriage. It gives prestige to heads of families and the elderly, and it supports their authority. It portrays adult vocations as divine callings that must be exercised morally and cannot rightly be refused; they are parts of the pattern that makes each person within society a real self. These two sides of religion—the return to childhood and the sanctification of adult life—have some parallel to the equilibrium of ecstasy and constraints presented in chapter one.

Finally, religion contends that there can be religious parallels to the transitions of life. If one has found life after physical birth to be empty

The Jewish bar-mitzvah ceremony, when a young man first reads publicly from the scriptures and undertakes the spiritual responsibilities of adulthood, is typical of religious rites of transition from one stage of life to another.

and off-center, one can be reborn spiritually, start again, and make right what went wrong the first time out. If one has inadequately moved from childhood to adulthood, one can become an adult spiritually, doing right through a new process of spiritual growth what was done wrong when the process was only physical and social. Mystics talk of spiritual marriage to Christ or deities. Just as one can grow, learn, and marry in secular life, so can one do the same in spiritual life.

The greatest natural and spiritual transition of all is birth itself, apart from the equally great transition of death. Birth is the transition from nonexistence, at least in terms of this world, to existence. Beside the momentousness of this event, other transitions such as those of maturation or marriage pale.

It is no wonder, then, that religion has seized on birth and often made it the most important symbol of all of its dynamic side. The idea of rebirth is a concept around which the most powerful forces of religious psychology revolve. In this idea everything potent is pulled together. Through rebirth one is able to negate his or her previous life and to start again, doing right what then went wrong. This experience immediately suggests the reality of two contrasting modes of being and so of ordinary versus transcendent planes of reference. Rebirth suggests the return to childhood, indeed to the womb and the very roots of childhood, yet it also indicates sanctifying a new life here and now as an adult. It also infers a passing through a mysterious alternative reality, thereby indicating that one who is truly reborn has knowledge, if not mastery, of other realities. He or she is one who has spiritually passed through death and come back and has dealt with all significant corners of the sacred, has met the numinous and taken it into himself or herself, and has built the symbolic bridge from here to there. Above all, by being reborn he or she has been reborn as a real self.

Not all religion, of course, puts equal emphasis on the symbols and language of rebirth. But if it is interpreted broadly to include any extensive change in one's state of consciousness, whether sudden or gradual, rebirth seems an apt symbol for the dynamics of religion within personality. Rebirth can also be called initiation, and the rites of initiation are often full of rebirth symbolism. We do not speak of just those traditions in which spiritual rebirth is expected to be sudden and dramatic. In an arduous but gradual process like yoga, undertaken as serious spiritual training, much in the traditional literature suggests a psychic return to the womb, gestation, and reemergence as a new person with a new and powerful mode of being in the world. In all sorts of religion and amid all kinds of technique, however, the prevalence of initiatory and rebirth motifs reminds us that at heart religion is, in Frederick Streng's term, "means toward ultimate transformation."[6]

Indeed, virtually every religious tradition has some process of initiation, either for all members, for religious specialists, or for both. These are commonly rife with symbolism of dying and then coming to life again, or returning to the womb and being reborn.[7] One good example is Christian baptism. Going into the waters or into a grave and then emerging clearly represents, as the apostle Paul stated, dying with Christ and rising again with him. It also suggests returning to the watery depths of the womb and being reborn as a new person with new values and a new life.

Among American Indian tribes, such as the Algonquin of the Northeast, a young man undergoing initiation spends several days in a

[6]Frederick J. Streng, *Understanding Religious Life*, 2nd ed. (Encino, Calif.: Dickenson Publishing Co., Inc., 1976), pp. 7–9.

[7]Mircea Eliade, *Rites and Symbols of Initiation* (New York: Harper Torchbooks, 1965).

round sweat lodge. In its center is a fire, representing the center of the world, surrounded by rocks on which water is thrown to produce steam. While in this hut full of fire and steam, the initiate neither eats nor drinks nor sleeps. He does, however, occasionally smoke the sacred pipe and endeavor to travel to the realm of the gods, see a vision of his guardian spirit, and perhaps receive from him a new name. After this experience in the warm, dark, and mystical world of the lodge, he emerges, clad only in a blanket like a baby, and ritually receives his first food and drink.[8]

Yoga in India and elsewhere is a comparable process but enacted more within the self—although sacred environments and regimens reminiscent of the Algonquin are not unknown to yoga. Indeed, yoga as we know it has partial roots in ancient sacrificial rites centering on fire. Its main emphasis is on inward control of the mind and senses, and inwardly the yogi strives to pass through a mystic death and rebirth. After mastering techniques of posture and breathing that give him tranquility together with mastery over his moods and desires, he is able to withdraw his senses from the outer world and become unaware of external events. He then finds developing within himself a whole new equivalent of the nervous system and the mind, as though a new person were forming. The power of the new yogic man compared to that of the old is as a superman to a baby; he has access to marvelous psychic senses (the tradition tells us) that enable him to know and control things near and far, and his consciousness is bathed with a calm light beyond the keenest joy of ordinary folk.[9]

These examples suggest deliberate techniques for inducing subjective rebirth, or moving from one state of consciousness to another more desirable one. It is important to realize that much of religion consists of just such techniques and of the concepts that go with them.

It is equally important to balance that realization with the understanding that although experiences of transformation can be prepared for by prayer, study, meditation, psychosomatic procedures, and association with spiritually significant people, when religious experiences occur they feel unexpected and spontaneous. They are a breakthrough that liberates something previously dammed up within the self. Far from feeling induced, they may feel like the most free and genuine being the self ever had. One thinks of the great conversion accounts, from those of Paul and Augustine in the West and Chaitanya or Shinran in the East to modern converts like Charles Finney and John Newman. The experience may have been sudden or gradual; in many cases it can be convincingly argued there was unconscious preparation; it may also have been

---

[8]Evelyn Eaton, "Towards Initiation," *Parabola*, 1, 3 (Spring 1976), 42–46.
[9]Eliade, *Rites and Symbols of Initiation*, pp. 106–108

strongly suggested by factors in the cultural environment or by specific events in the individual's prior life. The fact remains, however, that conversion differs from something planned. It feels like a new and unexpected gift, a grace. Instead of merely employing a technique based on an already accepted world view (though this may come later, as the convert endeavors to hold or recapitulate his experience), it moves the recipient into an altered world view and behavior pattern along with the new state of consciousness.

This does not mean conversion needs to be a surge of uncontrollable feeling. Many of the most famous converts have, in their sensitive spiritual questing, eschewed mere feelings in favor of intellectual conviction or a calm, sure certainty beyond emotion. This quality is evident in the following letters of John Henry Newman, the distinguished nineteenth-century clergyman of the Church of England who became a convert to Roman Catholicism and later a cardinal in that church. The following was written during the final stages of his rather prolonged and inwardly agonizing process of decision to enter the Roman Catholic Church:[10]

> 1. *November 7, 1844. I am still where I was; I am not moving. Two things, however, seem plain, that every one is prepared for such an event, next, that every one expects it of me. Few, indeed, who do not think it suitable, fewer still, who do not think it likely. However, I do not think it either suitable or likely. I have very little reason to doubt about the issue of things, but the when and the how are known to Him, from whom, I trust, both the course of things and the issue come. The expression of opinion, and the latent and habitual feeling about me, which is on every side and among all parties, has great force. I insist upon it, because I have a great dread of going by my own feelings, lest they should mislead me. By one's sense of duty one must go; but external facts support one in doing so.*

> 2. *January 8, 1845. What am I to say in answer to your letter? I know perfectly well, I ought to let you know more of my feelings and state of mind than you do know. But how is that possible in a few words? Any thing I say must be abrupt; nothing can I say which will not leave a bewildering feeling, as needing so much to explain it, and being isolated, and (as it were) unlocated, and not having anything with it to show its bearings upon other parts of the subject.*

> *At present, my full belief is, in accordance with your letter, that, if there is a move in our Church, very few persons indeed will be partners to it. I doubt whether one or two at the most among residents at Oxford. And I don't know whether I can wish it. The state of the Roman Catholics is at*

---

[10]John Henry Newman, *Apologia pro vita sua* (London: Longmans, Green, and Co., 1887), pp. 230–31.

present so unsatisfactory. *This I am sure of, that nothing but a simple, direct call of duty is a warrant for any one leaving our Church; no preference of another Church, no delight in its services, no hope of greater religious advancement in it, no indignation, no disgust, at the persons and things, among which we may find ourselves in the Church of England. The simple question is, Can I (it is personal, not whether another, but can I) be saved in the English Church? Am I in safety, were I to die to-night? Is it a mortal sin in* me, *not joining another communion?*

*P.S. I hardly see my way to concur in attendance, though occasional, in the Roman Catholic chapel, unless a man has made up his mind pretty well to join it eventually. Invocations are not required in the Church of Rome; somehow, I do not like using them except under the sanction of the Church, and this makes me unwilling to admit them in members of our Church.*

*3. March 30. Now I will tell you more than any one knows except two friends. My own convictions are as strong as I suppose they can become: only it is so difficult to know whether it is a call of reason or of conscience. I cannot make out, if I am impelled by what seems clear, or by a sense of duty. You can understand how painful this doubt is; so I have waited, hoping for light, and using the words of the Psalmist, 'Show some token upon me.' But I suppose I have no right to wait for ever for this. Then I am waiting, because friends are most considerately bearing me in mind, and asking guidance for me; and, I trust, I should attend to any new feelings which came upon me, should that be the effect of their kindness. And then this waiting subserves the purpose of preparing men's minds.*

The following, somewhat different account, much more fervent and sudden, is that of the American evangelist Charles Finney, a contemporary of Newman:[11]

*I went to my dinner, and found I had no appetite to eat. I then went to the office, and found that Squire W— had gone to dinner. I took down my bass-viol, and, as I was accustomed to do, began to play and sing some pieces of sacred music.*

*But as soon as I began to sing those sacred words, I began to weep. It seemed as if my heart was all liquid; and my feelings were in such a state that I could not hear my own voice in singing without causing my sensibility to overflow. I wondered at this, and tried to suppress my tears, but could not. After trying in vain to suppress my tears, I put up my instrument and stopped singing.*

*After dinner we were engaged in removing our books and furniture to another office. We were very busy in this, and had but little conversation all the afternoon. My mind, however, remained in that profoundly tranquil state. There was a great sweetness and tenderness in my thoughts and*

[11]Charles G. Finney, *Memoirs* (New York: Fleming H. Revell, 1876), pp. 18–21.

*feelings. Everything appeared to be going right, and nothing seemed to ruffle or disturb me in the least.*

*Just before evening the thought took possession of my mind, that as soon as I was left alone in the new office, I would try to pray again—that I was not going to abandon the subject of religion and give it up, at any rate; and therefore, although I no longer had any concern about my soul, still I would continue to pray.*

*By evening we got the books and furniture adjusted; and I made up, in an open fire-place, a good fire, hoping to spend the evening alone. Just at dark Squire W——, seeing that everything was adjusted, bade me good-night and went to his home. I had accompanied him to the door; and as I closed the door and turned around, my heart seemed to be liquid within me. All my feelings seemed to rise and flow out: and the utterance of my heart was, "I want to pour my whole soul out to God." The rising of my soul was so great that I rushed into the room back of the front office, to pray.*

*There was no fire, and no light, in the room; neverthless it appeared to me as if it were perfectly light. As I went in and shut the door after me, it seemed as if I met the Lord Jesus Christ face to face. It did not occur to me then, nor did it for some time afterward, that it was wholly a mental state. On the contrary it seemed to me that I saw him as I would see any other man. He said nothing, but looked at me in such a manner as to break me right down at his feet. I have always since regarded this as a most remarkable state of mind; for it seemed to me a reality, that he stood before me, and I fell down at his feet and poured out my soul to him. I wept aloud like a child, and made such confessions as I could with my choked utterance. It seemed to me that I bathed his feet with my tears; and yet I had no distinct impression that I touched him, that I recollect.*

*I must have continued in this state for a good while; but my mind was too much absorbed with the interview to recollect anything that I said. But I know, as soon as my mind became calm enough to break off from the interview, I returned to the front office, and found that the fire that I had made of large wood was nearly burned out. But as I turned and was about to take a seat by the fire, I received a mighty baptism of the Holy Ghost. Without any expectation of it, without ever having the thought in my mind that there was any such thing for me, without any recollection that I had ever heard the thing mentioned by any person in the world, the Holy Spirit descended upon me in a manner that seemed to go through me, body and soul. I could feel the impression, like a wave of electricity, going through and through me. Indeed it seemed to come in waves and waves of liquid love; for I could not express it in any other way. It seemed like the very breath of God. I can recollect distinctly that it seemed to fan me, like immense wings.*

*No words can express the wonderful love that was shed abroad in my heart. I wept aloud with joy and love; and I do not know but I should say, I literally bellowed out the unutterable gushings of my heart. These waves came over me, and over me, and over me, one after the other, until I recollect I cried out, "I shall die if these waves continue to pass over me." I said, "Lord, I cannot bear any more;" yet I had no fear of death.*

*How long I continued in this state, with this baptism continuing to roll over me and go through me, I do not know. But I know it was late in the evening when a member of my choir—for I was the leader of the choir—came into the office to see me. He was a member of the church. He found me in this state of loud weeping, and said to me, "Mr. Finney, what ails you?" I could make him no answer for some time. He then said, "Are you in pain?" I gathered myself up as best I could, and replied, "No, but so happy that I cannot live."*

Many conversions, particularly those as apparently sudden as Finney's, have involved significant symbols that seemed to trigger the transformation. St. Augustine heard a child chanting in a singsong voice from some neighboring garden, "Take and read, take and read," and opened a New Testament to a passage that deeply changed his life. Hui-neng, a Ch'an or Zen patriarch of the seventh century A.D. in China, sold firewood to support his mother after his father's death. One day he carried wood to a customer's shop. As he left he saw a man reciting a sutra. It was the Diamond Sutra, with such lines as the following: "As the raft is of no further use after the river is crossed, it should be discarded. So these arbitrary conceptions of things and about things should be wholly given up as one attains enlightenment. So much more should be given up conceptions of non-existent things, and everything is non-existent." Hui-neng was immediately awakened. He talked with the man and found he was a monk from a certain monastery. After provision was made for his mother, the young Hui-neng left to joined the monastery and eventually become one of the most influential figures in the history of Chinese Buddhism and Zen.[12]

A modern spiritual figure of India, Meher Baba, first awakened to his spiritual vocation from a rather ordinary student life when, at the age of nineteen, he passed a famous and very aged Muslim female saint called Hazrat Babajan. She was sitting under a tree but silently arose and embraced the young man unexpectedly. Not a word was spoken, but from then on the youth's life was deeply changed. He visited her every day for a time thereafter and soon was spending many hours in deep meditation.[13]

---

[12]Charles Luk, *Ch'an and Zen Teaching* (London: Rider & Co., 1962), vol. 3, pp. 19–20.

[13]C. B. Purdom, *The God-Man* (London: George Allen & Unwin, 1964), pp. 18–19.

## AWARENESS OF SELF

So far our reflections on the psychology of religion have led to the following observations: (1) human beings are capable of different states of consciousness; (2) religion accepts this fact enthusiastically and is concerned with distinguishing the states and giving them differing values; (3) religion offers techniques and symbols for inducing or giving meaning to changes in consciousness of religious significance. These operations of religion work against the background of the changes of consciousness that inevitably occur with human growth and alterations in life. Life is a series of initiations—of developmental changes, natural or induced, that produce lasting changes in one's *patterns* of states of consciousness, or at least in the meaning and symbolization one gives them—from birth through education, marriage, and parenthood. Religion relates itself to this process of initiation both by providing occasions of release from its inevitable tensions and by providing parallel ritual or psychologically transformative initiations with religious symbolic completion—rites for transition in life, rebirth, and conversion experiences. We next look at some important states of consciousness to see what meaning religion gives to them.

First, we must look at who will be doing the looking. The examination of one's own states of consciousness is in itself something like a discrete state of consciousness, one of introspective mood. It demands that we begin the exploration by awareness of what we are and through what filters we perceive ourselves.

How do we think about what we are as selves? What is the meaning of self in an expression such as scenarios for the real self? Most of the time most of us undoubtedly hold a commonsense definition of self. We see it as a center of sensory and emotional awareness illuminated by conscious cognition and bounded in time by birth and death. You know that you exist because you are able to see, hear, touch, smell, and taste things outside yourself, can feel emotions within yourself (the self being spatially identified with the body), and have a center of awareness that is conscious of all this and reflects on it. Together with this comes an awareness that the self came into being through a process called birth at a specific point in time and terminates at a point called death. Furthermore, you are aware that your own self is given distinctiveness within the human race because you have a unique pattern of memories; even though some other people may be quite a bit like you, no one else has had exactly the same experiences as you.

Moreover, within certain limits, you have a unique pattern of probabilities in emotional responses and thought-sequences. Owing to a complex interaction of memories, heredity, culture, and happenstance, no one else is going to think or respond to things exactly as you do.

Finally, you are a self because you can make free choices and decisions and doing so makes you feel like a self. Precisely to what extent one's choices are free can be debated endlessly, but most of us feel that despite all the conditioning we have significant freedom.

Yet it is also the ways in which we are bounded—being tied down to a particular body located at a particular point in space and time, caught between birth and death—that make us feel like selves. We may be limited by these factors, but we are also each aware that no other self occupies exactly that same place. We are finite but unique as separate humans.

When we reflect on our own natures as selves, it is likely to be with results like these, excluding the input of philosophical or religious tenets. Further reflection, however, shows that many of these ideas are not really given out of one's inner nature but acquired by an intricate interaction of self with others, beginning with parents, in the context of one's culture.

For example, the notion that one is bounded by birth and death is not immediately self-evident (no one remembers his own birth or can literally foresee his own death) but is a concept socially learned and rationally deduced by analogy of oneself with others. Parents and others tell one about birth and death, and one deduces from observation that he too is susceptible to them. Birth and death, then, as facts known about oneself, are really constructs of language, culture, and reason, not the immediate awareness of knowing one has fingers and toes and can be hungry or sick. This is a fact not without significance—all the more so since religion, as a means of social construction of reality, seems to be greatly concerned with birth and death and gives them all sorts of symbolic transmutations.

The same is true, though, of other aspects of one's self-awareness (or better, one's self-construction—that is, telling oneself a story about oneself and developing a vocabulary that explains, to oneself above all, who one is). Memory, out of which all self-construction is built, is an acquisition partially taught (children are told "be sure to remember this") and partially created by subjective selection of those things to remember that in some way help one to know who one is (meaning in large part who one is in the culture within which he or she must function). We neither remember *everything* that ever happened to us, nor consciously think of *everything* that is characteristic of us when we try to think about what kind of person we are. Only certain things that seem important are remembered. The selection is for the purpose of constructing a coherent story, or personal myth, that explains on the basis of the past who we are today (memories of religious experience can be a very important part of such a story) or gives each of us an identity both relational and distinctive in the context of the culture. We usually want both to find identity in our culture and to maintain ourselves as a self by having some areas of distinctiveness from it. Thus, we think especially of things that place us in the culture—degrees, job, and so forth—and personality quirks by which we rub against it. These components of self-awareness extend from obvious things such as clues of one's social or educational class to memories that enable one to give oneself such subjective tags as "I'm a person who likes beefsteak."

The point is that self is not really a given, except perhaps as raw material, but is a construction always in progress, derived from a complex interaction of environment, biology, society, and personal history. Out of all this the self is making itself. Because the process goes on through several stages (the experience of self is not identical in infancy, childhood, adolescence, and adulthood), the idea of a real self other than any of them, or perhaps absolutizing the stage one liked best, becomes possible. It is what we feel all these changes are moving toward or trying to express. Here it is that religion, with its symbols and techniques for inducing new, or lost, stages of consciousness can come in. Again, religion finds its advantage in the fact that states of consciousness are continually changing, both developmentally and around daily cycles.

Nonetheless, who we are in everyday life is the result of self-awareness and self-construction, of trying to put down some anchors in this sea of change and process. They influence the way we make ordinary decisions in life—how to spend money, plan a career, enjoy a free weekend. Because they pervade what for the individual is an ordinary outlook and state of consciousness, they provide something that consciousness wants to alter; as we have seen, every state of consciousness wants to call up something to contrast with it. Many of these contrasting states are not understood as religious, but some may be. Even though they work through some of the constructs of self-awareness consciousness, such as knowledge of birth and death, the contrasting states —especially religious ones—may seek to negate the finitizing meaning of that knowledge through states of consciousness of higher value than those that merely *know* of birth and death, that is, states transcending them.

## RELIGIOUS STATES
## OF CONSCIOUSNESS

Psychologist Abraham Maslow has called one state of consciousness that favorably contrasts with self-awareness consciousness the *peak experience*. [14] While Maslow's peak experience is not explicitly

[14]See Abraham Maslow, *Toward the Psychology of Being* (New York: Van Norstrand Reinhold Company, 1968); and *Religion, Values, and Peak Experiences* (Columbus, Ohio: Ohio State University Press, 1964).

or necessarily a religious state, he has taken pains to show its general similarity to the experiences reported by religious mystics in the past. It is primarily the feeling of joy and creativity that comes to anyone at high moments, whether in something done well, love, or spiritual ecstasy. It is a state suffused with absolute being, sufficiency, wholeness, and effortlessness. In a peak experience, Maslow says, a person feels integrated, able to fuse with the world, at the height of his or her powers, spontaneous, natural. Creativity flows out of the person and he or she needs nothing outside of himself or herself. Because the person has no sense of dependence or goal - orientation toward anything outside, he or she is complete within and so has little sense of time or space since there is nothing to drag the person out of where he or she is. It is akin to joyfully playing a piece of music one has mastered, so that the performance seems effortless. The person in a peak experience often has a sense of luck, fortune, or grace.

The ways in which this state can offer a contrast to ordinary self-cognition should be obvious. Here is a condition in which, for the moment, meaningful awareness of bounding by birth and death, and the stress engendered by unfulfilled needs, falls away. When you are swimming, skiing, loving, writing, painting, reading, or just contemplating and there wells up a sense of deep fullness in the here and now so great it needs no outside justification, that is the peak experience. Give it a religious content, call it an experience of God, and it is explicitly a religious experience. Intense conversion and mystical experiences have peak experience qualities (although they may include others too, such as intense awareness of guilt, especially related to the religious content). Both involve a melting down, so to speak, of the ordinary structures of thought shaped by self-cognition or self-awareness, thus enabling these structures to be reformed. One emerges from the experience with new systems or states of consciousness and new symbols to stimulate them interiorized.

This is what really happens psychologically during an initiation, rebirth experience, or conversion such as those previously described. The anthropologist Victor Turner, following the classic work of Arnold van Gennep, has distinguished three stages of initiation: separation, liminality, and reaggregation.[15] The Algonquin Indian initiate, for example, first passes through a process of separation from ordinary life—he undergoes a preliminary fast and purification, then enters the hut. Next followed the most interesting state, the liminal, or marginal, state of the novice during the heart of the transition, when he was in neither his former nor his new status, but was cut off from both as well as from the

[15]Victor Turner, *The Ritual Process* (Chicago: Aldine Publishing Co., 1969), chs. 3–5. See also Arnold van Gennep, *Rites of Passage* (Chicago, Ill.: University of Chicago Press, 1960).

mode of existence on which ordinary self-awareness or self-cognition is based. He was in a place with virtually no contact with the structural world but open to the depths of his consciousness and to the gods. The liminal state is tomorrow's knight during his nocturnal vigil, a future king during his coronation, the novice in the initiatory lodge.

In a broader sense, Turner points out, certain categories of people are in a permanent state of liminality against the structures of society: outcasts, monks, hoboes, unassimilated minorities, alienated youth, or whoever finds his or her role to be on the borders or margins of structure. Often this role, as in the case of the monk or holy man, may be a symbolic gesture toward antistructure accepted and semiritualized by society, and so (like initiation) is a part of its structure in a larger sense. Nonetheless the liminal person is in principle not bound by all of society's rules or a participant in all its privileges and thinks thoughts of a different sort since he or she is oriented toward different values. The liminal person serves as a standard symbol of the possibility of alternative ways of life and climates of consciousness, as do all sorts of people in American life from Trappist monks to black jazz musicians. Also, at certain times or occasions, groups of people, or society as a whole, enter a state of liminality in comparison with ordinary life—in festival or carnival, in pilgrimage, in revolution.

The ordinary initiate, however, only briefly passes out of structure into antistructure, with the aim of returning to the same structural world as a person changed within. The initiate is, as we have seen, spiritually reborn; he or she has returned to the forge of his or her making and has built new structures out of the breaking-down of previous ones. The new structures include the purport of the divine vision and the new name. The initiatory experience, in other words, functions to induce a transition state comparable to that of a peak experience. Both provide an alternative to ordinary self-cognition.

The conversion experiences already discussed, which could be called spontaneous initiations, are an important subcategory of transformative peak experience. Regardless of their cause, they also break down previous self-cognition, as do peak experiences, and facilitate new identity constructions. What seems to happen *psychologically* in conversion and related experiences (much more can be happening on other levels, of course) is that a buildup of emotional stimulation caused by conflict, anxiety, depression, or simply the excitement of something new causes an overload that blurs the ordinary self-cognition self, with all its sense of limits and qualifications. Issues are reduced to very simple, strong, primordial choices; symbols emerge with decisive power. In this fluid situation, the personality can be turned around to focus on a new symbol as representative of the new self; choices that before seemed too complex can now be made because they are simplified into polarities. For the mind, then, conversion is a kind of rebirth; it goes some distance back toward the unshaped plastic of the newborn's mind and is remolded.

At the same time, it should be observed that the conversion process can be more apparent than real. Important subsystems of consciousness can remain in place, with only their direction and conscious symbolization changed. A Dwight L. Moody's drive for success in business, for example, can be changed to a drive for evangelistic success.

Another state of consciousness related to the peak experience is the meditation state. Meditation is basically a pleasant and restful quietness or stillness of mind. It may involve imagery (of a religious nature, if the meditation is religious), or it may be focused on a chant, point of visual concentration, or a formless mental quietude. Claudio Naranjo and Robert Ornstein have defined meditation still more broadly. It is, they say, a quality that infuses whatever is done, be it worship, sitting, dance, or play, through a *dwelling upon,* that is, a stopping of the mind on a single thing.[16] This singleness makes one feel he or she is living close to the ground of consciousness and so is a real self. Meditation, whether in prayer or dance, is a common religious way of perpetuating or recovering or, one could say, enjoying the effects of a transformative experience.

Still another religious state of consciousness, related to the foregoing in a negative way, is guilt. A sense of guilt—that is, of severe dislocation between what one feels oneself to be and one's ideal self-image—is a state of consciousness markedly different from both ordinary self-cognition and the peak experience. It implies an intense, feeling-laden state of introspection. In it, as in conversion, values are polarized into broad-gauged blocs of feeling, essentially good versus bad, with the present self identified with the bad. One can continue in a state of moderate guilt for some time and be motivated by it to a high level of religious activity that simultaneously activates and alleviates it. The guilt state can also lead to conversion, especially as it becomes intense. It is perhaps less likely, psychologically, that a person with a strong sense of guilt would be successful in meditation or other peak experience, since they fundamentally require a positive valuation of the accessible self. It can be observed that religious traditions in which the guilt state is prominent tend to stress active or emotionally intense forms of religious expression more than meditation.

[16]Claudio Naranjo and Robert Ornstein, *On the Psychology of Meditation* (New York: The Viking Press, Inc., 1971), pp. 8–12.

Often, religion is also connected with a state of consciousness centered on a sense of immense power. One may emerge from initiation or conversion feeling that he or she has transcended all ordinary limits and is full of great power, immune to what can hurt and able to do almost anything. The power state of consciousness may result from the very close identification of self with the paramount symbol that the rebirth experience can afford, so that symbolically one *is* Christ or Buddha and is as immune and transcendentally powerful as he; or it may simply be that because one has enjoyed the sort of peak experience that alternates with ordinary self-cognition, he or she is infused with the alternative consciousness's indifference to the normal awareness of bounding and finitude.

Another characteristic religious state that can be psychologically defined is attachment or dependency. The religious personality frequently attaches itself in an emotionally powerful way as a disciple to a particular person, a savior, teacher, or guru. The attachment can also be to a particular symbol, idea, or slogan that is emotively powerful, perhaps one that emerges in a transformative process. One can see religious dependency psychologically (again, much else may be operative on levels beyond the psychological) as a process interiorizing something initially outside the self as a pivot around which the consciousness system revolves. Because the symbol is still outside as well, continual contact with it is needed to maintain the pivot in a central place, at least until it is well fixed. Thus, desciples may spend several years in almost continual attendance upon their master, then leave and not see him again physically for many years. Yet they continue to keep him in mind and heart, worship him from far off, and perhaps believe he is still teaching and guiding them in their thoughts.

Two very common religious beliefs are clearly affirmations of the peak experience. The nearly universal belief that, in some way or another, one's existence is not exhausted of meaning with physical death has psychological relationships with those higher states of consciousness that negate the ordinary sense of bounding by birth and death. In nearly all religious tradition there is a concept of continuing personal existence, in heaven or hell, in a reincarnate state, or in a realm of continuing spiritual growth. (This is true even in Hinduism and Buddhism; most people have many more lives to lead before attaining the ultimate transpersonal Nirvana state.) It is a way of affirming the awareness, especially strong in peak experience or even guilt and dependency states, that there is more to life than the ordinary, that one's real self is unbounded. The internal awareness is perhaps deeper and stronger than the formal doctrine or belief, but however the latter is put, it is a way of affirming the primal and normative value of certain states of consciousness.

The dependency relationship between master and disciple is suggested by this modern Chinese print of the sage Confucius and seventy-two scholars of his school.

The same can be said, psychologically, about another very basic religious affirmation, of the existence of a God or gods. If one looks at God or gods from the perspective of the psychological meaning of belief in divine beings, one can see that they can represent models of the unbounded or peak state of consciousness, since that is the consciousness that deities themselves are generally said to have—unbounded by birth or death and without human limits on knowledge or power. It is as though a deity, or a figure like a Buddha, lives in the peak experience state all the time and wholly fulfills the promise of one's moments of sensing power and immortality. Insofar as one identifies with the deity, the object of much traditional religious devotion, one shares in his or her plenitude of consciousness. Even if one is simply attached to the divine figure, the latter becomes a symbol around which one's own high experiences can form.

## PSYCHOLOGICAL INTERPRETATIONS OF RELIGION

For the father of psychoanalysis, Sigmund Freud (1856–1939), religion was a symptom of an incomplete or pathological development within a personality. Religion is individual in its roots, although it took social form since civilization itself is an expression of neuroses (that is, the channeling of drives within the self in ways that may be socially necessary but that create frustration, tension, and anxiety). Religion comes from a lack of a full, well-resolved relation of self and environment. It perpetuates childish or repressive attitudes toward the world in place of the reality principle. Religious notions are retentions of childhood concepts of father, magical omnipotence, and so forth, as means of rationalizing to oneself adult behavior that has neurotic rather than reality motivation.

For example, a person facing a difficult problem in adult life might turn to a divine father figure, recalling the time in childhood when the father seemed able to solve all problems, or he or she might turn to a magical rite or mystical state of consciousness, harking back to the infancy in which cause and effect or the limits of the self were not well understood. It is an assumption of the Freudian tradition, so basic as to be almost unspoken, that what we have called the ordinary self-awareness or self-cognition view of the self is the most accurate one, that is, the one that best corresponds to the reality principle. An equally basic Freudian assumption is that the sane adult is wiser in assessing reality than the child, and indeed the mature personality as a psychoanalytic ideal and goal seems to take the mentally healthy adult male as model.

Freudians would suggest that most religion endeavors to go in other directions; it denies one's best perceptions of reality to return to the comfortable misperceptions of childhood. While these misperceptions may be of limited benefit to some people, they cannot ultimately solve one's problems of adjustment to life because they are based on false premises. Since they conflict with other aspects of oneself that have to be perceived as reality, religion may well induce those deep-seated tensions and anxieties known as neuroses even as one tries through religion to alleviate them.[17]

A more positive assessment of religion was made by a student of Freud who later broke with him, Carl G. Jung (1875–1961). Jung taught that life is a quest for *individuation,* that is, for unifying the various constituents of one's mind into a harmonious pattern. These constituents are basically aspects of masculinity and feminity, together with the dark negative principle, called the Shadow, and the emerging ideal self. Each of these parts has a root image called an archetype. Traditional religious myth and ritual, together with dreams and fantasies, are seen by Jungians as treasure troves of images that represent these archetypes. The feminine side, for example, presents itself to us as the elderly and wise Great Mother (goddesses like Cybele or Isis) or as the eternally young anima (youthful maidens such as Persephone or the Virgin Mary). The masculine may be the Wise Old Man, like Merlin, or the Hero. The emerging individuated self may be represented by the archetype of the Marvelous Child or by a Hero triumphant through struggle, such as Christ.

The archetypes and the psychic force behind them are normal constituents of the mind. Everyone has something of all of them, and if any are repressed it may cause trouble. Equally unhealthy is inflation by an archetype, so that one acts *only* as the Great Mother or the Hero. They must instead be arranged into a pattern, a Mandala, so that they balance each other off and the ideal self emerges in the center. Religious rites, myths, and art (as well as those of traditions such as alchemy) are seen by Jungians as able to help one greatly in the process of getting the archetypes rightly placed and the individuation process attained. They give one symbols for understanding aspects of him or herself that correspond to the dynamics of the Great Mother or the Hero. Traditional rites can help insofar as they are basically aimed at aligning the archetypes and enabling a true self to emerge out of them.[18]

[17]See Sigmund Freud, *Totem and Taboo,* trans. James Strachey (London: Routledge and Kegan Paul, 1950); and *The Future of an Illusion,* trans. W.D. Robson-Scott (Garden City, N.Y.: Doubleday & Company,Inc. 1957).

[18]For summaries of the position see Carl G. Jung et al., *Man and His Symbols* (Garden City, N.Y.: Doubleday & Company, Inc., 1969); and Frieda Fordham, *An Introduction to Jung's Psychology* (Harmondsworth, England: Penguin Books, 1956).

We have alluded to the approach to the psychology of religion of Abraham Maslow (1908–70), Charles Tart, Claudio Naranjo, and others. This approach is grounded in the movement known as humanistic psychology, though a significant wing of it has come to be known as transpersonal psychology.[19] Maslow's fundamental premise is implicit in his exposition of the peak experience; one is most fully *actualized* (that is, what a human being should be and potentially can be) in peak moments, when one is most full of a sense of sufficiency and creativity, and least aware of needs outside the self. To know the truth about human beings, then, we should proceed from these states and what they tell us, not from pathological states as Freud was accused of doing. Maslow's approach has obvious philosophical and religious ramifications. Many have used the work of humanistic psychology to present a view that religion is grounded in the peak experience and is a resource of methods for inducing it.

A word should also be said about the very influential work of Jean Piaget (b. 1896), a Swiss psychologist who has concentrated on the problem of how children learn. While Piaget has not explicitly addressed questions of the psychology of religion, his structures for understanding the development of intelligence and world views are of considerable interest in connection with it.

Piaget has outlined four stages of the child's intellectual development. The first, covering roughly the first two years of life, is the sensorimotor stage, in which knowing is inseparable from sensing and responding through activity; the child knows the bottle by drinking from it. Knowing is mostly nonverbal but involves the child's total sensory and physical being in a complete act of knowing. Cause and effect are "condensed into a single mass centered around the effect perceived; the feeling of efficacy was merely one with the result of the act."[20]

The second stage, from two to seven, is called the preoperational. It is the stage in which objects come to be represented by words; the child gradually learns to manipulate words in his mind in order to put things in relationship to each other. This process is schematization; it is not yet real logical thinking, but experiments with associating things. The tran-

[19]There are several anthologies that provide an introductory sampling of the literature of these movements and particularly stress their interaction with traditional mysticism and religion. These include John White, ed., *The Highest State of Consciousness* (Garden City, N.Y.: Doubleday Anchor Books, 1972); John White, ed., *Frontiers of Consciousness* (New York: Julian Press, Inc., 1974); Robert Ornstein, ed., *The Nature of Human Consciousness* (San Francisco: W.H. Freeman and Co. Publishers, 1973); and Charles T. Tart, ed., *Transpersonal Psychologies* (New York: Harper & Row Publishers, Inc., 1975).

[20]Jean Piaget, *The Construction of Reality in the Child* (New York: Basic Books Inc., Publishers, 1954), p. 231.

sition from sensorimotor to preoperation begins with a sort of conceptual internalization. In the first stage, when an object was out of sight it no longer existed for the child. Now the child understands that it is still there even if unseen, and so looks for it. He or she distinguishes individual things by pointing—a prerequisite for language that requires the separating out of discrete objects that remain the same. The child loves to count things, which is almost a ritualization of seeing them as separate. He or she is, however, still egocentric and has trouble relating to objects that do not have to do with him or herself. Gradually, though, the child relates possessions to other people.

The third stage, from seven to twelve, marks the beginning of logical operations and of classifying things according to systematic similarities and differences. The fourth stage, up to adulthood, starts formal logical thinking and shows the beginning of understanding the symbolic nature of thought and the abandonment of identification of word with thing that marks one who is new to the use of language.[21]

Throughout the whole process the child is constructing a world view—a way to understand what the universe is, how it works, how things are interrelated in it, and above all how he or she fits into it and what kind of thinking is most useful in coming to terms with it. Piaget emphasizes that the world view is a *construction*. The child's mind neither sees reality as it is nor makes it all up; he or she gradually constructs reality on the basis of immediate impressions, on the ways of knowing possible at his or her stage of development, and on previous experience as remembered. The child's reality, then, is truly different from the adult's; he or she is not just a miniature adult. Reality is constructed by the mind as an artist paints a picture, with something of both outside existence and the artist in it. Piaget stresses that reality construction is a long process for the child, based on much experimentation and many mistakes. Along with verbalization, the construction of trial and alternative worlds in play is invaluable in the process.

The significance of Piaget's work for understanding human religion has not yet been adequately explored, and we can here only propose a few highly tentative lines of thought. First, it is evident that the process Piaget describes is really the process of developing a world view. Therefore if religion is part on one's world view, this process would have to include the acquiring of religion. Second, Piaget's process is not a wholly cerebral one, although he has perhaps underemphasized the interaction of physical and emotional development with thinking after the infancy stages. He does, however, stress that the process begins

[21]See Herbert Ginsburg, *Piaget's Theory of Intellectual Development: An Introduction* (Englewood Cliffs, N.J.: Prentice-Hall, Inc., 1969).

with holistic, sensorimotor knowing. Religion also involves, and some would say begins with, sensorimotor knowing through dance, ritual, or ecstatic motor responses.

Finally, in preoperational thinking a workable world view is being developed through trial and error, and through the use of associations. The moon may be shining through the window on a night when the child is frightened or hungry; for a long time after, the moon is sinister. A tree in the yard may be the center of the play area; the child might touch it whenever he goes out and think up stories about it as his or her ability to devise narrative and fantasy develops. One can see some parallels between this stage of thought and some kinds of religious myth and symbol.

Another psychologist, Ernest G. Schachtel, has presented further refinements of this line of thinking. In an essay dealing with the question of why we do not remember earliest infancy, he points out that conscious memory generally begins at about the time the child learns to speak fairly well. Until we have words and the schemata that go with them to relate thought in some way, we do not have the vessels with which to carry meaningful discrete memories into later life. This is another way of saying that the consciousness of the preverbal child is so different from the consciousness of those who have words that we cannot enter it again, except possibly in those feelings and symbols that are utterly transcendent over words.[22]

Schachtel also tells us that early development involves a transition from concentration on the "proximity senses" (touch, taste, and smell, the three senses for which one has to be very close to the object) to the "distance senses" (hearing and sight). That transition creates a new and more extended environment, one that opens the way for the verbal thinking and communication that is for humans probably the most important gift of hearing and seeing. The transition also makes the person less immediately involved with what he or she senses as a psychophysical organism.[23]

Putting stress on proximity versus distance senses, like sensorimotor versus verbal and conceptual ways of relating, can provide interesting ways of classifying religions and some insight into their views of human nature. Magical rites, for example, tend to involve a pungent, evocative use of the proximity senses, just as does sex. One

[22]Ernest G. Schachtel, "On Memory and Childhood Amnesia," in *Metamorphasis: On the Development of Affect, Perception, Attention, and Memory* (New York: Basic Books Inc., Publishers, 1959), pp. 279–322. Originally published in *Psychiatry* (February 1947).
[23]Ibid., pp. 298–301.

thinks of Tantric rites within Hinduism and Buddhism and certain practices in some Taoist and Western magic, with their heavy incense, sacred food or drugs, elaborate gestures, and simulated or actual sex. Catholic and Eastern Orthodox sacramental worship employs a rather genteel token acknowledgment of the proximity senses in the use of bread and incense and the kissing of holy objects. Traditional Protestant worship usually suggests, however, a vehement denial that meaningful religious communication can come through senses other than hearing and seeing.

## RELIGIOUS DEVELOPMENT

We have observed that life is a series of initiations that religion can help to correlate. We have also noted—and this could be very richly substantiated—that religious traditions tend to idealize various stages of religious development in a person. The following is a brief discussion of the major stages of development and of what, at least in modern American culture, tends to be characteristic of religion in each of them.[24]

### Stages of Development

*Infancy.*    In infancy and early childhood there is, of course, little if any separation of religion from the rest of life. Yet in the eyes of many psychological theorists, this is the age that is really all-important for religion. According to Freudians, it is the locus of the oceanic, infantile omnipotence and the parent-dependency stages one later endeavors to recover through mysticism, magic, or personal gods. Motor activity at this age is also one of the main ways of knowing, which could be the basis of religious ritual, dance, and ecstatic release. On the other hand, if religion really is a matter of knowledge acquired through philosophy, scripture, and tradition—media of the distance senses, a matter of words and cognition—then infancy would have very little relevance for it. Perhaps we can at least say that the quest for a real self begins in infancy and is continued through every stage by whatever means are accessible.

*Childhood.*    Many stages are really contained within childhood, but we must here collapse them all into one. The basic operation is reality construction, pursued in many ways, such as stories, fantasies, games, learning, and relating to parents and peers. Religion may be learned and practiced but is not likely to be a genuinely distinct area of life so much as

---

[24]An older but classic book on the psychology of religion, which provides a useful discussion of stages of typical development, is Gordon W. Allport, *The Individual and His Religion* (New York: The Macmillan Company, 1950).

The play world of children.

a matter of acquiring the ways of parents and friends. At the same time, however, the child through stories and imaginary games (though he or she does not distinguish clearly between imagination and reality) is also acquiring an interest in alternative realities and moving in and out of them. With sensorimotor knowing still very important, even though the child also is coming to know through words and concepts (the adult way), he or she has a strong capacity for ritual and dramatic experience. If these capabilities become attached to religion, as is often the case, religion becomes very much a live and precious thing, and this attachment can easily continue into adulthood.

*Adolescence.* For many people, though certainly not all, adolescence is the golden age of religion. It is first of all a time of intense feeling that indicates a lively capacity for religious experience. It is also a time when one is striving desperately to find one's place in life, to sort out difficult relations with parents and the opposite sex. The adolescent has strong sexual drives, sometimes so disturbingly strong one would like to transmute them into something else or to have other drives just as strong to counterbalance them. He or she also has a new capacity for logical, abstract thinking and wants a logical, coherent picture of the world and his or her place in it. He or she wants something highly persuasive to which an intense emotional commitment can be made. All of these drives together make the religious commitments and intense personal experiences characteristic of adolescence very understandable. For many, of course, these drives find other outlets and adolescence is not especially religious. Indeed, the strong drive for self-identity that underlies all other drives may well take the form of deeply felt rebellion against one's past; and if religion were included in that past, it may be one object of rebellion.

*Adulthood.* Early adulthood is often marked by a greater flexibility of thought than in adolescence. If one explores the nature of religion more deeply, he or she may be led to a fuller religious commitment or to a greater inclination to see the relativity and symbolic nature of religious language. The emotional commitment side of religion may diminish as he or she moves further into adulthood, but the importance of religion as a social construction of reality (that is, its rich meaning in family and community) and its ability to help one manage the tragedies, frustrations, and emptiness of adult life become more important. Religion becomes a vehicle for the interpersonal expression that undergirds adult society; it is like a vocabulary, to religious persons, for expressing the meaning of family and community and for finding meaning in the absurdities of a good deal of adult life.

*Old Age.* Finally, in old age, religion can sometimes grow in importance. Not because it is easier to believe then or because one is closer to death (which is, perhaps surprisingly, often less of a problem to old people than to children or adolescents), but just because one finally becomes more emotionally contained and better able to live in the present. One can enjoy more calmly the beauty, sociality, and wisdom of religion. A rigorously logical interpretation tends to matter less, with emphasis shifting to a symbolic environment that links one to one's own past and present.

### Religion and Childhood

This scheme of the religious importance of stages of life is, of course, very general. Undoubtedly the reader can think of numerous exceptions. Moreover, one final problem that should be discussed is the relation of religion and childhood. Much of what we have said could create an impression that religion is little more than a perpetuation of childish things. The matter is not that simple. While the importance of childhood experiences for religion is immense, this may not be the same thing as saying religion is childish.

The affinity between religion and childhood is, in fact, generally accepted. Great religious personalities, such as Jesus when he admonished his disciples to become like little children, acknowledged it from one point of view, even as those who discredit religion as immature do from another. While some may say that one should leave behind all childish or immature areas of life, it can be argued with equal force that it is crucially important to accept and unify within one's total personality all of one's past as well as one's present. The person who does not wisely and knowingly give place to the child within may find that child expressing itself in highly undesirable ways

Even more important, the assumption that what is earlier in development is necessarily less adequate than what is later is only an assumption. Religion around the world, through innumerable myths, symbols, and rites, has commonly made an opposite assumption that however valuable adulthood may be, there are ways and occasions in which children have a far keener perception of right values and truths than do adults. (Thus, the savior is a babe, the youngest son is a hero, or a boy or girl opens a religious rite or divines in a sacred oracle.)

It needs to be understood that when we talk about mysticism and the infantile oceanic consciousness, or childhood fantasies and religious myth or alternative realities, these words should be taken only metaphorically. The child within may open for an adult the capacity for mysticism or understanding myth, but he or she is still an *adult* mystic or myth-maker, not literally a child again. The adult brings to the experience everything that has happened since he or she was a child, including perhaps considerable education, and this makes the experience quite different from what it would be if he or she were still a child.

## SUMMARY

The psychology of religion, then, is a complex matter deeply interwoven with the psychology of development, language, and states of consciousness. We began with a simple reflection on the fact that we have differing states of consciousness, like concentration and lethargy, and observed that the mind needs to alternate between them. We noted that this alternation is fundamental to the psychology of religion, for religion values some states more than others, making some in effect into subuniverses in which reality is far better perceived. It provides ways of making the transition into those and of avoiding the undesired states.

These alternatives do not necessarily just circle around and around the same track. For religion, and its psychology, is also linked to human development. It parallels, with its rites and feelings, natural development from childhood to adulthood. It can also set in place its own separate pattern of open-ended change—through initiations, conversions, and growth that make a person new and different, even if they may draw on motifs of returning to childhood or birth and repeating it again.

We then looked at certain states of consciousness that religion employs as it constructs its real self: meditation, the peak experience, and states such as guilt, power, and dependency. We discussed the psychological meaning of beliefs in immortality and deity and examined some important psychological interpretations of religion. Finally we dealt with typical relationships to religion in various stages of life and with the perennial problem of the childhood motif in religion.

We have examined the psychological aspects of religion, the intricate dialogue between childhood and adulthood, and the ever-changing states of consciousness needed for functioning in this world, with their irresistible need to change into an alternate state. Next we study some of the symbolism employed in these various states.

The doorways of this restored twelfth-century Buddhist temple at Angkor, Cambodia, suggest the role of religious symbols, including symbols in architecture, as portals to mysterious other worlds.

## CHAPTER FOUR

# MAGIC DOORWAYS: SYMBOL, RITE, AND RELIGION

### SIGNS AND SYMBOLS

Perhaps you have read a story in which a very ordinary entryway, a closet door or a garden gate, turns out to lead into a fabulous other world. Sometimes even the flick of a television dial, when it moves to a drama like *Star Trek,* can do this. This chapter is about symbols in religion, and symbols for religious believers are like such doors, gates, and television channel controls. Even the plainest symbols can open up a virtual universe of transcendent feeling and meaning for those who understand. They are magic portals into the other world where the truth of one's religion is visible, felt, and far overshadows the inconsistent ordinary. A symbol may be a work of art, the architecture of a temple, a church service, or a sacred book. The Ise shrine and the figure of Jesus, as described in the first chapter, are good examples of religious symbols that have this kind of magic doorway power for people.

To comprehend how all of this works, several distinctions have to be made. There is a distinction between a *sign* and a *symbol,* and there is a distinction between the *religious* and *nonreligious* use of both terms. All sorts of indicators bombard us from all sides, and the structures of our thought processes continually construe them to tell us things not literally contained in the words as noises or the objects as things. We constantly make out certain squiggles of ink, like those before you now, to be more than just black-on-white patterns, just as we read significance into colors, gestures, and even the arrangement of the stars. We understand significance through associations we have been taught or that the mind makes on its own from past experience or from its own intrinsic structures. Language itself is sign and symbol; the noise of most words has no relation to the meaning, yet words immediately call to mind, to one who knows the language, what is being communicated. *Cat* does not sound or look like the animal, yet when we hear or see the word we call up a visual and even audio idea of the furry creature that meows.

Many such verbal units as well as countless nonverbal indicators, from traffic lights to the dial tone on the telephone, come to us as little more than signs. They are just indicators that have no essential relation, except convention, to the thing signified. Susanne Langer speaks of them as *references*. They may be, she suggests, a very truncated form of the original, such as the code word or gesture in some game. Unlike a true *symbol*, however, they are not necessary to the *completion* of some experience, much less a miniature of life itself as would be the "miniature" eating or washing of a sacrament such as holy communion or baptism.[1]

The sign can be thought of as the traffic light, and the symbol as the cross or holy communion (though, as we shall see, matters may not in the end be quite this simple). Signs are generally taught, or based on language that is taught, since they have little intrinsic relation to the thing signified. Signs saying STOP, EXIT, KEEP RIGHT, NO PARKING, THIS SIDE UP, HOTEL, CAFE; gestures of pointing, guiding, or even hostility; and footprints one is following are all examples of signs.

Some indicators, however, are more than this. If you come to a restaurant featuring the cuisine of a particular nationality, and you are familiar with that culture, the sign might do more for you than just reveal the existence of the restaurant. It would probably evoke in your mind the whole world of the culture—memories of travel, of the smell of the kitchens of relatives who came from that country, of a few bars of ethnic music heard with the inward ear, maybe even of a few scenes from a childhood long past.

Recall from chapter one Alfred North Whitehead's statement that the mind is functioning symbolically when some components of its experience elicit consciousness, beliefs, emotions, and usages respecting other components of its experience. The former set are symbols, the latter the meaning of the symbols. If the restaurant sign evokes the sort of emotions and nostalgia suggested, the sign would clearly be a symbol, and the culture of the evoked nationality, as you had interiorized it, would be the meaning of the symbol for you.

The theologian Paul Tillich has also discussed the distinction be-

---

[1]Susanne K. Langer, *Philosophy in a New Key* (Cambridge, Mass.: Harvard Press, 1957), pp. 153–59.

tween sign and symbol, defining the latter as that which participates in what it symbolizes.[2] One could argue that the restaurant sign is still not quite a symbol in this sense. However positive the feelings it elicits, it is not really a participant in the culture it evokes, any more than would be the colored blotch representing the country on a map.

If you were to enter the restaurant (just as you might enter a religious building or service, attracted by the sign or token outside), any doubt about the extent of real participation in the culture would likely disappear. You would see decor representative of the homeland, hear its music, smell the spices used in its cooking, and perhaps notice a patron or two in the corner reading a foreign language newspaper. The restaurant would become for you a symbol, indeed an experience, of the culture in the fullest sense.

The distinction between sign and symbol is intricate but important. What is a symbol to one person may be only a sign to someone else. If you are Hungarian, a Hungarian restaurant may function as a major symbol for you, evoking memory and meaning. For another person, who never eats there and has no particular interest in Hungary, it may be only another routine building along the street. Meaning is not a quality inherent in events or objects themselves but a product of what is brought to the objects by the associations, memories, and psychological makeup of the observer, especially if he or she is also a participant.

Thus there are situations in which even the traffic light becomes a symbol that participates in what it symbolizes. It is a part of modern technological society and representative of the way the authority of the state must operate in such a society. To this extent it is a *bona fide* symbol of authority in a society that depends on immensely powerful vehicles and must regulate their movements, even when they are under individual control, with a precision unknown in the streets of ancient Athens or medieval London. Fortunately, the same society that produces powerful private automobiles can also mass produce traffic lights. The latter can evoke responses that are really responses to the whole meaning of modern technological society and the sort of state authority that goes with it.

Every part of a culture is a symbol of the whole of the culture.[3] Advertisers constantly tell us that how one brushes one's teeth or what kind of soft drink one imbibes can identify the person's whole life style and generation. The principle behind such claims, however excessive they may be, contains some truth. For a cultural style, like a personality, is made up of a thousand details that are interrelated, reveal something of

[2]Paul Tillich, *Systematic Theology* (Chicago, Ill.: University of Chicago Press, 1951), vol. I, p. 239.
[3]For example see Claude Lévi-Strauss, *The Raw and the Cooked* (New York: Harper and Row Publishers, Inc., 1969).

the totality, and are capable of serving as a symbol of the whole that participates in it. Toothpaste tubes and carbonated soft drinks, like stop signs, are significant symbols of modern American civilization. They participate in it, not only metaphorically but also as million dollar industries with high-advertising visibility. They reveal important attitudes in the culture toward health and happiness. They could not have existed in the same way in any previous culture. Trivial as they may seem, without them modern American civilization would be something different.

If the part serves as symbol of the whole in ordinary society, it does so to the highest degree in religion. (It is, however, sometimes misleading to regard the religion of a society as a part that symbolically reveals the values of the whole. That relationship is often complex, with the religion being more dialectical than continuous with the cultural values.) Religion is the greatest of all redoubts of symbolism, especially if the vast realms of art and music associated with religion are included. Everything in religion is a symbol, since the object of religion is the transcendent and the real self, and these are beyond immediate representation.

All the forms of religious expression, the theoretical, practical, and sociological, are symbols of the total message and experience of the

*Hugh Rogers/Monkmeyer Press Photo Service*

A modern American highway scene with its multitude of signs and symbols—advertising, traffic instructions, license plates, endless words.

religious system in which they coexist. Each participates in that total experience, but each is only a part of it. For example, the doctrinal statement of a religion tells us something about its vision, but the message for the actual participant is modified by what is told him or her through the kind of worship and the kind of group experienced.

Religious symbols, however, are not merely passive clues to identity or meaning. They are also aids to thought, and so to decision, just as are language symbols. Encapsulating a total world or experience in a single symbol or a discrete symbol system can sometimes be misleading, but it also helps one to clarify distinctions, make choices, and so find or create one's own identity. In any case, for better or worse, that is the pattern of human thought.

## DISTINCTIONS AND PATTERNS

There is general agreement between logicians and those who study how infants begin to learn to think that making distinctions begins with recognizing pairs of opposites and choosing between the two poles represented by them. It starts simply by distinguishing between what is (something) and what is not. The infant makes his or her very first act of discrimination in this world of many things by distinguishing between breast or bottle and all that is not breast or bottle and turning toward the former; the toddler reaches out for the red flower, singling it out from the bush that is only the background of the red flower.

It is then only a short step to the next important launching platform of thought, one that the child probably never really leaves: thinking in terms of pairs of opposites, such as hot or cold, the light on or off, black or white, in or out, me or outside of me, cause and effect. The last leads one to think in terms of causation and so leads to mechanics and science. Rationalization and religious thought, as they struggle to make usable sense out of the overwhelming mass of experienced reality that sweeps around and through one, follow the pattern and use the same basic sets— hot and cold, male and female, me and outside of me. Pairings may be a handy tool for getting a blurry chaos into order, relieving one kind of tension the same way as does focusing binoculars until the view becomes sharp. However, almost immediately another, and even more insidious, tension presents itself. When reality is reduced to pairs, it is also reduced to poles. This means decisions; poles mean choices.

For the infant to see and distinguish is to act; the child goes toward one end or the other, to feel, grab, or eat the side he or she favors, rejecting the other. When it is breast or bottle versus nonbreast or nonbottle and if the child is hungry, there is no question which will be chosen. Easy also are the cases of hot versus cold (or both versus lukewarm in the middle) or bright versus dull. Others are harder, for example, in versus out. Is it better to be in mother's arms or out walking around? Toddlers often run to and from their parents to try to affirm both sides, and to establish that they can come and go as they please. Even more difficult to sort out completely is "me versus outside of me." It takes a long time to establish exactly what the parts of the body are and where they begin and end—for awhile, blankets may be dragged about as extensions of "me."

These problems are hardly resolved when baby blanket and doll are finally laid aside. Every day we are forced to make decisions that boil down to one action instead of another, emphasizing one side instead of another. Even if the choices first appear multiple rather than twofold, when we try to think it through we find that the mind wants to bring them down to two to facilitate decision—wise versus foolish, right versus wrong, good versus bad. If the mind succeeds in identifying the options with these poles, the rest is easy. The most decisive and effective people seem to be those able to do this most positively. Computer-like, they translate a complex series of variables into a set of binaries and then grind it all out into an optimum solution.

In other words, we want maps to chart the separate polarities we encounter into a simpler, comprehensive polarity pattern, as scrambled iron filings leap into line when a magnet is brought near. We want a *pattern* that fits over them and lines them all up—right versus wrong, good versus bad. Then, as we easily pick up the right ends, we feel part of the pattern too—a somebody, a real self, who also fits in. The pattern, thus, is really a way of *seeing;* it is not necessarily out there in the world. (It may be, but that is not the point at the moment.) The important thing about the pattern is that it is a grid laid over the world by the percipient as a result of the human way of thinking in terms of pairs of opposites and of the need to know how to make choices between opposites.

This is where religions, with their construction of universes of symbolic meaning, come in. We have talked about transcendence in religion. It means experiencing oneself as having a definite place and valid identity in the context of infinite being itself. First, though, it means laying a pattern or grid of symbols over the world to facilitate decision derived from the highest perspective. What is transcendent does not come from out of the material itself or from one's biological equipment, but at the least (if we follow Luckmann) from the uniquely human and at the most (if we follow Berger's concept of what is distinct in religious transcendence) from a level of experience above the ordinary human. Let us see how humans impose a transcendent pattern of the world.

If a cat sees two equidistant birds at the same time, it may freeze, bemused and unable to leap at either. For once its well-tuned biological equipment, programmed to pursue the most likely prey, is stymied. Incapable of making a truly free choice that is not guided by instinct, the animal cannot move. A human being, in the same dilemma, would at least have the ability to select one or the other arbitrarily and would have lunch sooner than the cat. This decision is scarcely a religious one, but it illustrates in a very practical way the real and invaluable trancendence of human over animal minds.

It is this practical transcendence that, in its agonies of decision, cries out for help and makes religious transcendence possible. It makes religious transcendence possible because it affirms that the human can and must choose. The way to go is not given to us by nature, either the world's or one's own, in the direct way it is to animals (though we may sometimes wish it were). The way to decide must somehow be given to us on our own level, the human. We intuit that there are many possible patterns. We may and do affirm that one is the right one, one revealed by God or history. While it is necessary to feel the pattern one uses *is* the right one—it must *be* right to *feel* right, to make one a real self within it—it also represents a choice. We always know we can opt out, even while we know this will probably not happen, especially if the pattern is so deeply ingrained in culture that we never have to make a really self-conscious choice for or against it. For the side that cries out for religious transcendence, and siezes upon it when it appears, is just as strong as the fact of freedom. It is not so much that we do not want the human gift of free choice as that we want a choice to be made and so put behind us. We do not want animal determinism or humanness facing unbearable absolute choices without map or compass but a third state past them both: free human choices made boldly and rightly because we know our ultimate identities and destinies.

Religions, then, are patterning spotlights that facilitate choice by illuminating the correct poles. In this respect, religion is part of a total cultural pattern that enables choices in all kinds of matters large and small. They all run into each other and reinforce each other. In looking at a particular culture, one can often see parallels between the way meals are eaten, politics are conducted, stories are told, and the gods or God are conceptualized and worshipped. The worship at Ise was stately and decorous, full of emotional restraint; any familiarity with Japanese culture will remind one that it is continuous with one whole side of it. The American girl's conversion experience, on the other hand, would be continuous with an American emphasis on what seems, at least, to be individual autonomy—on doing what one feels is sincere, even at the expense of role-playing courtesy or emotional repression. All this shows up both in the more haphazard meals and manners of Americans over Japanese and in the more moralistic tone of American politics.

When religion is important in a culture, it plays a more distinctive part. It is like the percussion in an orchestra. In practice, religion follows more than it leads, but it does reinforce the loudest notes, indicates continuities of rhythm with what has gone before, and points up the exuberance of the trills by contrast. More important, a solid drumbeat has a once-for-all absoluteness and finality about it unmatched by the resonances of any other instrument. So religion and its symbols in a culture—whether highly audible or not, whether anyone much pays attention or not, so long as it is there—suggest the possibility of access to the largest possible context for human life, the most transcendent perspective, the most unconditioned real self. This seems to be the continuing role, for example, of Christianity and Judaism in the countries under communist rule.

Of course, there are times when religion, in direct or indirect ways, is highly creative culturally. It can facilitate innovation precisely because the access to the past and transcendent offered by its symbols helps people to break out of the constricted patterns of the present.

Religion's overlaying or undergirding patterns are actually expressions of the fundamental pairing way of symbolic thinking. They indicate inner and outer, good and bad circles to the religionist. Like the infant turning to breast or bottle, religion knows there is a source of life and goodness and an outer area of meaningless confusion. Like the child learning to avoid touching a hot pan, the religionist knows some patterns of behavior work and some do not. For religion, the places and patterns that work do so because they are those in harmony with the most transcendent and unconditioned reaches of reality. These patterns, and the values represented by the poles of pairings in the religion, are represented by religious symbols.

## CATEGORIES OF RELIGIOUS SYMBOL

Let us now look at some of the major types of religious symbol, which are major tools in religious thinking, used for making the kinds of pairings and distinctions—between the sacred and the outer realms, and between one religion and another—that the religious mentality wants to make. What we deal with are symbols in the most exacting sense of the word; each is a specific, discrete object that is seen, like an image or diagram, or heard, like a story or a piece of music, and is distinguishable from other objects. The sociological structure of a religious group can also be highly symbolic, but this is a symbolic statement of a somewhat different type from that communicated by discrete visual and audio objects and is considered in the next chapter. Later in this chapter

This large representation of the Jewish Menorah, or seven-branch candlestick, in Jerusalem, Israel, recalls the focal symbols of religion.

religious rites as orchestrations of symbols are discussed. First, it is useful to examine some categories of religious symbol.

### Focal Symbols

To start with, there are focal symbols in religion. Some of these are the cross in Christianity, the image of the Buddha in Buddhism, or Mecca for Muslims. While the details of their function and meaning may be different, they have qualities in common: each is specific to the religion, is obvious in its role as a symbol, and serves as a standard focus for worship and identity within the religious community. Focal symbols convey a central and generally recognized message about the religion—the importance of Christ's death on the cross, the importance of the Buddha's enlightenment—that even outsiders can identify with the religion if they know anything at all about it.

Focal symbols, however, should not be reduced to the bare signs by which places of worship are marked. A religion may well have several objects that serve obviously as focal symbols. In Judaism there is not only the Star of David and the Menorah but also the Torah and the Ark within the synagogue; in Hinduism, all the principal deities are focal symbols, as is the sacred Ganges River.

Focal symbols generally have some specific visual form by which they are remembered and recognized, but there is more to them than a visible shape. When we say the Torah in a focal symbol in Judaism, do we mean the elaborate scroll on which it is written, and which will probably spring to the minds of those accustomed to synagogue or temple worship when the word is pronounced, or do we mean the actual words of the first five books of the Bible and the commandments therein? When we say a Hindu deity like Krishna is a focal symbol, do we mean the image of Krishna in a Hindu temple, myths and teachings related to Krishna, the concept (or reality) of Krishna as a transcendent deity, or the name Krishna chanted in a formula mantra like the "Hare Krishna"? Obviously, we have to mean all of these together because in practice they go together. A characteristic, in fact, of major symbols is ability to work on several levels at once, so the composite experience says in a moment what it would take many pages to express in writing. Each level of meaning supports the others and adds to the others' symbolic power.

Focal symbols are not necessarily visual. The cry to prayer five times a day by the muezzin from the minaret of a Muslim mosque is as powerful a focal symbol as any. So are the organ music and church bells of Christendom.

Focal symbols contain suggestions of other parts of the religion's full symbolic constellation; they are undoubtedly related to its most important myths or narratives and to its central doctrines, and have an important role in its major acts of worship and in legitimation of its principal sociological structures. The image of the Buddha is not enthroned passively on the altars of Buddhist temples but receives flowers and incense in private and public worship. Seated in meditation, it suggests the major act by which spiritual realization comes. Standing to teach, the form of the Blessed One recalls the sutras that contain the basic doctrines of Buddhism and are attributed to his lips. Finally, the image of Buddha serves as the model and spiritual master of the monastic brotherhood that is Buddhism's fundamental sociological expression.

### General Symbols

Another category of religious symbols could be called general symbols. These are constructed forms, like the cross and circle, or natural objects, like the tree and moon, that recur over and over in the religious world as components of symbolic constellations. These symbols move from one culture to another or appear independently in many cultures. The meaning may be somewhat altered in each use, yet the general symbol also retains something of what might be called the core meaning of the symbol. To what extent symbols are universal, and to what extent their recurrence is independent and accidental, is a hotly debated issue.

Also subject to much debate is the related issue of the precision with which the universal meaning of general symbols can be specified. Some, perhaps following a Freudian or Jungian school of psychological interpretation of religious motifs, would say, for example, that a symbolic circle is bound to represent female sexuality and the womb—even if only unconsciously—and that on a more abstract level it represents wholeness and eternity. Others would say that the meaning of each symbol can only be determined in the context of its own culture.

As in most arguments over such abstract matters as these, some truth can be rightly claimed by both sides. The cross in Christianity is a symbol of Jesus Christ and of redemptive suffering. Both of these meanings, one historical and one conceptual, are highly specific to Christianity and are by far the most important meanings of the cross in that faith. Cross symbols, however, appear widely outside of Christianity, from the sand paintings of Navaho Indians to the mandala diagrams of esoteric Buddhism. Outside of Christianity, the cross characteristically suggests the earth with its four directions and access to a mystic center integrating the four corners of the earth and of one's psyche. This meaning is not stressed in Christian discussion of the cross but is consistent with the central Christian meaning. It has appeared in the past as a minor theme, related to the lordship of Christ over the earth and his place at the spiritual center of the world providing the way of access to heaven.

The tree is a widespread symbol suggesting life and access to transcendence. Compare the tree under which the Buddha sat at his enlightenment and the old tradition of referring to the cross of Christ as the "tree." The moon as a symbol has a highly specific meaning in Islam: it suggests the flight of Muhammad from Mecca to Medina, which marked the turning point in his career and is the beginning date of the Muslim calendar. In Christianity it is associated with the Blessed Virgin Mary and particularly with the annunciation. In Chinese and Japanese popular religion it is a heavenly abode of immortals. In all its uses as a religious symbol, the moon seems to suggest or mark renewal, the triumph of life over death, and supernatural aid—no doubt suggested by the phases through which the moon goes as it seems to die and then to return to life, by its relation to the female cycle, and by widespread belief that the moon gives rain and fertility. This combination of near universality, versatility, and broad but deep underlying themes illustrates the nature of general symbols. They often provide elements, or even the basic idea, of much more particularistic focal symbols.

### Secondary Specific Symbols

Still another class of symbols could be called secondary specific. These are symbols specific to a particular religion but not as important for identification with the religion as the focal. Examples are the triangle or three interlocking circles that symbolize the Trinity in Christianity, the many arms of the bodhisattva Kannon in Japanese Buddhism, and the mace and discus of Vishnu in Hinduism. Secondary specific symbols are typically those of particular doctrines or religious figures such as saints, gods, and bodhisattvas, but they may well incorporate simpler general symbols as do focal symbols—the circle representing eternity (or the womb) multiplied *three* times to express the trinitarian Christian God.

## AUDIO SYMBOLS

Focal, general, and secondary specific symbols may be either visual or audio. Most people think of symbols mostly as something seen, but it is important to realize that sounds, not to mention stories and ideas, can function just as powerfully as visual symbols. When a worshipper enters a church, he or she is lifted into the religious world just as much by the organ music, the choir, the words of prayer, and the sermon as by what is seen. Now we turn our attention to the religious symbolic role of what is heard. The symbolic role of the written word is included in this discussion because in religion it is never wholly detached from its parentage in the spoken word and shares its meaning.

It should not be thought that visual and audio symbols work together in religion in mutual reinforcement and grand harmony. In fact, an underlying dynamic aspect of the history of religion that might seem very puzzling to the proverbial man from Mars has been a seesaw war between the respective symbolisms of the two distance senses—a war sometimes only latent but sometimes rising to furious battle in which men have killed and died for the sake of the word against the picture, or the picture against the word. Sometimes religion has been most conspicuous as the patron of sacred painting and sculpture, has made the fruits of this patronage the foci of worship, and has communicated to most people a preeminently visual suggestion of the sacred. Medieval Catholicism and Mahayana Buddhism veered in this direction. At other times religion has generated iconoclasm (the destruction of images) in favor of upholding the spoken and written word as the most reliable conveyor of truth. Protestantism and Islam are examples.

The written word in religion is an extension of the spoken word and shares its psychological attributes. Reading may be visual but is not usually mistrusted by those who suspect visual symbols of a nonverbal nature. The origin of writing in the spoken word is more decisively recognized in religion than anywhere else; reading is rarely allowed to stand alone as the formal expression of one's relation to the verbal symbols of faith. In Protestantism one is certainly encouraged to read the Bible and religious books, but doing so does not take the place of formally hearing the Bible read in church and a sermon preached.

Audio symbols fall into three categories: nonverbal—music and sound; nonconceptual verbal—words such as chants and spells used chiefly for effectiveness in the word itself rather than the concept it conveys as verbal communication; and conceptual verbal—story, myth, rhetoric, and doctrine.

### Nonverbal

Music is virtually universal as an important accompaniment of religion, except in Islam in which chanting and rhythmic recitation take its place. Music's importance in facilitating the basic task of religious symbolism, helping the participant to make the transition from ordinary to sacred reality, is unsurpassed. Whether the solemn and mystical Gregorian chant, the fast-paced hums of Buddhist sutra reading, or the gladsome notes of gospel singing, music in religious worship sets the altered emotional tone and universe of meaning of the rite and does much to bring the participant into it. Religious music is mostly a secondary specific symbol. Despite its immense and pervasive importance, there are few instances of single discrete pieces of music having quite the status of the focal symbol, and there are surprisingly few musical motifs that, like general symbols, find their way into the worship of a diversity of religions with a core meaning intact. Rather, the music of a religion is mostly specific to its cultural context and drawn from it, although a great religion may spread across many cultures and carry musical traditions with it along with other cultural baggage.

### Nonconceptual Verbal

Although it may be less familiar to some Westerners, sacred words as nonconceptual verbal expression are extremely important in the history of religion. In some cases, such as the distinctive chants of Japanese Pure Land and Nichiren Buddhism, they rise to the role of focal symbol.

Very often the nonconceptual feature is not absolute. Religious scholars within the tradition may appreciate the meaning, and it may in fact be known to ordinary practitioners. Nevertheless, as in the case of the Nichiren chant *Namu Myoho Renge Kyo* ("Hail the Marvelous Truth of the Lotus Sutra"), the literal meaning is not as important to ordinary devotion as the mantic or evocative power of the formula, which just through the vibrations of the sounds themselves is believed to align one with rich spiritual forces.[4] Examples are the mantra of Hinduism and Buddhism, recited in formal prayer and private meditation to create an atmosphere of the presence of divinity and peace; the *dhikr* or chanted ascriptions of praise to Allah in Islam; and such comparable Christian devotions as the Jesus prayer in Eastern Orthodoxy, the rosary in Roman Catholicism, and the repeated utterance of familiar prayer-phrases and hymns in Protestantism.

The use of special or sacred language, from Latin and Sanskrit to the archaic English of the King James Bible, is a closely related matter. Most nonconceptual verbal expression is predominantly secondary specific symbolism, although the *idea* of some of its modalities, such as the use of sacred language, rosary, or mantra, has spread through several religions.

### Conceptual Verbal

Conceptual verbal expression in religion takes several different forms. As one grows older, the words about religion that he or she hears change. He or she may at first be told stories about religious heroes, later may learn the faith's creeds and catechisms and be taught something about the abstract meaning of the doctrine, and finally may have it expounded in mature philosophical form. Without implying that one or

---

[4]See, for example, the description of Nichiren chanting in Robert Ellwood, *The Eagle and the Rising Sun: Americans and the New Religions of Japan* (Philadelphia, Pa.: The Westminster Press, 1974).

the other forms is better, most religions have words that fit all these categories.

## MYTH AND DOCTRINE AS SYMBOL

Myth is one example of conceptual verbal expression. Myth in religious studies means a story that expresses in narrative form the basic world view of the culture. Myths are of two basic types, the cosmogonic and the hero/savior. The first tells how the cosmos came into being, and the second tells how a way has been found back to the primordial unity of mankind with the transcendent.

How one says that the world came into being tells a great deal about how one thinks of the world, and his or her place in it, today. In India one of many accounts of the beginning of this world tells of a primal man who is also God dividing himself up in a sacrifice to make the many things. The Judaeo-Christian account in the Book of Genesis relates that God literally created the universe as something outside of himself and subject to him. These two narratives suggest two views of the total meaning of the world in relation to God. In the first, God is hidden in the world. All parts of the cosmos, stars, mountains, trees, and people, are really God in veiled form, self-sacrificed so their multiplicity can flourish. In the second, God is not the same as the world but views it as a craftsman views the exquisite work of his hands and as a sovereign views his subjects, expecting love and obedience from them. In both cases, the myth implies that if we know the real origin of something, we can understand it now. In this light, the myth is indeed a symbol, because it both participates in what it symbolizes and is part of the conceptual reality that interprets the meaning of the whole.

The hero and savior narrative tells the way back to this beginning. It presents a model of the accomplisher of the way who is a pioneer of salvation, opening and demonstrating the path for others. Examples are warrior-heroes such as Rama in India or more peaceful figures such as the Buddha and Jesus. Religions may advance both classic examples that are part of its memory from the past and recent saints and heroes who exemplify its way of life in the present. People such as Albert Schweitzer, Mohandas Gandhi, Martin Luther King, and Mother Teresa of Calcutta have been widely regarded as religious heroes of the twentieth century.

Regardless of whether it is classic or modern, the hero-savior story comes to be told according to a fairly predictable structure (which makes the hero-savior myth per se a general symbol, even though of course the specific contents vary widely). The mythologist Joseph Campbell, for example, describes the pattern of what he calls the *monomyth*—the basic structure of the myth of the hero that is repeated over and over behind a thousand names and settings.[5] Simplified, his scenario can be compared with the three initiatory stages of van Gennep and Turner, previously discussed, of separation, liminality, and reincorporation.

There is first the *departure* of the hero—his call, the crossing of the first threshold of trial and temptation, and entry into what Campbell calls the "deep sea journey" or (from the example in the Book of Jonah) the "belly of the whale," a long and arduous passage out of ordinary reality to the place of true transformation. The second part, the time of real *initiation* through struggle and triumph, has experiences such as those called the "road of trials," the "meeting with the goddess," the "atonement with the father," "apotheosis," and the "ultimate boon." It would be the Buddha's enlightenment, the passion and resurrection of Jesus, or, in J. R. R. Tolkien's *The Lord of the Rings,* the struggles of Frodo from the last meeting with Galadriel to the destruction of the Ring and the coronation of Aragorn. Finally, there is the stage of *return*, at first perhaps refused, when the hero is reincorporated into society as a changed person and one able to change others to enable them to go more easily through what he or she experienced.

There are other kinds of structural patterns that can also be seen; Claude Lévi-Strauss made three basic points about myth in his essay, "The Structural Study of Myth."[6]

1.   Myth is a kind of language—that is, it has a message and is trying to make a statement.

2.   A myth is composed of all its variants—to know what the message is, one does not only look, as a historical scholar might, for the earliest form but also at every way the myth is expressed. To know the full message of the Buddha in human experience, for example, one would not only look at the life of the historical Buddha but also at all the ways he has been represented and talked about down through two and a half millennia of Buddhist history.

3.   The movement of myth is from awareness of opposites to mediation. Polarities like male and female, man and nature, youth and age, or locality and world are reconciled. Lévi-Strauss shows how this is done in one way by the "trickster" figure, like Coyote in North American Indian mythology, who manages by his wits to make his way among gods and men, alternately bamboozling and

[5]Joseph Campbell, *The Hero with a Thousand Faces* (New York: Bollengen Foundation, 1949).

[6]Claude Lévi-Strauss, "The Structural Study of Myth," *Journal of American Folklore,* LXXXVIII, 270 (October–December 1955), 428–44. Reprinted in Richard and Fernande DeGeorge, eds., *The Structuralists: From Marx to Lévi-Strauss* (Garden City, N.Y.: Doubleday Anchor Books, 1972) pp. 169–94.

befriending them. The same task of mediation is done more formally by the hero in his initiatory adventure.

Doctrine is also a symbol of the religious world one is in. It differs from myth and narrative in that it usually comes later and sums up in more abstract language what they said in story format. Doctrine asks and answers the question, If such and such is what the divine did on this and that occasion, what can we say about it that is true all the time? Responses are such general statements as that God, or the sacred reality, is always near at hand, knows all things, can transform people, and so forth. Specific religious doctrines are discussed in a later chapter.

Religious rhetoric, language that is conceptual but intended to persuade or to construct religious reality through its interweaving of concepts, is found in preaching and inspirational writing. It blends the second and third forms of audio symbolism, verbal nonconceptual and verbal conceptual, and perhaps even has a hint of the first, music, when the rhythm and intonation of a voice are used to create a special state of consciousness. Chiefly, though, preaching and other rhetoric is the use of words and concepts not so much as doctrinal statement or sustained logical argument but as triggers to enable the hearers (and perhaps the speaker) to make the leap of transition into the religion's alternative worlds where its values are plain and true. Key words, phrases, and ideas potently recall the root images and metaphors and experiences of the faith, bringing them back if one has known them before, suggesting their transformative power if one has not. Religious rhetoric constructs religious reality rather than describing it and enables experiences of it rather than mere knowledge about it.

## PUBLIC AND PRIVATE SYMBOLS

One last categorization of symbols that ought to be made is between public and private symbols.[7] Symbols pervade both outside social landscapes and the private landscapes within each person's head. They affect both the way one relates to the community and the way one lines up ideas in his or her own mind.

Symbols that chiefly relate people to larger social units and are widely known and understood, at least in terms of their social role, are public symbols. Examples are the flag or the cross. They are accepted in the society as symbols of its identity. They can also, of course, dwell within one's mind as an interiorized public symbol—a soldier may die with an image of the flag in his mind, a devout Christian may bear the

[7]Kenneth Boulding, *The Image* (Ann Arbor, Mich.: University of Michigan Press, 1956).

cross in his or her heart and mind even when he or she is not seeing it visibly on steeple or altar.

Between public and private symbols is a realm of what may be called conventional symbols. Such symbols are widely understood and almost a kind of language but have no official status in any community as does flag or cross. Examples are such favorites of editorial cartoonists as the dove of peace and the sword of war.

Private symbols in the strict sense are most meaningful just to one individual because they have come out of one's personal experience and imagination. Every person, however plain and unpoetic he or she is, must have some mental image—a special place, a scene from some significant dream or fantasy, a favorite picture or memory—that has importance as a symbol for that person but no one else. For that person, the image participates in an important greater reality, and one may look at it, go to it, or recall it from time to time.

Symbols in the original creative work of artists and poets are basically in the private category and may derive from each artist's personal roots. They have a fuller destiny as they become known and bring others into the poet's or artist's private world. They do not, however, become official in the public symbol sense, though a few may become conventional.

Of course, it is a relative matter; to be a symbol in a religious or poetic sense the entity must have a communicable meaning. It cannot be purely and flatly personal. It must call up some kind of response in the minds of percipients. Many of the most effective symbols in religious art and poetry are based on general symbols (tree, moon, circle, and so forth) but are used in such a fresh way as to seem novel and evocative.

## SYMBOLS AND MEANING

Let us look again at what religious symbols are. They are discrete visual or audio objects or sets that offer a paradigmatic concept of the real self and the way to it. Ultimately, stories and pictures of gods, religious heroes, or other religious topics are powerful because they suggest oneself at his or her highest, the real self. They are like seeing or hearing outside of oneself, or perhaps recognizing outside of oneself, what one would most like to be, in rapport with ultimate reality. Alternatively, symbols can be said to become most powerful when one is already in a state of being in touch with the real self—they are like doors to the infinite divine reality accessible only to the real self.

Moreover, symbols are triggers facilitating transition to an alternative reality in which the real self, or infinity, is actualized. Visual symbols, words, or music may express tremendous reality to some people and be just a passing entertainment to others, but for those to whom the other world behind them is part of life, the symbol is enough. Seeing or hearing the symbol can work almost like a posthypnotic suggestion, calling up emotional and conceptual responses of immense power. At the least, these images or tones make entry into the other world seem inviting and serve to make the person open to it. That achievement depends on the evocative ability of symbols to reconstruct times past, to simplify emotional attitudes, to provide the sort of mental rearrangement around a new center that makes this world look different. Symbols energize such shifts through jolting one with a transitional shock.

Let us now look at some symbolic functions. Symbols recall the past as public or private memory jogs. S. G. F. Brandon has spoken of religion as "ritual perpetuation of the past."[8] To a great extent this is an accurate characterization. Religion's services and festivals, like the secular rites of societies, are based on events that happened, or are believed to have happened, at some point in the past and are of vital importance to the present. They are moreover events that go a great way toward giving the people of the present their identity. Rites are a kind of collective memory, and memory and the story it tells is important to identity.

Because the past cannot be recreated completely, it must be done symbolically, even as the individual consciously recalls only a few representative moments from the distant past. Just as one does not remember everything he or she did in his or her ninth summer, recalling just one trip to the beach or one baseball game that encapsulates and represents the whole, so the founder of a religion or a nation may be represented by just celebrating his birth and death or by just one characteristic gesture, such as Jesus at his Last Supper or Muhammad returning to Mecca for his final visit. Through such joggings of the collective memory, Christianity and Islam perpetuate their pasts with symbols to recall to the minds of their present followers who they are. Through rites like the holy communion or the pilgrimage to Mecca, they make the entire past live symbolically in the present.

It could be argued, of course, that the ritual reenactment of single events in the lives of men as spontaneous and original as Jesus or Muhammad grossly distorts their lives. That may be, although perhaps no more so than our own memories distort our past lives, but it must also be acknowledged that to a religion the meaning of its own past is more than simply historical. The ritual repetition of keys to the religion's spiritual meaning is essential to unveiling the larger meaning of the past. The further meaning is that the past evoked is a sacred time, when a special divine power and wisdom were available. The symbol, music or rite or image, becomes a way of getting into that past time. The very fact

[8]S. G. F. Brandon, *Time and Mankind* (London: Hutchinson, 1951), p. 19.

that it is familiar and perhaps repeated makes it most effective for this purpose: time travel (even if only subjective and even if only back to a stylized version of the original time) is not an easy gambit and so is best done over familiar roads. One becomes accustomed to responding to familiar clues or concepts.

Religious symbols can also recall one's own past. Some symbols clearly suggest the world of childhood. It is religiously valuable to be taken back into it, since memories of happy childhoods always have a glow about them that reinforces other concepts, whether paradises or divine maternal or paternal figures. Religious symbols may also recall the intense religious experiences of one's past. To hear the music once played at one's most meaningful religious service or to again see the place of one's conversion or warmest devotion can understandably strengthen a desire to remain loyal to those moments.

These reflections evoke another feature of symbols. Symbols have the capacity to simplify feelings and ideas into strong, undifferentiated monoliths that can easily be seen as polarized to their opposites—the sacred and the profane, the good and the bad, our world versus the outside. By simplifying religious decision to acceptance or rejection of the symbol, worship or nonworship, the symbol makes commitment easier. That is particularly the case when the symbol represents a god, Buddha, savior, patron saint, or teacher who personifies an absolute divine claim or is the center of identity for a city or culture.

It is important to remember, though, that even as symbols simplify they are also complex. Every symbol conveys a complex set of messages. This is because symbols are able to handle several matters at once. The same symbol—say the ancestral tablets of a Chinese family—can suggest at once loyalty and commitment to the family watched over by these ancestors, adherence to the traditional Confucian system of values that so emphasizes ancestral piety, and transcendence over ordinary life indicated by the supernatural aspect of the ancestral spirits. More developed symbols, such as the Buddha who dwells in a family or community temple in Thailand or Japan, might even suggest conflicting values that the individual would have to resolve—for example, between loyalty to the family supporting the temple and to the Buddha's call to his followers to free themselves from all worldly ties. Within Christianity, some have felt the same kind of conflict between the message of Jesus and the church as they know it.

Nonverbal symbols may oversimplify issues, compared to the kinds of nuances and qualifications that can be raised by verbal discussion, although we must remember that language too is symbolic and words as symbols also oversimplify the realities behind them. Symbols, however, bring out certain complexities, either resolving them in the symbol or presenting them to the individual to resolve, by bringing together in one discrete point several otherwise different areas of experience—self, family, community, the past, the numinous, the transcendent.

All these are important aspects of what is contained in most religious symbolism. The symbol's purpose is to put them all together or to lead the individual to do so. Thus loyalty to the past and the family, or leaving the family for a holier life and rejecting the past to build a brighter future, may both be tinged with numinous, transcendent value.

## THE ORCHESTRATION OF SYMBOLS
## IN RITE

It remains to say a few words about symbols in relation to the practical form of religious expression, that is, expression in acts such as worship, pilgrimage, art, architecture, or private prayer and meditation. Rite or public worship, the fullest of all these practical forms, is an orchestration of symbols to evoke the religious alternative world through several media simultaneously—vision, hearing, perhaps also smell, touch, and taste. The most effective worship is a network of many small things, all of which converge to bring the participant into the alternative reality of the religion. It becomes a total perception. When such a total environment is constructed, there is no objective reference point from which to judge it, and even one's inner thoughts are brought into alignment with it.

These concepts have recently been applied to theater by the dramatist and critic Richard Schechner.[9] His approach to theater, centering on the ideas of environment and performance, depend heavily on studies in traditional religion, especially shamanism, and in turn do much to illuminate the meaning of rite as orchestration of symbols. Schechner emphasizes the theater experience as a total experience—a "total immersion" in the drama, which therefore becomes transformative for cast and audience alike. For there to be a total environment, of course, the audience cannot be just spectators *outside* the drama but must be participants, a part of the environment that makes the drama. The fact that there are people present is a major factor in what goes on.

In the same way, a religious rite (whether a shaman's trance, a high mass, or a Protestant service with sermon) may be an effective performance by the religious specialist, but the total experience for those present is affected also by the presence of the whole group of participant-observers. The rite is probably the act of a community of some sort, and its meaning is completed by the fact that there are others besides the

[9]Richard Schechner, *Environmental Theater* (New York: Hawthorn Books, Inc., 1973).

performers present and by the transformative impact it has on those others.

Transformation means subjective movement from one world or reality to another in which one becomes a real self. This must finally be done by a communication of the reality of the alternative by a person or setting for which it *is* real. The alternative reality cannot be feigned; while human motives and consciousness may always be mixed, if religious specialists or players on the stage are *only* acting and have no involvement in the reality of what they are doing, that strange and indefinable but real sense of entering another world through their operations is likely to be missing. For this reason Schechner speaks of performance, not acting, in the theater.

Notice, though, that the term "performance" does imply actions done according to definite patterns for which one can prepare and that can indeed be a highly programmed break with the diffuseness and unpredictability of ordinary life. Doing something that seems real and that points toward another level of reality is likely to be *more* controlled and structured—in a word, cultural—than the ordinary. (Even such spontaneous-seeming worship as speaking in tongues and falling to the ground in ecstasy usually occurs within the structured situation of a service in which it is expected.) It is Peter L. Berger's social or cultural construction of reality, in which the human capacity to change reality as we perceive it by symbols and management of time and environment is carried to a high degree. This is often done by gestures whose point, in fact, seems to be reversing the natural to show the power of culture and, thence, of the gods transcendent over it. Claude Lévi-Strauss has set up several transformation pairs of opposites:

| | |
|---|---|
| continuous | intermittent |
| spoken | sung/chanted |
| profane | sacred |
| everyday | mythic |
| unadorned | masked |
| nature | culture[10] |

Consider how often the transformative movement of religious rite is from the first column to the second—singing when in ordinary life one would speak, being masked (or otherwise dressed in special garb) when in ordinary life one is not, doing something that happens only occasionally instead of any time or all the time. All this suggests a cultural and sacred reversal of the natural and ordinary. Precisely by performance (doing things in the second column) rite begins the transformative process. When a shaman or priest comes out robed in rich colors to begin a

[10]Cited in Schechner, *Environmental Theater*, p. 171.

dance or rite, that immediately tells us something different is about to happen and begins the transition to, in Alfred Schutz's term, another province of meaning.

All rite and worship involves a combination of symbols. Even worship as simple as a Quaker meeting speaks through several symbols and senses—silence, the spoken voice and words, austerity of surroundings, the presence of other people. There is a message about any religion in the structure and symbolism of its worship, just as much as in what is outwardly said. All religion has a worship form of expression. It is simply a matter of ascertaining *what* its message is wordlessly saying about how one best comes into rapport with the transcendent through this form of expression. If it is an elaborate and traditional rite, it says one best transcends finitude through participation in something with strong aesthetic appeal and a sense of getting beyond the present through forms that come out of the past. If it is very plain or free-form, it says one achieves the same end best through a minimization of impediments to knowing the divine inwardly or to freely expressing oneself. The same can be seen in the messages carried in whether worship has strong centralized leadership or widespread participation, largely visual or largely verbal communication, and so forth. The messages about the nature of mankind and God on this level, while surely there, are not often fully articulated and have to be felt or intuited.

We shall now look at some of the stages by which worship as orchestration of symbols typically enables the transformative process. The order of the internal stages may vary.

*Opening.*   The rite begins with a gesture that marks and enables a transition from the ordinary to religious reality. It may be a rite of purification, such as the Shinto priest waving a wand over the assembly of worshippers. It may be a hymn, a dramatic procession, the beat of drums or the sound of a conch, but it marks a transition and may even induce a sort of shock to assist the subjective shift.

*Prayer or establishment of rapport with transcendence.*   The next stage is likely to be a verbal process of becoming synchronous with the sacred—chanting, praying, or reading of sacred texts. It is quieter but more prolonged than the opening drama, indicating a more deeply meditative adjustment to the other reality.

*Presentation of offerings.*   This is many things, such as placing of food on Shinto or Hindu altars, offering the sacramental bread and wine in Roman Catholic and Eastern Orthodox liturgies, offering money in Protestant churches. Some rather ceremonial collection or presentation relates important material symbols to the divine. This is a somewhat more active and dramatic moment than the preceding.

This scene from the rich and tradition-laden worship of the Eastern Orthodox Christian churches suggests the power of the orchestration of symbols in religious rite to bring the worshipper through the portals of another world of deep meaning.

*The Message.* In most, but not all, worship there is a sermon or at least the reading of a sacred text by a religious specialist as instruction or inspiration and the use of religious rhetoric in the very supportive setting of temple and rite. This is a reversal of the previous action—the people then communicated to the divine, now the divine communicates to them.

*Participation.* In this the culminating stage, the people and the divine come most together and are thoroughly mixed. Divine life comes into the people, perhaps altering behavior, and people feel closest to God. There is likely to be some motor activity and the use of some of the proximity senses. This is the point of holy communion, of pentecostal speaking in tongues, of the Shinto

112

festival climaxing in sacred dance, carnival, and the rapid procession of the deity through the streets.

*Closing.*   At the end there is another shock of transition in the termination of the sacred experience and return to ordinary life, though it may be eased by blessing, music, final prayers, and socializing among participants.

Practical expression is not limited to worship settings. It can also be done individually. A person alone can move himself or herself through these stages and enter the alternative world or actualize the real self in prayer and meditation. The process can be done with the aid of sound or visual accoutrements, such as a sacred picture or image upon which one concentrates, or it can be done with only the evocation of what is within one's mind.

The process of transformation through orchestration of symbols can be accomplished geographically. Pilgrimage—travel for religious renewal to a special place that is itself a sacred symbol, such as Rome, Jerusalem, or Mecca—is a prolonged and spatially expressed rite. Traditional pilgrimage customs have the same sense of opening, transition, offering, learning, and participation, but they may go on over days or weeks, and each stage is done at a different place along the route. The entire journey is like a rite and amounts to a temporary movement into the religious alternative world or into liminality, to a place where the map of the alternative world coincides with geography as we know it. The pilgrimage site is a place where one can be a real self.

For example, the well-known Muslim pilgrimage to Mecca begins with separation from ordinary life as the visitor dons simple pilgrim's garb at the port of Jidda several miles from the holy city. From then on he will take no life, cut neither hair nor nails, and abstain from sex. At Mecca, he will circumambulate the shrine of the Kaaba seven times, stand on the side of Mount Arafat (where he will hear a sermon) all afternoon, and then, leaving the sacred state, ritually sacrifice a goat or sheep and have his hair cut—all over a period of two or three days.

Traditional pilgrimage sites, like Mecca and many others, are themselves complex symbols. Their buildings and temples reproduce the organization of the heavenly realm of the gods or God. In Mecca, for example, the throne of Allah above is said to be directly over the Kaaba, and angels continually circle around it even as do the faithful below. Kyoto, the ancient capital of Japan, is patterned on a mandala or Buddhist sacred diagram of the relationships of cosmic Buddhas and has monasteries or temples guarding its approaches.

Religious symbols, then, are magic doorways into worlds where religious meaning becomes the overt and apparent meaning of things, rather than the hidden meaning as in our ordinary world.

This congregation of Muslims praying in unison in the direction of Mecca suggests the social and corporate nature of religion.

## CHAPTER FIVE

# TRAVELING TOGETHER: THE SOCIOLOGY OF RELIGION

## ALL RELIGION IS SOCIAL

Religion as we know it is always social, inseparable from the fact that we humans live in societies and in a matrix of interpersonal relationships. Therefore, for every religious concept, experience, or practice there is a social form of expression—a group formed, or at least a modification of certain relations between certain people. True, people may have subjective yearnings and intuitions and even ecstasies homologous to those of religion and independent of any dealings with other people. If our understanding of religion is valid, however, these remain only subjective feelings or musings or even ritualized gestures, such as those of Konrad Lorenz's duck Martina, unless they are given symbolic completion through words and the experience is related to the social environment.

In this environment we humans inevitably find ourselves, and we cannot ignore it in the completion of any intuition or drive. Even the way we explain the meaning or nature of an inner experience to ourselves is an expression of interpersonal being: postinfantile human mentation without words and concepts could scarcely get beyond feeling. We use words and ideas to understand things about ourselves in our own minds as well as to explain them to others. Conceptualization and reasoning are products of society, since they are products of language. Thought and consciousness themselves, of any sort of which we can possibly conceive, are results of our living in societies, though the separate individual has an innate biological potential for them.

Religion, then, is bound up with the fact that we live, talk, and learn in groups. Human groupings are immensely varied and overlapping, ranging in size from a married couple to an empire. Some, like a family, are based on biological relationships; some, like a state, in part on territory; some, like a club, on voluntary association; some, like a monastic order, on conceptual commitments. They have different balances of male and female, young and old, rich and poor. Even what we mean by a "society," a grouping that shares a distinctive culture and so defines the basic world view and values of its members, is notoriously hard to pin down in practice, and can vary from a tribe of two or three dozen souls to the half the world we know as Western civilization.

However varied and elastic our groupings, we have them and cannot live without them. Moreover, all groups are organized in some way, formally or informally. That is to say, there are patterns in the relationships between the members. In most cases the pattern or structure includes some division of labor and some relation of authority and subordination. In all cases, though, there is a structure; one can see some consistency in the role of each member and some rhythm and repeatability in the configurations of the group as a whole.

Further, the nature and structure of the group is not just incidental but itself is a symbol and gives a message about what it means to be human. In the case of a religious group, the group structure also gives a message about what it means to be a real self and about the nature of the transcendent and how it is known. The realm of a sacred king (like the pharaohs of ancient Egypt) who provides a direct and visible link between his people and the gods gives a different message about the meaning of human life from a modern democracy, which says through the symbol of its own structure that one finds his or her meaning within society through some degree of individual freedom, and that in principle it is the individual rather than the leader or the society that is sacred. Comparably different messages are offered about what it means to be human by other arrangements, from the primitive clan to the twentieth-century totalitarian state, and by different economic and political systems, from barter to feudalism to modern capitalism and socialism.

The picture is made more complex by the fact that one actually lives in several concentric social structures at the same time—family, local community, nation, culture area. Together with them, one is probably involved with several subsystems—religious group, clubs, educational institution, informal friendship affiliations. All of these also have their own implicit messages about what it means to be human, about what is important and what is not. These messages may be far from consistent with each other, and the individual has to sort them out as best he or she can.

It is all these groupings working together that determine who we are and what we do, even in the most seemingly trivial matters. Consider an American girl of ten swinging in a playground. She is there because the city provided the playground, her friends asked her to go with them, a church group meeting for that afternoon was cancelled, and she lives in a culture in which swinging in a playground is what children do—doing what children do being very important to children in every culture.

## RELIGIOUS GROUPS IN SOCIETY

Religious groups are parts of this complex. They take shape within the context of a society's articulation of what it means to be human, but the relation of the religious group to the larger society and its message—whether it accepts or rejects or modifies it—varies as vastly as do the kinds of religious groups. Sometimes the religious group is virtually identical with the society as a whole, as in ancient Egypt where the sacred king was also high priest and nearly all his subjects worshippers of him and his gods. Other groups have seen surrounding society as very sinful and have withdrawn as far from it as possible, or have even fomented violent revolution under the aegis of religious symbols.

Obviously, these two extremes and all the possible variations in between give very different messages about the meaning of being a real self and how the self can establish rapport with the infinite. To say this is done best by accepting the established structures of one's society and following devoutly the spiritual ways of one's fathers and neighbors, or to say one can best relate to the infinite by withdrawing from general society and associating instead with a small minority of like-minded believers, would be to say two very different things about oneself and about God.

Indeed, it is important to note that the nature of the group, like the nature of the worship, modifies experienced meaning even of doctrinal beliefs. A teaching that looks the same when set down on paper can come across very differently in different social settings. To say that Jesus is Savior, for example, in a large mainline church, a small and intense Christian sect, and a tiny mission in a non-Christian land is, in social context, to make a statement of conformity, rebellion, and alienation, respectively.

Before going on to the different kinds of religious groups, let us emphasize again that religion always has an interpersonal or social aspect; a message resides in this aspect of the religion that is just as important in what it says about self and God as what the doctrine or

worship says. Even a withdrawal from society, even a refusal to participate in any group religious activities at all, is a social statement that has
meaning because of the prior fact that humans are social creatures.

What legitimates a religion, both in its own eyes and those of
others, is its social structure and its relation to the larger society. Some
social expression is necessary in religion because the construction of a
universe of meaning we can really accept must be a social act. We feel
uneasy with purely independent views of reality, whether in ourselves
or in someone else. Since we cannot live apart from society, interpersonal
agreements about the limits of reality are very important. We have
already observed the importance of language and the givenness of family
and community. We cannot travel down a road together unless we agree
on where the road is.

Those whose perception of reality varies greatly from the social
construction are characterized as either heretical or insane and dealt with
accordingly. Paranoid or schizophrenic persons frequently develop elaborate religious symbol systems that differ from the socially accepted ones
chiefly in their private nature. They are often of remarkable beauty and
meaning, at least for the individual, and may reconstruct classic motifs of
myth and symbol. It is, however, the inward isolation of the insane
individual that leads him or her to make a new construction of reality.
His or her construction is usually not accepted by others—and indeed
may seem profoundly disturbing to them—just because the others know
that a legitimate view of reality has to be social, has to be shared by
several people, and the insane person's is not. It does not have social
completion. If a person of new vision is able to control the solipsism of
his or her transcendent opening well enough to acknowledge the meaning of the social environment—that it is part of completeness, that the
vision can only be finalized and legitimated when it has found social
symbols of expression as well as those in the individual's own mind and
art, and that to be so it must use some common expression and mediate
between a visionary and a socially pragmatic way of being—far from
being merely mad, he or she may be recognized as a person of immense
value to society. The history of religions suggests that it is not so much
the objective content of the message as the relation of it and especially of
the messenger to society that determines whether it is successful or not in
the terms of this world.

This means that the messenger must express his or her indebt-
edness to the prior social matrix and accept his or her position as within
the range of accepted human possibilities by following some standard
means of social expression. As did Jesus when he proclaimed that his
teaching was not a denial but fulfillment of the Jewish law, he or she must

show some symbolic acceptance of the social milieu as well as dissidence from it. In an archaic shamanistic society, the role of visionary shaman should be taken up in a more or less normative way—getting the right training and sponsorship, seeing visions only within the outer limits of the culture's expectations, bringing his ecstatic capacities under control so that they emerge only at proper times. They should finally appear only in shamanistic seances, not usually in berserk behavior. In modern American society, the visionary should express himself or herself in accepted times and means—through preaching, lecturing, writing books —and should maintain an ability to relate warmly and without har- angues to people outside the vision-communicating situation. It helps if the new vision can be shown to be in some way a subsystem of what is already socially accepted—a new revelation of the God the others already acknowledge.

Above all, the prophet should be able to legitimate his or her activity by forming a group, if possible setting up the group legally with articles of incorporation. Getting even one other person to accept and share the reality of a religious construction of reality makes the experi- ence vastly different for both parties from a purely private vision. It becomes social, even if it is only two against the world. They can talk about it and practice it together, making it of a piece with language and society rather than with inchoate subjectivity and isolation. The differ- ence is beyond mere calculation.

Indeed, even in the eyes of the disbelieving remainder of society, acceptance by one or more other persons changes the nature of the visionary's view. If it is a closed society, it gives him or her the dubious honor of being a heretic instead of a madman; in more tolerant circum- stances it may afford him or her the marginal legitimacy of being a tolerated exerciser of religious freedom instead of a "nut." Societies that pride themselves on freedom can tolerate and even encourage a wide spectrum of independent world views as long as each in turn accepts the priority of the social construction of reality and its message about what it means to be human. For some societies, such as modern democracies, society's message includes a statement that humans may have some differences in religion. Pluralism within society is part of the total state- ment the society is making. If the new visionary is to compete with older churches, this may well mean that the modern shaman is put under all the more pressure to establish a formal group structure with formal papers and to abide by all the unwritten rules.

If the modern shaman is able to handle the legal details and ac- counting of the group, as well as to see invisible realities, that person is generally left undisturbed. The shaman shows ability to move between two social constructions of reality, that of the small groups and that of society as a whole—and in modern pluralism, the most effective people of all are those who can operate in several realities at once.

## RELIGIOUS GROUPS

What is a religious group? It is a set of people whose interpersonal relations complete for one another the symbolic expression of religious experience. Since the group itself is a religious symbol, it also stimulates further experience. For one who has been converted to a particular religion, a prayer group made up of like-minded people is a congenial fellowship that both completes the initial experience by supporting it and by showing that it is, after all, a shared experience, and stimulates more experiences along the same line as the initial one.

The group legitimates the religious experiences of individuals in it by incorporating them into a *social* perception of reality and ultimately into *the* social construction of reality of the culture in which they live, whether as mainstays or dissidents. As a group it has some kind of participation (even if only through withdrawal) in that culture. So any religious group through its very structure and relation to the cultural environment communicates significant messages about self and reality.

The group also establishes a sense of religious power in the individuals within it. When functioning well, religious institutions and groups of all sorts bring together not only heaven and earth, but also the individual and effective power. Religious institutions and groups are like miniaturizations of a hard world and an inconceivably vast cosmos in which the hardness and the vastness are replaced with human warmth and manageability, as well as transcendent wonder. Through religion the average person can feel effective and important, close to power and ways of changing things the nonreligious world does not know.

The Chinese peasant prayed in temples to gods who were deified high Mandarin officials. In the flesh he or she would hardly have approached these personages with humble requests, but now that they were elevated to temple gods they were, paradoxically, more accessible to the common man who, though he or she may not be heard by earthly officials, could be heard in heaven.

Ordinary American churchgoers, troubled by news of hunger and revolution in less fortunate areas of the world, mention these places in prayer groups and contribute to missionaries overseas. They believe these gestures help even if, when they look at the suffering of the world from the perspective of numbers and politics, matters seem almost beyond help. Religion creates a human-sized, individual-sized world and universe in which, through the religious group, individuals can find not only meaning for themselves but also may be effective in the larger world and universe.

Let us now examine some styles of religious sociological activity. These range from vast international religions numbering hundreds of millions to private visions shared with one or two others. We can mention only a few representative categories—notice that they actually overlap.

## GREAT AND LITTLE TRADITIONS

Anthropologist Robert Redfield distinguishes between *Great Traditions* and *Little Traditions* within a culture and religion, using these terms to point to the fact that, within every culture, there are two ways of expressing its motifs.[1] One, the great tradition, has been the way of books and scholars and intellectuals; the other, the little tradition, has been the way of the common people. In older societies, the latter is called folk religion; in modern societies like the American, it is called popular culture.

To comprehend the great tradition, think of scholars at universities and chaplains at the courts of great kings, or, in many cases, all those who can read and write and do actually read the major books of the cultural heritage. The great tradition is that of the literate elite. It takes a long perspective; it is oriented toward history and the past out of which the present comes. Intellectual and emotionally cool, it is likely to be the way the religious tradition is presented in the centers of learning, the major cathedrals or temples, and (unless political considerations mandate a closer relation to the popular traditions) the palaces or centers of power. The great traditions of the world's religions are immensely important. It is to them that we owe the preservation of most the world's heritage of religious literature—the scriptures, the great commentaries like the Talmud and the Laws of Manu, and the rigorous philosophical defenses of faith such as those of Thomas Aquinas, al-Ghazzali, and Shankara that have made religion able to compete with other kinds of thought. It is also to them that we owe the continuing perception that a religion has historical conditioning. It appeared at a particular point in history, which orthodoxy regards as the pivot of historical time—the place where "the hopes and fears of all the years are met"—and has undergone certain stages of change and development. This is knowledge both hopeful and

---

[1]Robert Redfield, *The Little Community and Peasant Society and Culture* (Chicago, Ill.: University of Chicago Press, 1960).

dangerous but in any case not widely known (or if known, understood) by the masses, who for all practical purposes know things only as they are in the present.

That gives an insight into the nature of the little tradition. It is essentially nonliterary, is oriented to the present and to cosmic time rather than to history, concentrates on worship and experience more than theory, and is basically transmitted within family and community rather than through books and academic teachers. For people oriented toward the little tradition, religion centers around the seasonal festivals and the ways things are done in the community, rather than around philosophical teachings in books. Religion is not unemotional; it may become fervent, yet the fervor is associated with pilgrimage, devotion, conversion, or festive joy as venues that have always been there. More often than the great tradition, the little tradition understands that differences in worship and social context make religions different as surely as differences in theory—in fact, it is likely not to understand differences in theory save as they are expressed in differences in worship. All religions are the same on the popular level, except as they *do* different things and attract different people.

I recall that some years ago, when I was clergyman of the Episcopal church in a small town in the Midwest, a lady told me that the Methodist and Presbyterian churches in the same town combined their services during the summer. She added that she did not see any reason why they should not do so all year round, since there was no real difference in their manner of worship. That attitude, centered on worship-experience and the perspective of the local community, was very much from out of the little tradition mentality. Elites of the Methodist and Presbyterian great traditions would immediately have realized that, although it is true their forms of worship in America have come to be quite similar, the historical background and theological heritage—the literary and historical time dimensions—of the two churches are very different. Among other things, one comes out of the Calvinist tradition with its emphasis on the fallen state of mankind, while the other says that after conversion true holiness and Christian perfection are at least lively possibilities. For most people in that small town, those were the issues of long ago and far away, while what sort of people attended worship in each church and what they did there were close at hand and well known. On this score, the Methodists and Presbyterians seemed little different. If the lady to whom I spoke had visited the local Roman Catholic, Lutheran, or my own Episcopal church, whether the doctrine as actually preached and taught was familiar or strange, the differences in worship from Methodism or Presbyterianism—with people standing at altars in colorful

The great tradition in religion is brought to mind by England's lovely medieval Salisbury cathedral. This magnificent church was built by cooperative community effort and was the seat of a bishop of the predominant faith.

vestments and making ritual gestures and so forth—would probably have been enough to convince her that it was a different faith.

In America in general, the distinction between great tradition and little tradition follows lines parallel to this discussion. Defenders of the great traditions tend to have a background in theological seminaries or to be influenced by people who do. They have an extensive, if perhaps partisan, knowledge of church history and use arguments from out of it about what the true teaching of a tradition is. Nonetheless, their awareness of the whole matter of history and the ambivalences inherent in it suggest, on a deep level, a less than intense identification with every faddish contemporary religious movement and an affirmation of the whole tradition instead. At the same time, these people have important links to the great traditions in the culture of art and music. (In the contemporary European and American scene, this means they have more feeling for what Bach and Palestrina represent than for country-western gospel music.) Characteristically, it is this tradition that has control of the major temples, churches, and cathedrals and has ties to the centers of political power.

In American religion today, especially in Protestantism, the little or popular tradition does mean an orientation to the Bible, but not one greatly informed by the historical or scholarly study favored by the great tradition. Rather, the Bible is more a matter of immediacy and a religious symbol; the orientation is toward seeing it as a direct stimulus to conversion, devotional fervor, and psychological collapse of intervening time on behalf of identification with first-century roles in Christianity or Judaism. (The surest sign of difference between great and little tradition in any culture seems to be whether historical perspective has any meaning or not. That is not to say that one approach is better than another; the lack of consciousness of historical time of the little tradition is repeated, in another mode, in the thought of the profoundest mystics.) In America, the differences in styles of worship between great and little traditions is evident in the less intellectual and more emotive quality of the latter. The typical little tradition enthusiasm for pilgrimage is not so apparent but may be reflected in the popularity of conferences, missionary work, and choir tours that involve travel.

Turning to another culture, the distinction of great and little tradition in India is even more marked. There, the great tradition has been essentially that of the brahmins, the hereditary priests and intellectuals who have been chaplains of wealthy and aristocratic homes and custodians of the profoundest spiritual lore of India. Every brahmin young man was expected to learn by heart a portion of the Vedic scriptures and to be able to perform the sacrifices around the sacred fire by which initiations and marriages were sanctified. The brahmins had a mixed reputation in India. On one hand, they were widely accounted arrogant and avaricious; on the other, their blessings were greatly desired and their curses feared, and their collective assent was ultimately required for any spiritual development to be regarded as orthodox. Books such as the Upanishads and Bhagavad-Gita, now considered part of the spiritual heritage of the world as a whole, have been given to the world chiefly because of brahmin preservation of them over many centuries.

Conversely, the Hindu little tradition has not been greatly concerned about what it might give the world centuries from now, because it does not think in terms of historical time. Rather, even as with the little tradition in America, its focus is on different dimensions of time—the seasonal cycle of festivals in the village; the inner psychological time, or timelessness, of worship, devotion, and sometimes fervor or mystical ascent as it is actually experienced by the ordinary, nonliterate people and those priests and holy men close to them. This tradition takes its fundamental structures—the caste system, the gods and their names and temples, the roles of wandering entertainers and holy men—as given, as having been that way without change at least back to mythical time. It is not concerned with understanding or questioning them intellectually but with enforcing them and also garnering from them what intensity of experience one can, which may be quite a bit. This is the religion of temple, wayside shrine, home altar, careful observance of caste, and village festival, which one learns not from books but through growing up —and which, however unsophisticated, will always be linked with one's earliest childhood memories of maternal arms and cattle byres and holidays.

Of course, strong links exist between great and little traditions, and the line separating them is often fuzzy. Probably for this reason, some of the most influential religious personalities and movements have been those able to relate convincingly to both sides and to borrow freely from both. In eighth-century Japan, Buddhism was seriously divided between the learned, wealthy, aristocratic, and officially recognized temples of Nara, the capital, and a popular Buddhistic religion of the countryside that was unorthodox, but closely involved in the lives of the peasants, and under the leadership of shamanistic, charismatic priests who served as country healers, prophets, wonder workers, mystics, and leaders of such practical enterprises as constructing bridges and irrigation projects. It was a classic case of the split between great and little tradition. The great tradition was scholarly and patronized undying art. Indeed, millions of tourists a year go to Nara to appreciate the glowing cultural legacy of that era. That richness, however, was paid for by the rents and taxes of laboring peasants who themselves had little access to it. The peasants' shamanistic priests sometimes minced few words in

Procession in a popular Hindu festival in Madras, India.

decrying the sins of the ruling class and its priests and were in turn sometimes persecuted. Then, in the middle of the century, the Emperor Shomu, aware of the gap and eager to reconcile the countryside so that he could raise money to pay for the Great Buddha he desired as a national shrine, took the step of appointing Gyogi, a leader of the shamanistic Buddhists, chief priest of all Japanese Buddhism. Gyogi was able to bring both groups together through his links with the two sides, and he also helped reconcile Shinto and Buddhism by receiving oracles at the Grand Shrine of Ise favorable to building the Great Buddha. The Great Buddha was erected and is now the noblest of all the cultural attractions of Nara.

Other figures like this who have linked both traditions could be named, including St. Francis, Gandhi, and many of the great American evangelists. They are people who have some learning representative of the great tradition, yet have come out of a popular background or are able to relate deeply to it, so that the ordinary people feel instinctively, "This man is one of us—he or she thinks and prays like us, yet more effectively.

We can understand and trust him or her." In a word, this person is able to enter the timeless, nonhistorical mood of popular culture by taking the present seriously. He or she can play the role of a folk religion saint or prophet and be appreciated as such, yet also has goals and levels of understanding from the great tradition that motivate his or her actions and may make him or her a motivator of reconciliation and dynamic change.

For obvious reasons, political leaders, such as the Emperor Shomu and many others down to the present, are especially concerned about maintaining links with the little tradition of their country's religion—more so usually than the great tradition's priestly or academic leadership. Rulers may show great favor to such popular religious leaders and linking figures as are deemed politically reliable. This patronage is not necessarily insincere—the leader may be someone who genuinely prefers popular religionists or may earnestly want to reconcile and befriend all segments of the population for the best of motives. Its political value to the leadership, however, is far from negligible. It should be realized that, although courts and governments may also patronize the great tradition, the real locus of the great tradition in a religious culture is not so much in its aristocratic and political milieu as in its upper priestly and academic circles. In India, for example, it was not found in the circles of emperors or maharajahs (save for the occasional Ashoka or Akbar) but among learned brahmins or mullahs who might accept the gifts of kings but whose lives were very different from theirs.

## ESTABLISHED RELIGION

The great and little traditions together represent only one side of religious life. Seen in themselves, they suggest a static sort of spiritual life, tied in with ponderous institutions—whether it is the way of scholars studying the same texts generation after generation or of peasants passing on immemorial folklore for age on age. While religion is never really changeless, it does have a side that, whether scholarly or folkish, likes to think of itself as unchanging and that is closely related to the most deeply rooted structures of the society. This kind of religion can be called *Established Religion*.

There is, however, another side of religion and another manner of religious social experience. It was hinted at in the discussion of the linking religious figures and movements that often seem to supply the impetus for change. It leads us into the world of new religious movements—movements typically centering around remarkable persons, breaking into the placid waters of established religion to denounce many of its beliefs and practices and perhaps especially social structure, to propose radical alternatives, and to make *their* religion a vehicle for protest on many levels. In time, of course, some of these movements may sink back into established religion or become the bases of new established religions. For the time they are at odds with the dominant pattern and show a disjuncture in the spiritual fabric, they are something else— finally a whole different way of being religious. This way may be called *Emergent Religion.*

Each of these two ways, established and emergent religion, has its own message about the nature of a real self and the way to transcendence. Established religion says that one can find ultimate meaning through living within the religious traditions of one's community. It says that sufficient religious truth can be known by most people, not just an elite. It indicates that even though the great tradition version of the religion may be more ample and accurate, the way it is practiced by the little tradition is adequate and perhaps even more devout; while it may seem superficially superstitious, it is informed by what has been called *implicit faith* in the central religious truths. Established religion then says it is better to participate in the normative religion with one's relatives, neighbors, and friends than to break with them for the sake of some individual calling.

Established religion comes in many shapes and sizes. We cannot mention every kind of sociological expression it takes, but only a few representative categories.[2] First, there are the international and intercultural religions. The major faiths that are truly intercultural are Buddhism, Christianity, and Islam; within Christianity the Roman Catholic church stands as a unique example of a very large religious institution that is highly international yet centrally administered. Each of these religions has been a bearer of culture to many lands, and so has generated there a particular cultural tone, usually working its way down from the religion's great tradition, which is more international and intercultural than most aspects of the little tradition. They have also appeared in each place as something that has come in within historical time, and thus, each exhibits a degree of tension with the indigenous culture.

The message of these religions is that to be a real self and in rapport with infinity, it is better to be aligned with a culturally rich and very numerous movement. Truth is not just for a handful and is not even just the possession of one nation or one culture. One must disdain absolutizing one's own land or way of life for the sake of the higher absolutes

---

[2] These categories are based on Ernst Troeltsch, *The Social Teaching of the Christian Churches,* trans. Olive Wyon (New York: The Macmillan Company, 1931) vol. 2; and especially J. Milton Yinger, *Religion, Society, and the Individual* (New York: The Macmillan Company, 1957).

of the international religion; one must be detached from any single culture, though far from anticulture.

These faiths are overwhelming majorities in most places where they are found, though minorities in some—as are Christianity in Japan and Buddhism in America. They have the experience of being both broad-based religions and tiny withdrawal groups, depending on circumstances. Where they are greatly preponderant, they are examples of established religion.

Besides such international institutions, established religion can also be manifested as national religions shared by the majority of the population, whether predominant churches, such as the Church of England or Lutheran churches in north Germany and Scandinavia, or one-culture religions, such as Hinduism in India or the traditional religious complexes of China, Japan, and some African states.

Finally, established religion can be expressed through denominationalism. A denomination is a particular institutional and sociological organization within a larger religious tradition. In effect it ministers mostly to the spiritual needs of its members, probably a minority of the total society. Collectively in a denominational society, a number of parallel denominations comprise the great majority and represent the society's established religion. America, of course, is a denominational society, as are some British Commonwealth nations and, in many respects, Japanese Buddhism.

Conversely, it is mainly in connection with denominational societies that another manifestation of established religion, called *Civil Religion*, has been discussed.[3] This name pertains to a belief that society as a whole has a sacred meaning apart from individual religious groups. In America, for example, it is the "religion" (cutting across many denominations of our pluralistic society) of patriotic holidays, such as the Fourth of July and Thanksgiving, and the belief that the nation as a whole has a calling from God and a divine destiny. It has been argued, in fact, that there is a civil religion interpretation of American history that parallels biblical history—the coming of the Pilgrims corresponding to the call of Abraham, the Revolutionary War comparable to the Exodus, Washington like Moses, the Civil War the redemptive suffering of this new Israel, and Lincoln like Christ in his wisdom and sorrows. Whether one goes this far or not, there is something spiritually American yet nondenominational that many feel and that expresses itself in certain attitudes, holy days, and places like the Arlington National Cemetery.

---

[3] See Russell E. Richey and Donald G. Jones, eds., *American Civil Religion* (New York: Harper & Row, Publishers, Inc., 1974).

Whether international, national, or denominational, a church connected with established religion tends to have certain characteristics.
Because it has a long tradition and an institutionalized structure, it
generally has strict, clearly defined doctrinal and moral positions in
theory. In practice it has to be fairly tolerant as long as the integrity of the
institution is maintained. Since it is the nominal religion of the great
majority of the people—of those who have not made a self-conscious,
deliberate choice to be something else—it must find ways to accept
people in all stages of spirituality. It has ways of incorporating infants of
all families into its symbolic network through baptism or comparable
sacraments; it has a conspicuous role in traditional festivals and community celebrations; its architecture is old and monumental; its leaders are
spokespersons for and to the community on moral, and perhaps political,
issues of general concern.

The established religion enforces, probably through some pattern
of constraint and reward, the normative values of the community. While
offering paths to sainthood for those called to follow them, it provides
ways for those of more modest ambition to pursue meaningful spiritual
lives in some hope of commensurate reward. Thus, in predominantly
Buddhist countries, the Buddhist institution offers monks opportunity
to make the ultimate meditations that lead to nirvana and laymen opportunities to gain merit through good deeds and devotional practices that
will result in a desirable reincarnation.

Structures of the established religion tend to parallel those of society as a whole, especially on the national and denominational religion
level. Thus in America they have democratic-parliamentary forms, in
Japan hereditary leadership, and in India they center around the charisma of saints.

One could ask whether established religion as a concept still has the
meaning today that it did in the past. Modern institutional secularism,
loss of belief or interest in religion, and revolutionary changes like those
in China have greatly altered the meaning of a notion such as the
normative religion of a society. But there is a sense in which religions
traditionally considered the national religion have very different roles
and meanings in their societies from those long considered non-
conformist. One is identified, at least symbolically, with the whole
society in national religion, with a minority segment within it in other
groups.

Finally, let us consider again the meaning of the little tradition and
folk religion as part of established religion. Its usages are called little
tradition because, being nonliterary, they seem on the surface limited to
small areas and time as counted in generations. In a deeper sense,

however, folk and popular religion is greater than any great tradition; it is a sea out of which great traditions rise and fall. Ultimately, most of the symbols, motifs, and ideas of the great traditions have come out of common little tradition patterns, and even the most appealing aspects of the great traditions—its festivals, rites, social roles—are usually only specific adaptations of common little tradition practices such as having seasonal rites and sacred places. If one can so speak, perhaps 80 percent of all religion is essentially "just religion"—that is, the little tradition or popular religion kind of activity that does not differ much in role from one culture or faith to another but only in detail—this symbol or this name instead of that. A family gathering with prayers, feasting, and games for the children is not much different whether it is on a Jewish, Christian, Muslim, or Hindu joyous holy day. Only the "top 20 percent" represents the specific ideas and doctrines of each faith—over which, because of the particular kinds of identification and experience they may provide, great polemic is sometimes waged.

## EMERGENT RELIGION

It is with this whole pattern of ongoing established religion that emergent religion contrasts. Of course it has roots in it, but it bends away from its environing established religion. If established religion in a culture is a pervasive sea, emergent religion is a volcanic island breaking through its surface and roiling the waters around it.

The definitions of the word emergent suggest several salient characteristics of the sort of religion of which we are now speaking. As an adjective, *emergent* defines something arising out of a fluid which heretofore has covered or concealed it, or suddenly appearing, or coming as a natural or logical outcome of a situation (such as a war), or appearing as something novel in a process of evolution. As a noun, the word indicates something that stands out, as a tree above the forest.

These definitions, if applied to religious life, really apply quite well to the counterpart of established religion. New religions emerge out of the fluid sea of popular religion, perhaps suddenly, perhaps in response to situations that impel change such as wars or conquest or new cultural contacts, perhaps as an inevitable result, like a mutation, of a process of evolution. They are likely to be recent, for the tendency is for an emergent religion to become a new established religion, or a part of an ongoing complex that makes up established religion, within a few generations. Some emergent religions, like the Amish, remain emergent in the sense of maintaining a distinctive visibility indefinitely; they do not mix and never really become part of the establishment.

An example of emergent religion is Tenrikyo, one of the new religions of Japan, although it is now over a century old.[4] Tenrikyo traces its inception back to 1838, in the last years of old Japan before its phenomenal modernization that began in 1868 under the Emperor Meiji. The final decades before the end of the old regime were times of increasing economic trouble and civil unrest. The traditional popular religion, more than anything else a perpetuation of the shamanistic Buddhism already discussed, persisted, but popular frenzies of dancing and pilgrimage, especially to Ise, swept through from time to time, more and more associated with prophecies of immense change.

In 1838 the son of a prosperous farmer near Nara suffered intense pain in his leg, but a series of shamanistic healing sessions seemed to give him temporary relief. The shaman's female assistant would go into trance and be possessed by a god, whom the shaman would then worship for healing. On one occasion the shaman's usual assistant was not available, and Miki Nakayama, the farmer's wife, substituted for her. When she went into trance, however, a very unexpected thing happened: a voice spoke through her lips saying, "I am the true and original God," and declared that he would use Miki as his residence in this world.

From then on, according to Tenrikyo belief, Miki Nakayama was the instrument and shrine of God. She lived a busy and holy life; she healed and gave forth words and writings that are believed to be messages of God. Above all, she taught a sacred dance that reenacts the creation of the world by the one God and indicated the sacred spot where the creation of mankind began. A fundamental Tenrikyo belief is that by knowing and dancing-out the creation of the world by God the Parent, as the Creator is called, mankind can be brought back into the original harmony with God. Now there is, as Miki instructed, a pillar over this spot, and it is the heart of a vast temple, which in turn is the hub of Tenri City, a religious city with administrative headquarters of the faith, pilgrimage hostels, training schools, and a university. Pilgrims come from all over the world to this site, and the sacred dance is performed around the pillar.

This indicates that belief in the revelation of God through Miki Nakayama has grown and prospered. It began with a small and often-

---

[4] On Tenrikyo and other Japanese new religions, see Harry Thomsen, *The New Religions of Japan* (Rutland and Tokyo: Charles E. Tuttle, 1963), and Robert S. Ellwood, Jr., *The Eagle and the Rising Sun* (Philadelphia, Pa.: The Westminster Press, 1974). On Cargo Cults, see Peter Worsley, *The Trumpet Shall Sound* (New York: Schocken Books, Inc., 1968). On new religions in America, see Robert S. Ellwood, Jr., *Religious and Spiritual Groups in Modern America* (Englewood Cliffs, N.J.: Prentice-Hall, Inc., 1973). See also Bryan Wilson, *Religious Sects* (London: Weidenfeld and Nicolson, 1970), for a worldwide perspective.

persecuted band around her. Since her passing in 1887, it has become a large and well-organized institution, with an ample structure of classes, churches, and services, as well as missionary zeal.

Other emergent religions could be cited, from the twentieth-century Cargo Cults of some colonial areas to a number of well-known religious movements in modern America. Nevertheless, the story of Tenrikyo adequately illustrates several of the most important features of emergent religion.

First, it emerges in a time of change, when many people feel that traditional values are being shaken and the future is uncertain. (This is not too much of a qualification, since most periods appear as times of transition and uncertain future to the people actually living in them, seeming eras of calm and stability only in the retrospective vision of later generations caught up in their own times of change.) In times of change, some classes of society feel left behind or want ways to comprehend and relate to the changes. Emergent religion usually first takes root among groups of people who are relatively powerless within society, or not at the center of change—peasants in Japan, colonial peoples, minorities, the young, women. It provides them, as an elect who are in on a divine secret, with a compensatory even greater power. The emergent religion says that God is doing something in the changes that only they know about, or else that he is doing something even greater than what is happening in the outer world and that this will be climaxed in the near future. This teaching enables the believers to accept change by understanding it in the religious language familiar to them from the older popular and established religion, but with a new twist. As the institution grows, it enables believers to take part in something with a new and modern feel, similar to that of the modern government and business to which they may be outsiders, but *theirs* and for the sake of a faith they can understand.

Second, the emergent religion typically makes the jump from established religion to something new by selecting from out of the amorphous sea of tradition *one* person, place, teaching, practice, and group as its focus, to give it a new, crisp, distinct shape. Established religion tends implicitly toward multiplicity and even polytheism. Whatever the official position, there are likely to be a number of saints and heroes as sacred personalities, of charismatic preachers, of possible institutional affiliations, of sacred churches and places, but when emergent religion breaks through in that scene, it is reversed. As in the case of Miki Nakayama, emergent religion singles out and absolutizes particular examples of these manifold forms. It selects one shaman or spiritual person out of many candidates, one God out of many polytheisitic or attributional candidates, one sacred place out of the many shrines of established religion, one religious practice or rite out of many possibilities. This selectivity gives it a unique identity within the prevailing religious complex but at the same time sets up the likelihood of conflict. Conflict, however, is the stuff of life for emergent religion, since it enhances the distinctiveness that it craves.

Another characteristic of emergent religion is that it is likely to emphasize a future orientation. It will probably teach that in the near future a utopian kingdom, or a divine judgment that will vindicate its claims, will occur. This sort of prediction can only enhance its appeal to people caught in a time of rapid change when the future is unsure. It is also an expression of the fact that the religion, because it surfaced in a time of rapid change, really represents a discovery, in a new and radical sense, of historical time. Eschatology, or religious teaching about future events, suggests that what the God whom one already understands can do about the future is greater than what any human changes (about which one may in any case feel dubious) can bring about. It says that what you have already seen is nothing compared to what God or the gods will bring to pass.

Emergent religion usually centers around a charismatic personality —an individual who by the radiance of his or her own personality and the appeal of what he or she is, rather than any structural authority, draws the people to him or her. The centrality of the charismatic person, rather than the institutional appeal of the faith, is very important. Unlike established religion, which can depend on the allegiance of all those not sufficiently moved to protest against it to make a self-conscious adult choice to be something else, emergent religion is mainly made up of converts who *have* made such a choice—which gives it a reservoir of highly committed persons but also means that it must maintain a level of intensity sufficient to counteract the natural pressures of family, community, and inertia that keep people within the established religion of their particular place.

The upshot is, in fact, that after two or three generations most emergent religions become established religions or, at least, a part of whatever established religion is prevalent. This is a result of the process called by the sociologist Max Weber "routinization of charisma"—when the grace and teachings communicated in unexpected ways by the religious founder come to be channeled, or are said to be channeled, through an institution in particular times and places. What he or she did spontaneously now comes through sacraments; what he or she said on odd occasions now comes through preaching, at regularly scheduled services.

Two basic kinds of emergent religion should be distinguished. They may be called *intensive* and *expansive* religion. This pair corresponds with what some sociologists of religion have called respectively *sect* and *cult*, but those terms no longer seem to have appropriate connotations.

Intensive emergent religion groups withdraw from ordinary society in favor of a more intense and rigorous commitment to major symbols of the established religion. Within American Christianity, they would be groups such as Seventh-Day Adventists and Jehovah's Witnesses; within Judaism, extreme Hasidic groups. They tend to be legalistic, feeling ordinary followers of the same religion are lukewarm or hypocritical and not really serious about the religion in which, for cultural reasons, they find themselves. Sometimes, as in the case of the Amish or Hutterites, intensive religionists are communal. More often they are not, but their members tend to have a high involvement with the group and relatively little relationship, except perhaps for evangelistic purposes, with the society outside of the intensive circle. The intensive religion communicates a message that, apart from a very high level of group involvement and intensity of commitment, the full realization of religion's ability to make one feel like a real self and have access to infinite life cannot be realized.

Expansive emergent religion, on the other hand, withdraws from ordinary society in order to found what is, in its adherents' eyes, a more broadly based experience than that of the monochrome religion of the society. It seeks to combine elements of the established religion with new ideas and teachings from science, from far-away places, and from inner vision. In America, examples would be movements such as Spiritualism, Scientology, and various meditation and devotional movements brought in from India or Japan. Expansive religion is generally centered more on mystical experience than on the truth of particular rules or tenets. It is, however, just as likely as intensive emergent religion to be centered around loyalty to a particular charismatic leader and some simple, sure technique for spiritual transformation. It may also be just as much a withdrawal group. Expansive groups, though, are more likely to have outer, diffuse circles of followers of milder fervor, since it is possible to study the teachers and practice the meditation or whatever with greater or less degree of separation from the ordinary world.

It should be emphasized that no specific religion is established or emergent per se; these categories are dependent not on the nature of the religion but on role. A religion can be emergent in one place and established in another, or it can be one at one point in its history and the other at another. Buddhist faith is established in Thailand and Japan but likely to be emergent in America. Buddhism and Christianity were both emergent at the time of their inception but became established within a few generations. As has been indicated, most religions become established within two or three generations because of the routinization of the original charisma and because more and more of their members are born within the faith rather than converted.

The denomination and its founder, who is generally the sort of personality who links great and little traditions (and also links established and emergent religion) are often bridge phenomena. The denomination's founder—for example, Luther, Wesley, Shinran, and Vivekananda—is typically a reformer within a great, well-established religion who emphasizes a particular aspect of or attitude toward it as a key to the whole. As does emergent religion generally, he or she singles out one simple sure key to the essence of its immense experience and mystery, whether faith, scripture, one certain rite, or one doctrine. At the same time, his or her appeal is usually affected by social factors; it serves as a means of identification for a particular nation, social class, immigrant group, or personality type. Methodism appealed particularly to the working classes in England and to frontiersmen in America; denominational Lutheranism in America represents the heritage of both state churches and pietistic movements in northern Europe.

Denominationalism says that individuals and movements within the long history of a great religion can provide adequately definitive expressions of the religion's heritage, even though they come late in its history and only in particular places. Those individuals and movements can in fact nearly eclipse the rest of the religion. Pure Land Buddhists in Japan, like denominational Protestants in America, know the history, teaching, and ethos of their version of the religion far better than any other. These movements started as emergent religion within an established version of the same faith and have finally become, for all intents and purposes, established themselves. They nevertheless retain a sense of being a sort of spiritual commonwealth, given to activism and belief that activity is good, all the more so because the denomination is not ultimately responsible for the whole faith. In a way, the denomination has the best and worst of both established and emergent religion. It can combine the solid sociological base of established religion with the venturesomeness of emergent religion, being able to take risks it could not if it felt itself responsible as an institution for the whole of the faith to which it is committed. It may, however, also suffer the conservative caution of an established religion, together with the new religion's hypersensitivity to criticism and precarious sense that it must always justify itself.

## TYPES OF RELIGIOUS PERSONALITY

Intertwined with different kinds of religious groups are different sorts of religious personality.[5] Each of these, in its own way, communicates a message about what it means to be religious. The number of conceivable types of religious personality is very great; perhaps every religious person is in the last analysis his or her own type. Several that are largely shaped by distinctive and well-known roles within religious history are listed here. These are not so much psychological types as role types that generally reflect or call forth certain attitudes and styles of behavior toward religion that amount to at least a public personality of a certain sort.

The following are what may be called objective types, types determined by structural role:

*The Shaman.* The shaman really transcends both objective and subjective categories since, as we have seen, his or her lot is a complex mixture of inner call, spiritistic experience, and socially defined role. Generally the shaman is an individual in primitive or archaic religion who, having become master of spirits that initially seemed likely to drive him or her mad, now uses them in public and private seances to heal, divine, and perhaps guide him or her to the worlds of the dead and the gods. The shaman's performances, which will follow traditional patterns, are centers of the experience of transcendence for the community and reinforce the sacred view of the universe.

*The Priest.* This category includes religious categories of other titles, such as bishop, minister, or rabbi. It embraces religious specialists, commonly professional, who hold office through heredity or training and whose primary function is to perform customary religious rites or services in expected ways. While he or she may be personally devout and have had a personal call, is the priest's position that assures his or her status. The priest mediates the sacred, without necessarily interiorizing it, objectively through rite and word and thus grants his community the necessary ongoing symbol of its presence afforded by institutions and their reliable custodians. Some religious specialists combine attributes of shaman and priest, fervor being a part of their role.

[5] These lists are suggested by those in Joachim Wach, *Sociology of Religion* (Chicago, Ill.: University of Chicago Press, 1944), and *The Comparative Study of Religion* (New York: Columbia University Press, 1958); and G. van der Leeuw, *Religion in Essence and Manifestation* (New York: Harper & Row, Publishers, Inc., 1963), 2 vols.

*The Monk and Nun.*   This category includes many sorts of holy people as well, such as the sadhus of India and some Sufi mystics of Islam. Unofficial approximations of its way can be found among the likes of some Protestant missionaries and members of contemporary religious communes. Not all approximations of the monk/nun type are even celibate, but the point of the type is to live a life outside the ordinary structures of society (yet in reality accepted and provided for by the religion) that exemplifies the ideal spiritual life as understood by that tradition. The way of the monk and nun has three goals: to save one's own soul; to exemplify the ideal way of perfection; and to support the tradition through prayer, teaching, and service. It is often (though not always) lived communally for mutual help in this difficult way and to exemplify the ideal social as well as individual model of perfection. Because its ideal is total dedication, this way may have (when well lived) an aura about it of poverty, abstinence, and inward holiness.

*The Layman.*   The layman is one who lives in a community and participates in its religious usages but is in no way a specialist or professional. He or she is the farmer, fisherman, or townsperson who is the ordinary worshipper. His or her place in the religion is not to be defined only negatively, by what he or she is not. Rather, it is a definite and distinctive role, with its own pattern, and is structurally essential to the religion as a whole. His or her religious life has, in practice, different goals and self-interpretation from that of the priest or monk. It is more related to supporting family, community, and ethics and to limited but specific benefits from the deities, as well as ultimate transformation or salvation. In the total life of the religion, the layman's role is to provide its material support, to make its rites and teachings practically possible by serving as their recipient, and to show the universality of the religion's world view by manifesting how it structures society and how it can have some kind of effect on the life of everyone.

*The Philosopher and Theologian.*   These are likely to be priests or monks, but some have been laymen. Their special role is to interpret the religion in terms of the intellectual tradition of their culture. (That tradition may in fact derive from other sources, just as Western intellectual culture derives largely from the Greeks.)

More subjective and spontaneous religious types are types that appear out of a person's inner need rather than out of a wish to fill (even if on the basis of a deeply felt calling) a role or niche already existent in the tradition. The following are some subjective types:

*The Founder.*   The founder of a new religion (the vocation commonly ascribed to persons such as the Buddha, Jesus, Confucius,

This modern Roman Catholic monk suggests one definite type of religious personality and lifestyle.

and Muhammad) is, needless to say, very rare. He or she must have an especially comprehensive religious personality, together with a special charisma and the right historical setting. The founder must become a symbol in his or her personality of both complexity and clarification. The great founders have had a reputation for being able to cover enough of the diverse roles of religion to provide models in themselves for all the strands a great religion needs to have: a spiritual way, an attitude toward society, a common touch, deep wisdom. The founder must also appear at a point of historical transition when religious symbols are still persuasive, but new ones or new arrangements of old ones are needed. The founder must be able to facilitate the transition because he or she has links with past, present, and future. People were reassured by Jesus, for example, because he did not reject the tradition, only its abuses; yet he also gave new symbols, himself and his cross, for a new age and suggested meaning to the future as well, in the kingdom of God. An important aspect of the founder is the fact that he or she has a small band of disciples. The disciple is a special type of religious personality in his or her own right and is essential to the founder to transmit his or her message as well as to provide an intimate audience for it allowing for the lasting institutionalization of the newly founded religion.

*The Mystic.*   The mystic is usually within a particular religious tradition, although sometimes, like Kabir in late medieval India, he or she is on the borderline of two and occasionally may seem genuinely independent. The mystic's emphasis is on attaining special states of consciousness considered direct, immediate experience of the religious reality. Understandably, to the mystic these states are more important than religious structures or rites, although their attainment is not necessarily inconsistent with the latter. Within the religion, the mystic has a role as an exemplar of its spiritual reality. He or she may be a teacher and writer, though of course many mystics have not been literary.

*The Reformer.*   The reformer works within a tradition rather than starting a new one, but he or she shares with the founder some sense of a new historical situation that requires a new application of the tradition, particularly in relation to the structures of the social order and the religious institution's own structures. While the reformer feels these structures ought to be changed, he or she does not believe that the essential doctrines of the faith should be altered. Rather, the reformer has the tradition highly interiorized; he or she does not need to depend on its outward forms and so can urge their extensive modification. In interiorization the reformer may be like the mystic, but unlike the mystic the reformer is critically aware of outward structures and wants to make them conform to his or her interiorization.

*The Popularizer.*   This category applies to a wide gamut of effective and charismatic preachers, Sufi saints, Buddhist missionaries, and Christian evangelists. The popularizer is not particularly a reformer or necessarily a mystic (though some have been these, too) but is a dynamic and attractive person able to appeal to the masses as well or even better than the founder. He or she makes no pretense of being original but is a transmitter of faith from out of his or her inner and contagious fervor, chiefly through rhetorical performance. The popularizer may well be an important link between great and little traditions.

Other types of religious personalities could be cited—saint, prophet, seer, convert, penitent, and mystagogue are among those that have been used in lists similar to this. These seem, at least to my mind, either overly imprecise or too restricted to particular traditions. Close equivalents to the types in the preceding lists can be found in nearly every religion.

On the other hand, it could be argued that the category of founder is not sufficiently distinct from the other three subjective types, especially reformer, since often the figure who becomes—from the perspective of historical hindsight—the founder of a new religion had no intention of being more than a mystic, reformer, or popularizer within the existing religion. From the perspective of his or her own time, the reformer may not have played a role much different from being a particularly successful exponent of one of those types.

I would contend that historical role as well as the psychology of the figure should be a factor in the typing of religious personalities. The founders did seem to have a psychology and self-understanding some-what different from mystics, reformers, and popularizers within tradi-tions, even if that difference may have been the product of the distinctive historical circumstances within which they worked and that also enabled their movements to take off as new religions.

All such lists of categories and types as this, in religious studies as in biology, contain elements of historical or evolutionary hindsight. Moreover, they are tentative and useful chiefly for the fact that working with them, rearranging them, and arguing about them can be an ex-cellent aid to study and understanding.

## THE TRANSFORMATION OF SOCIETY
## BY RELIGION

Having considered the effect of historical situations and sur-rounding society on religion, the reverse, which is equally important, must be noted. That is the transformative impact of religion on society. Religion and other social factors work both together and in reaction against each other to produce spirals of change. Here are some ways religions have affected change in society.

### Image of the Normative Nature
### of Society

All religions contain an image of the normative nature of society. It is not always explicit but is implied in the fundamental myths and symbols of the religion itself, especially in the life of the founder and his or her relations to disciples. For example, Buddhism suggests an aristocratic model of the social order in that the Buddha, however much he embraced ascetic poverty, did so as a prince who deliberately gave up riches. He was, then, always significantly different from a poor man who had never had wealth to sacrifice. In India, and also in China and Japan when it came there, Buddhism appealed most effectively (except in very modified devotional forms) to people of the upper classes, although it marvelously persuaded many of them to endow hospitals, orphanages, and hostels out of Buddhistic compassion. Even bodhisattvas were portrayed as crowned like princes. Buddhism has never succeeded on a large scale in relating to a society not basically hierarchical in the traditional aristocratic sense, and it may not so long as its fundamental human metaphor is of the prince who has everything but gives it up for the sake of enlightenment and universal compassion.

The case with Christianity is a little different. A fundamental image in it is *hidden kingship*. Jesus was the *hidden* son of David according to the tradition, and Jesus has often been thought to have known he was the Messiah or divinely annointed king who would establish a paradisal rule but to have kept this matter concealed for a time—the "messianic secret." This image suggests the possibility of royal legitimacy, and Christians have by and large been governed by kings, and have accepted them as parts of a divinely ordained pattern of society. The hiddenness of truth, the suffering of Christ at the hands of authority, and the early church's being the "offscouring of the earth" in Paul's term have all also placed in Christian minds a notion that in society things may not be what they seem. Christianity has thereby been the consolation both of authoritarian traditional regimes, such as those of the Bourbons and Hapsburgs in Europe, and of oppressed people, such as Blacks in the New World.

In any case, the implied image or images of society deriving from some of the most basic narratives and doctrines of the religion have profoundly affected societies to which the faith has spread.

### Normative Moral Literature

The normative moral literature of a religion—the Ten Commandments, the Confucian classics, and so forth—has an obvious role, but it needs to be understood that the impact of prescriptive ethics of this sort on a society may be less than straightforward. Confucian filial piety (sense of obligation toward parents) shaped the lives of billions in East

Asia and probably also led to the explosive rebellion against all that is old and paternalistic in modern China. Upwards of two thousand years of the Ten Commandments in Europe and America have not eliminated adultery, killing, or taking the Lord's name in vain, even among the ostensibly devout or the highly placed; they have instead forced the construction of elaborate explanations of what is and is not justifiable human slaughter and sex. They have produced much wrestling with guilt on these matters and have given sex and violence a double-edged symbolic power—they are both fascinating and forbidden. All this has made societies influenced by Judaism and Christianity genuinely sensitive to moral issues. The sensitivity is reflected in much legislation and in a literature shot through with guilt and justification, but it has not so much eliminated what it regards as sin as set the terms and tone of moral discourse; the same can be said for Confucian, Buddhist, or Muslim societies.

### Worship and Sociology of Religion

The worship and sociology of a religion offer models of how it conceptualizes the ideal community, and such models work on deep levels in the minds of people. Whether the worship and the style of leadership imply highly structured forms or mystical freedom, charismatic or routinized leadership, egalitarian or hierarchical patterns; whether worship has mainly verbal or nonverbal symbolism; whether participation is passive or active for most—all these deeply affect the social and political values of the community as well. One can see how Hinduism with its ideal of the holy man prepared India for a leader like Mohandas Gandhi. Denominationalism in America with its models of routinized, egalitarian, and democratic leadership, together with the nonrational charismatic styles of leadership that emerge especially in revivalistic evangelicalism and pentecostalism, help explain American social and political styles.

### Historical Impact of Religion

There is also the direct historical impact of religion, especially of the international religions that have conveyed cultures, literary heritages, and political systems across continents. Buddhism, Christianity, Islam, and Confucianism have influenced cultures outside the one in which they began, and not only through formal doctrine. They have come into new lands as models of a different, and often more advanced-seeming, style of civilization. Commonly they have either come together with new imperial rule from outside or been catalysts in major political changes internally. At the least, the new religion offers a sense of history, maybe even a discovery of history, that implies the possibility of change in many areas of life by showing that values can be revamped.

# RELIGION AND THE INTERPRETATION
## OF HISTORY

Finally, religions affect history because they affect the way history is interpreted, understood, and even remembered. So they affect the way history is written and the way we come to know it. Confucian historians in China, for example, taught their sense of morality through the medium of history by making good things occur during the reigns of virtuous sovereigns and bad things under evil ones.

The matter can be more complex than this. Donald E. Miller, a sociologist of religion, has done a study of the attitudes of Armenians living in southern California who were survivors of the genocidal massacres of Armenians in the Turkish Empire during World War I.[6] In a two-year period beginning in 1915, some one and one-half million Armenian men, women, and children—over half the Armenian population in Turkey—were slaughtered, often in circumstances of appalling cruelty. Miller found four basic responses among survivors—people now elderly who as children had seen their families killed before their eyes or suffered extremes of hunger and fatigue on forced marches, but by a seeming miracle managed to escape the fate of most of those around them and to reach a new and happier land.

One response of the survivors was denial. For some the memory was too painful. They did not want to think about it, and if they did discuss it, they reverted to a childish idiom as though it could only be handled by a subjective reversion to the other time and place.

Another response was desire for revenge. One way to deal with the trauma of unjust, nonsensical suffering is to seek restitution—that is, to reestablish justice. Some survivors were filled with such thoughts of revenge. (One respondent, a Christian minister, said he was glad he was a Christian because otherwise he would have delighted in killing as many of the other side as possible.)

For others the response was rationalization. They could not accept that their suffering was to no purpose and so tried to find a purpose. Some explained that the Armenians actually provoked the massacre themselves through their insistence on independence. It was better in the eyes of these people to see themselves and their people as guilty than to face a world in which there is suffering for no reason. These people often turned to religion to assist in this line of thought. They said the massacre was a punishment from God for the pride of the slain. They also spoke of its benefits to the survivors—that it led them to turn to God or strengthened their characters.

[6]Donald E. Miller, "Recalling the Past: A Case Study of Survivors of the Armenian Genocide" (unpublished paper presented at the Pacific Regional Meeting, American Academy of Religion, 1976).

Finally, there were those whose only response was resignation. They could neither deny the massacre, nor see any satisfaction in revenge, nor rationalize it in any way. They could only accept that it happened, but this resignation brought them no peace. Survivors in this category were often melancholic.

The ways in which religious concepts, vocabulary, and symbols are used to enable historical events to be interpreted in situations like these are obvious. Religious symbols, ideas, and practices can deny events by making them seem illusory or by returning one to childhood in confronting them; they can inspire revenging crusades and a sense of mythic national destiny; they can aid in explaining how a bad event was actually sent from God as punishment or to test and strengthen one; they can even facilitate a fatalistic resignation. In the Old Testament, for example, we can find all these responses, often eloquently expressed, as reactions to the various troubles of the children of Israel. These responses embellish history with interpretation; to say an historical event was an act of God is more than just describing the historical event. It is, however, really not possible to do otherwise, especially of events with which one is personally deeply involved. While historical events may be objective facts, the telling of *significant* history, like the evocation of memory, will for those for whom it is more than bare fact include interpretations that make it a story of who the teller or the rememberer and his or her people or generation are.

Thus religion is used to make historical events understandable, even as history is used to legitimate religion. It is not only evil events, of course, with which religion deals; it also glorifies triumphs and places in an eternal context the basic institutions of the society, the rulers and the social order. Kings may descend from gods; a nation's faith separates it from other nations.

Religion, and the culture of which it is a part, presents symbols and metaphors of self, but they are symbols and metaphors of the self as a member of society; there is finally no other way we know what it means to be a self than as a member of society. That is, religion and culture offer tools for thinking about what it means to be a self and how a self should act; they provide bridges between perception and interpretation and explain the self metaphorically. They tell us, so to speak, what the self is but in other terms—in the vocabulary of gods, myths, and liturgical drama. Politics and economics, in modern America, tell us what a self is in their spheres through the symbols of voting machines, money, houses, and clothes. Religion does this through its symbols for the self in relation to the ultimate, unconditioned environment, but its essential instruments for so doing come out of society, the relation of one self here below to another.

St. Augustine (A.D. 354–430), depicted in this fresco by Sandro Botticelli, was one of the most important of Christian philosophers and theologians. This picture suggests the intensity and importance of intelligent reflection on the meaning of truth in religion.

# TRUTH MESSAGES: THE CONCEPTUAL EXPRESSION OF RELIGION

## WHAT IS SAID AND HOW IT IS SAID

Now we come to the part of our study of religion that has to do with what religions "say" and the concepts with which they work: their doctrines about God or gods, the soul, divinely given rewards and punishments in this life and the next, and so forth. It may surprise some readers that it has taken so long to get to these matters, except through various hints and allusions, that to many are virtually the whole point of religion. Religion, they think, is principally a question of beliefs regarding God and life after death and the faith they inspire.

Certainly the verbal and conceptual theoretical expression of religion is extremely important, and the reality construction or universe of meaning that comes out of the interaction of all forms of expression can certainly be called faith. The discussion of religious ideas has been saved until this point to emphasize that they do not comprise the *whole* of human religion but are integral parts of religion as a total experience.

A particular belief may indeed seem to religious participants the main rationale for participation. But the nature of the total experience they have in religion is, however, deeply colored by the kind of worship that goes with it and the kind of group with which they worship. Immensely different styles of worship and sociological placement can make the same doctrine seem different, and similar styles of worship can make different doctrines seem compatible if not almost the same thing in different words.

One could argue, with the philosopher Ludwig Wittgenstein, that religious statements are "language games" with only internal reference within the circle using them. The corollary would be that all religions are equally true and false; you cannot really talk or argue with people outside of your circle but only preach at them—that is, try to bring them through conversion into the circle where that language pattern is meaningful because one has associated it with important experiences.[1]

Moreover, religious myth and doctrine, like other symbols, can be seen as codes; people argue that what they really mean is something other than what they say. To Freudians they encode the world view of the child within trying to retain the magical universe and omniscient father he or she once knew; to Jungians they express the diverse components of the psyche, such as the Great Mother and the Wise Old Man; to structuralists like Claude Lévi-Strauss they are, so to speak, a code just for the sake of being a code, the patterns of myth and doctrine telling us there are thinking human beings here.

Religious statements can and must also be looked at, and taken seriously, as what they obviously intend to be on the ordinary conscious level, that is, statements of real knowledge and real truth. Whether religious statements should be seen as statements of plain truth or as codes for something else is a decision each person has to make for himself or herself. Nevertheless, one never rightly understands religion and its importance until he or she has complemented a descriptive approach with endeavors to understand, and wrestle with, the claims of religious statements to be *true*.

Most religious people, then, have perceptions they believe to be true to go with their participation. These are ideas, stories, and mental images about invisible reality and its impingement on the visible. The clarity, logical consistency, and precision of these concepts may vary considerably between the professional elites and the ordinary members of the religion, who may be illiterate or at least religiously illiterate. The religious universe of the latter may be vague and haphazard, albeit deeply felt. However, this only reflects the haphazard way they were acquainted with it—through casual word of mouth, through family and

---

[1]See William C. Shepherd, "On the Concept of 'Being Wrong' Religiously," *Journal of the American Academy of Religion*, XLII, 1 (March 1974), 66–81. Shepherd argues that even the ontological argument and Thomas Aquinas's five proofs of God, to be discussed later, really fit the concept of "language game," since they are in the tradition of a particular religious culture and really serve to clarify their accepted language—they are "faith speaking to faith." At heart, religious authority does not depend on reason. It is the other way around, but Shepherd goes on to argue that it is now undesirable to use traditional arguments to defend faith because they are illusory and ignore enriching possibilities. In the situation of modern pluralism, he says we should rather accept polysymbolism.

friends, rather than through systematic training. In virtually every religion one finds the professional elite have a different perception, sometimes more liberal and sometimes more rigorous, of its truth statements than the ordinary lay members, though they are often wise enough not to communicate their perception in ways that would unduly unsettle the lay believers. (Even in America, anyone who has been to a divinity school and then worked as a minister in an ordinary church will know what I mean.)

This does not mean, however, that the elite perception is better or even more accurate in terms of the ultimate meaning of the religion; it is only different. The interpretation of Buddhism by its monks and philosophers, that it shows one a path to the cessation of desire and attainment of Nirvana, is immensely important to understanding the role of Buddhism in history and thought—but so also is the more popular role of Buddhism as a bearer of high culture to millions, the sociological meaning of belonging to a temple in Thailand or Japan, and even its role of occasionally providing symbols to revolutionary political movements in China.

It is a matter of messages. In doctrine and myth, as in other areas, there are two messages at once in a religious statement: the content message and the structural message. The content message is what is said; the structural message is what is said by the *way* it is said.

For example, two faiths may postulate the existence of God. One bases its belief in God ostensibly on a tightly reasoned logical argument that there must be a God, the other on visions or feeling-experiences of God its people have. The content is the same, but the tone, and so the total experience of these two faiths, is quite different.

As another example, imagine a religion in which the elite envision a systematic hierarchy of gods from the supreme ruler of heaven on down. They are arranged in phalanxes, each with its captain and lieutenant, each in charge of a particular area of earthly affairs. The laypeople are likely to know of just a few of the gods—the deity of one's village temple, or of one's personal occupation, or even the god of whom one once had a vision or miracle. Those gods, however, are very deeply embedded in local shrines and festivals, profoundly parts of daily life. Again, the content messages converge, but the structural messages differ. One says the spiritual universe is orderly and reflects the pattern of a well-tempered state, or of the reasoning powers of the seasoned philosopher; the other that the universe is as haphazard as the average man's lot is likely to be, but that there is such a thing as community and seasons and that there are points of glory in the cosmos that break through unexpectedly here and there.

The same difference between content message and structural message can be seen in American Christianity. A statement such as "God was in Christ" would be affirmed by all Christians in the same words but would have different meanings because of a different structural context in a traditional church doctrinal statement, in the discourse of a liberal theologian, and in the words of a conservative or fundamentalist theologian.

The adjectives *traditional, liberal,* and *fundamentalist* suggest in fact three different structural styles of speaking religious truth messages. While they are drawn from the situation of Christianity, close parallels can be found in Judaism and other major religions. Traditionalist religious statements give a tone to truth indicating that it is interlinked with deep family and ethnic ties, or a desire for their equivalents, and with the oldest and richest art, music, literature, and wisdom of the culture in which the religious tradition is based. Liberal religious statements indicate by their tone and structure that truth must be consistent in all areas of knowledge, including the scientific, and is apprehended through induction and synthesis. Liberals usually see truth as fragmentary, and to be held in a way that preserves large areas of inner and outer freedom. Fundamentalist or conservative religious statements are parts of highly consistent systems based on scriptural or ecclesiastical authority. The structural message of the way they are put is that there is absolute truth and absolute authority. The view that human nature has and needs absolute truth and authority may be reflected in family and social values as well.

The structural and content messages are both very important. They may or may not be consistent, but that fact only suggests another message about the ultimate importance of *consistency* in human experience; for there is much to indicate it is important and much to indicate it is not. However, the content message is finally a statement about the human need for consistency, or at least unity, from out of diversity. The religious content messages are intended to unify all aspects of religion and life— the group, the worship, the psychological states, the symbols—around a single meaning. It says we have this group, this form of worship, these experiences and symbols, *because* we believe in this kind of God. These religious statements articulate the meaning of it all; they are the points where religion breaks through on the level of the human capacity for reason, mental images, abstractions, and concepts.

These highly verbal articulations are still religion and have all the characteristics of religion. They are the sacred in the mind as surely as the temple is in the city. They are the real self in the realm of ideas as surely as dancing in a sacred place is in the physical realm. These ideas provide a real interpretation of the world different from the ordinary—though all culture and philosophy does this, religion does it more and relates it to the transcendent, that is, to invisible but more ultimate dimensions.

Fosco Marain/Monkmeyer Press Photo Service

The *ka-pa,* or wizard, is an important figure in popular Tibetan religion. He deals with the exorcisms and spells derived from the power of the mighty Buddhas and other beings who animate the Tibetan pantheon. His use of their power is eclectic; he moves with shrewdness among the infinite occult powers by which every Tibetan feels surrounded. Although as a popular religionist he may deal with these deities just one at a time, note that behind him are *tankas,* or meditation paintings, that show the Tibetan pantheon arranged in systematic, hierarchical, and symbolically significant order.

Religious ideas deal with issues such as suffering, value, and meaning in terms of symbolic forms that focus them and concretize them so the answers can be easily grasped and handled, but the symbols are now ideas and concepts, symbols in the mind. That they are called symbols is not to deny their cognitive value—that is, that they are an actual *knowing of truth* as far as this is humanly possible and as far as it can be known in ways that are transferable through the common coin of human language. Knowing, to oneself as well as in communication to others, requires the invisible symbols of words and ideas, but it may be that some symbols do correspond to absolute reality better than others, and even that some do so as perfectly as possible. Even so, this does not mean they are not also symbols. They are related to our central theme of the real self; as with other kinds of symbols, thinking certain ideas may authenticate one as a real self.

In the sections that follow we examine some common idea-symbols in religion, dealing largely, though not exclusively, with Western concepts, issues, terminology, and thinkers. This is not because the intellectual arguments important to other traditions, such as the Buddhist analysis of experience that leads to the denial of separate egos or the Hindu philosophical arguments for an undivided universal consciousness, are any less challenging or profound. Rather it is because there is not room here to deal with the intellectual life and the main concepts of all religions. Thus, the discussion is limited to some exemplary material that is mostly from the traditional Western theological tradition. There are several reasons for this. One is that since it is associated with the religion and culture with which most readers are familiar, it may be easiest to relate to at the beginning of religious studies. The second is that, for the same reason, it should be a part of the groundwork of religious studies. Comparative religion is certainly important, but every person educated in religious studies in the West should also have an acquaintance with such things as the classical arguments for the existence of God devised by the theologians of his or her own culture. Finally, this *is* in its classical form a highly rational and intellectual treatment of religion and as such is a fairly unambiguous example of religious expression on that level. As an example of the conceptual life of religion, then, the discussion focuses on the Judaeo-Christian God.

## GOD

Virtually all religion affirms the reality of being, knowledge, and joyful power greater than the human; that is the obvious expression of belief in transcendence and of a real self greater than the ordinary.

Generally, this belief is concretized in belief in a God or gods—self-conscious centers of being, knowledge, and joyful power superior to mankind. Even when this ultimate being is not personified, as the Tao, Dharmakaya, Nirvana, and Brahman of Taoism, Buddhism, and some expressions of Hinduism, respectively, are not personified, there are gods and buddhas who refract the power of the plenitude and so are symbolic manifestations of it. Significantly, however, in Taoism and Buddhism the superior beings who now hold this splendor were once human.

Three basic distillations of divinity can, in fact, be isolated. They may be understood in light of H. Richard Niebuhr's understanding of God as *center of value*—that is, as the touchstone of meaning beyond which one cannot go.[2]

First, God can be thought of as an *impersonal absolute*. From this perspective, personality such as you and I have is seen essentially as a limitation. Because we can think about only one thing at a time, there are millions of real things we are not thinking about, and in this way the nature of our consciousness identified with personality makes us terribly limited. Because our personalities are really constructed out of various human desires, anxieties, defenses, and cosmic ignorance, they provide poor models for God. Better, according to impersonalists, to understand God as pure being and consciousness without the hindrance of personality—let the Absolute be like an unstained mirror, out of which all things rise and fall, itself untouched by their vicissitudes. The human correlate is that it is those moments when individual personality is most subdued—in deep meditation, in scientific contemplation—that we best know, or realize, the divine.

Second, God can be thought of in terms of *personal monotheism*. As in the Judaeo-Christian-Islamic tradition, it sees the absolute power of the universe as personal but personality that transcends the human limitations. In its hierarchy of values, personality is at the top. Personal monotheism, therefore, can speak of God as having a sense of purpose, as loving, as being the eternal friend. Its best argument is this: although God may be infinitely greater than personality as we know it, personal

[2]H. Richard Niebuhr, *Radical Monotheism and Western Culture* (New York: Harper & Row, Publishers, Inc., 1970). Compare it with the following words of C. G. Jung: "The idea of God is an absolutely necessary psychological function of an irrational nature. . . . There is in a psyche some superior power, and if it is not consciously a god, it is the 'belly,' at least, in St. Paul's words. I therefore consider it wiser to acknowledge the idea of God consciously; for, if we do not, something else is made God, usually something quite inappropriate and stupid such as only an 'enlightened' intellect could hatch forth." (In *Two Essays in Analytic Psychology*, Bollengen Series, *Collected Works of C. G. Jung* [Princeton, N.J.: Princeton University Press, 1973], vol. VII, p.71.)

existence is the highest form of existence we know, so we can do no better than to start by thinking of God as personal on the model of our own personalities, and then try to expand this idea to infinity.

Finally there is *polytheism*, belief in many gods. Polytheism, as Paul Tillich sagely observed, is really a matter of quality rather than quantity —the point is that multiplicity of gods creates a cosmos of very different tone from belief in one center of value. It suggests that every old tree, golden grove, rushing stream, and ponderous mountain may have its gods of independent mood, as does every fertile field and city, and every changing human occasion, from love to war or business to contemplation. At best they may belong to some hierarchy; otherwise they may seem, as often does human life itself, to be running off in several directions at once. In any case, polytheism presents religion not as forcing all of life around a single center of value (something we may often desire if not deserve) but as reflecting our usual experience of it in fragments, with all its many fragments shot through with various inconsistent apertures toward transcendence.[3]

Let us return, however, to the Judaeo-Christian God, since that is the God with which most of us are familiar. As examples of religious statements of the most rigorously conceptual and rational sort, the attributes theological tradition has ascribed to him and the arguments for his existence are briefly discussed.[4]

∝  According to this tradition, God is omniscient; he knows everything. He is omnipotent; he can do anything. He has aseity; that is, he exists on his own, without any prior cause, and depends on nothing. He has personality; he is self-conscious and able to work out of his own volition or will. He is infinite; without limit, he is omnipresent or existent everywhere. He has unity; he is one, simple in the sense of being indivisible into parts. He is unique; there is no other like him or of the same order as he. He is changeless. He is pure spirit; there is nothing material in his essential being, for the creation is made by him but is not an essential part of him. He is the source of all life. Further, he has certain characteristics in addition to these attributes: goodness, righteousness, love, mercy, holiness.

This impressive picture of absolute God is drawn both from biblical statements and congruent categories of Greek philosophy, but that is irrelevant for the moment. Instead, let us consider what sort of arguments, derived from reason, have been adduced on behalf of such a God.

First, there is the cosmological argument. It says that for everything

---

[3]See David L. Miller, *The New Polytheism* (New York: Harper & Row, Publishers, Inc., 1974).

[4]The following discussion is based on Claude Beaufort Moss, *The Christian Faith: An Introduction to Dogmatic Theology* (London: S.P.C.K., 1954).

there is a cause and for every cause a prior cause, and these causes can be pushed back and back until one comes to a first cause; for every particular thing to have a cause but for there to be no cause for everything would be an absurdity. This first cause, however, is of a different nature than particular causes, since it has to have certain different characteristics; it has to be a necessary being, to be itself causeless, to be omnipotent and unlimited—in short, God.

Then there is the teleological argument, or argument from design. It points to the fact that one can see purposes throughout the universe—that the complex arrangements of cross-pollination of plants, the incredible arrangement of the human body, and much else seem finally beyond what could be attributed to chance alone. Although ancient, this argument has received new impetus from the discovery of biological evolution; to some philosophers the incredible march of life from simple organic molecules to millions of diverse species and human intelligence seems unbelieveable in purely natural terms, especially since some necessary adaptations along the way had little appreciable immediate survival value.

Two other traditional arguments may seem a bit more precarious to moderns but should be cited and are worthy at least of deep reflection. One is the moral argument. It claims that all sane people possess some sense of a distinction between right and wrong, however they conceptualize it or explain it. If this moral sense is universal among humans, it must be explained in terms of something more than human that is concerned about right and wrong as well as about human survival.

Another is the argument from general consent, as it is called. It says that some sort of religion and belief in transcendent beings is found everywhere among humans, and so some reality must lie behind it. Animals with features of no survival value, like the eyes of fishes in black caves, eventually lose them. Whey would something consuming as much energy and as many resources, both psychological and material, as religion continue if the spiritual universe were as void of God as the cave-fishes' physical universe is void of light? Perhaps this argument underestimates mankind's capacity for folly, but the persistence of religion is a remarkable fact. Even in countries such as the Soviet Union in which a determined effort has been made to stamp it out, a yearning for religion or spiritual values seems undying.

Finally, there is the ontological argument, in some ways the most intriguing and mysterious of all. Attributed to the medieval philosopher and archbishop Anselm, it has often allegedly been refuted, yet it never seems to die. Philosophers and theologians return to worry over it as dogs over old bones. At first glance it may seem incredibly naive, a mere game of words. Yet one does not entirely forget it and, after reading it, is left with a lingering suspicion that perhaps there is more to it than meets the eye, that Anselm was saying something we do not quite catch because it is too profound rather than too naive. The argument goes as follows: We think of God as the greatest being there is, but a being that has existence is greater than one that does not have existence. Therefore, if we think of God as the greatest being there is, he must exist.

Four related commentaries on this argument might be suggested. They are not *the* meaning of the argument or any sort of authoritative explication of it. More similar to a Zen koan than the usual Western sort of rational argument, the ontological argument can lead in many directions or none.

First, though, it suggests that an idea necessary to reasonable thought must have reality, or else thought corresponds to nothing, the universe is irrational chaos, and there is no point in thinking about anything. It does not matter, in other words, if God is provable by external arguments such as the cosmological; if he is thinkable, this is a kind of reality as real as anything else, since unless we assume ourselves partially or wholly insane and divorced from outside reality, what we think is real and correlates with something in the universe out of which we came. The ontological argument, then, is a bold endeavor (similar to pure mathematics) to show that the human mind itself, without empirical outside help, can create ideas indispensable to an understanding of being, cosmos, and our own minds, which separates us from sheer chaos.

Second, it suggests that finally it is through the mind knowing itself that what truth there is to be found is found—and this is necessarily so because all that comes into mind, such as the data for the other arguments, is filtered through the categories of perception we set up around ourselves. Philosophers such as Hume and Kant have shown, for example, that we may see cause and effect because the mind thinks in such a way as to expect to see it. When the mind turns inward it comes upon one segment of reality that it must assume to be unfiltered and undistanced, its own consciousness. Upon this reality, then, it should start to build its picture of absolute reality and assume that what consciousness postulates as required by the fact of its own existence is most real.

Third, the ontological argument, like the argument from general consent but with far more subtlety, suggests that the widespread and persistent quality of human religion points to some reality. One can, of course, say that human religion is merely due to cultural forms and psychological quirks. True, the mere widespread existence of religion does not logically prove its truth, or its falsity; the pattern could look about the same as it does and be either false or true in its assumptions. For that matter, it could be based on some reality but a reality other than God as ordinarily understood. The ontological argument, however, without proving anything, points out that those who say the religious pattern is without grounding in reality are saying that much of human life, thought, and creativity is divorced from any reality of universal significance, indeed from *existence* in an absolute sense. It shows they cannot escape the consequence that their humanity, and their universe, is both futile and largely deluded—for finally the ontological argument is over who is insane, who is lost to reality in fantasy. Basically, of course, it weights the case in one direction by stating reality can only be greater than any idea we have of it.

Fourth, let us return to the earlier statement that at first glance the ontological argument may seem to be just a word game. Still earlier, we indicated that Ludwig Wittgenstein would have called any religious idea system a word game, which one is either in or out of—though new players can be brought in, not by argument (since argument would presume the rules of a game the outsider is not yet playing) but by "preaching" (that is, making the game seem irresistibly necessary or attractive to him). Even as a word game, however, the argument of Anselm is not to be scorned; it proposes that even within such games there can be words that are trump cards. This may not, as is often alleged against the argument, prove anything outside of the game—but even that counter argument presupposes that there are some word and idea systems that are *not* games. Many people are now much more dubious of that proposition than we once were, and this makes Anselm's trump card as heavy as any other. It makes the word game that God wins as viable as the one that chance or blind fate wins. It depends on which game you want to play, and that comes down to how it correlates with the game for the stakes of reality beyond words within you.

## CREATION

The next step in a formal statement of content in religious messages is to get from God to the existing world. In any religious system, the way this step is accounted for, the description of the creation of the world, is extremely revealing of the world view. The following are some examples.

Some religious traditions, such as the Hindu and Buddhist, see the universe as essentially eternal, without beginning or ending in the stream of time as we know it. While the universe always stands over against timeless reality, from within the stream of time we do not perceive a moment of absolute starting or stopping, but only endless cause and effect. The cosmos, however, does undergo immense cycles of creation and destruction, each cycle leading to the next. This view carries with it the implication that conscious existence within this unending chain of worlds would finally become wearisome and sad, leading one to quest for the way to jump off the wheel altogether into unconditioned reality, to find life in God or Nirvana instead.

The way to God, while it may be difficult, would not involve going far; the same traditions show us that God or the Absolute is within all things, their true nature, an essence to which only our ignorance blinds us. Another account from India tells us the world as we know it was made when Prajapati, a primal god, offered himself as a sacrifice and divided up his body into the many things that make up our world. This myth indicates, as we have seen, that the multitudinous world is God hiding himself behind countless forms.

Still another account of creation is that of the Egyptian and Babylonian myths, among others. This might be called a genetic creation, and tells us that the world and its inhabitants are the result of a process of generation analogous to the human but between primal gods. Frequently there is a union of a god and a goddess representing heaven and earth, although in one Egyptian account a solitary deity generates the creation out of himself. In Japan, the primal parents both come down from heaven, and among the Hopi, both come out of the earth. These narratives emphasize above all the continuity of spiritual life with the biological processes and so integrate cosmology with the agriculture and biology of human society.

Finally, there is creation *ex nihilo*, "from nothing," the picture favored by Judaism, Christianity, and Islam. It says that God by an absolute decree called the universe into being, without having to use any preexistent material or any parallel to genetic process. The resultant picture is of God as different in an unqualified way from his creation—as the difference between a craftsman and the work of his hands. It establishes that God is sovereign though loving ruler of all he has made and that while his people, who are as grasshoppers in his eyes, have no natural claim to kinship with him, they owe him obedience and can respond to him with love.

The account of creation must explain the existence of that most unusual entity within it, humankind—a being who senses that he or she is part of creation, yet different from the rest of it and in some ways close to God, but in others farther from him than the nature that remains still as it came from his hand. A major tool of religious thought for dealing with these ambiguities is the concept of the soul or its equivalents, such as the Buddhist idea of an ongoing bundle of karmic forces. The soul is an immaterial substance within the individual that provides his or her ultimate identity and is in rapport with deity or infinite reality—a function that includes the capacity to receive the supernatural judgment or punishment and reward incurred by the individual's deeds.

Beliefs about the soul have varied. Some cultures have conceived of multiple souls having different destinies after death—some going to paradise, some lingering around the grave or the household shrines. Some very important cultures have thought that, according to its deeds, the soul reincarnates in human or animal or even ghostly or divine form. Others have held that it goes directly to a postmortum reward or punishment in heaven or hell or perhaps to an intermediate state, a purgatory, where the demerit of sins less than fatal can be worn away. Others emphasize the association of the spiritual principle in man with the physical body and do not expect the soul to live a meaningful life apart from it; they wait for God to raise the body and the spirit to newness of life on the Last Day. Still others stress the closeness of ancestral spirits to the living of their family; the departed remain near the living members of the family in tomb and altar to bless and watch.

In all these beliefs, the soul or something comparable to it is like a reflection of God in a small mirror; it shares the nature of God or the gods in that it is immaterial and deathless, yet it shares the nature of human clay in that it can receive the imprint of sin and suffer both finitude and punishment. At the same time, the idea of the soul has a splendid side; it reflects mankind's deeply rooted conviction that in some way we are more than mortal, that we have a true self capable of tasting immortality and infinity, and that we are worthy of commerce with deity. Indeed, even to be worthy of punishment from divinity is better than the lot of a creature born only to die forever, or so religion has generally thought.

The theory of creation also involves a widespread awareness that something after creation must have gone wrong. Somehow mankind, despite or because of the priceless possession of souls, has lost the closeness to divinity the original creation implied. The explanation of this lapse, like the accounts of creation, vary considerably. It may be due to some accident—a misunderstanding on the part of our primal parents or cantankerousness on the part of one creature out of all creation. It may be due to a fierce rebellion by the creation against its maker. It may stem from ignorance of the true nature of things because of blind attachment to the things of this world or to pet ideas and concepts. It may, as in some Gnostic myths, be because mankind has been enslaved by greater and more malevolent beings than ourselves. Each explanation suggests a different view of mankind and of the kind of God who is susceptible to each mode of human separation from him.[5]

## THE PATH TO SALVATION

Religion not only postulates that something has gone wrong since the creation of the world in original harmony with its divine source but also tells us the way back to the original union, for that is implied in the

[5]For a valuable discussion of how different theories of the origin and nature of evil correlate with different world views, see Paul Ricoeur, *The Symbolism of Evil* (New York: Harper & Row, Publishers, Inc., 1967).

description of the separation. If the separation is due to ignorance, it offers us the hidden knowledge; if due to rebellion, it enlists us in the armies of the commander of the counterattack. The method and the putative goal of the return vary.

The goal—a human order in absolute harmony with the ideal understanding of our origins—may be a supremely good society, cosmic consciousness, or the restitution of right relations to God in love and service. The diverse ways back are typically initiated by God and are exemplified by a paradigmatic hero who is pioneer of the return. Through identification with him or her, or with his or her vision of society, one may become a real self. The hero may be a great teacher such as Confucius, the wayshower of an ideal society, or Lao-tzu, the sage in harmony with nature and infinity; it may be the Buddha, Muhammad the emissary of God, or Jesus Christ the savior.

Whoever the teacher and whatever the way, the follower has to make a choice of priorities. It may seem easy or hard, but there must be a discipline that requires the subordination of some values to others. It is not a course one must pursue out of one's own power, though, for as one achieves closer harmony with the way things really are, he or she finds himself or herself aided by powers even more deeply in union with the way things really are: a Buddha totally enlightened into horizonless awareness of reality; a savior such as Jesus the Christ who is both God and human; even a wise sage such as Confucius who, though no more than fully human, saw with unparalleled clarity in the eyes of his followers the nature of an ideal human society based on right human relationships.

Finally, the way of salvation teaches that the final end of human life is ultimate transformation, in the expression of Frederick Streng, who defined religion as "means toward ultimate transformation."[6] As we have observed in chapter one, it moves toward a transcendent state of being beyond all qualifications and conditions, meaning in effect that one is unbounded. There is the path toward ultimate transformation—the total reversal of all boundings by either society or one's own psychology—if one has the wisdom and skill to lay hold of it.

Religious teaching about the way back, salvation, and ultimate transformation is not limited to this present world and an afterlife only. Many, if not most, teach that the world itself can change too. Someday, the powers of evil within the world shall be defeated, and it will be turned into a paradise. This is the well-known teaching of many faiths of an end to time as we know it, a last judgment, a final resurrection of all the dead, and the making of a new heaven and earth or the inauguration

---

[6]Frederick J. Streng, *Understanding Religious Life*, 2nd ed. (Encino, Calif.: Dickenson Publishing Co., 1976), pp. 7-9.

This relief depicts, from left to right, Osiris, Thoth, and Isis, three deities of ancient Egypt and Hellenistic times that were deeply connected with salvation. Osiris was a deity of agriculture and the Realms of the Dead; those who adhered to him shared in his immortality. Isis was his consort who restored him to life; in Roman times she became the goddess of a widespread salvation religion. Ibis-headed Thoth was god of wisdom, especially the mysteries of immortality.

of a paradisiacal era. If transformation is truly ultimate—that is, without any reservation, without any corner of self or universe left unchanged to what is totally good—then it must seem to affect the whole of the world. This is the case whether the world is changed outwardly and physically or only subjectively in the eyes of the mystic who sees it cleansed when, in Blake's phrase, the "doors of perception" are cleansed.

Transformation, and above all the sometimes contrasting role of religion to uphold the normative values of society, requires following certain standards of behavior in this life. The ethical teachings of a religion are not in isolation from its transformative goals but either create the necessary preconditions for inward spiritual advance—such as the *niyama* and *yama*, constraints and advice, that prelude serious yoga—or, like the Sermon on the Mount, suggest a perfectionist way of life that foreshadows here and now the Kindgom of Heaven.

In summary, then, an important part of religious doctrine is the manner in which it maps the return from separation to union with God or the absolute. The picture of return generally focuses on a symbolic individual who encapsulates and demonstrates it, such as the Buddha or the Christ, and associated with the individual are a pivotal time and event that open doors to return. The way to return combines the inner transformation and outward ethical aspects of religion; it requires both even as it enforces the quest for ecstasy and support of normative values sides of religion in society. Ultimately, these are pulled together in the teachings of the religion about the end of time as we know it: eschatology, teachings about the final times, or apocalyptic teachings that emphasize things will get worse and worse until the end, when God will intervene in a sudden, unexpected, and radical reversal of the way things seem to be, as in a Last Judgment breaking through in the midst of a cataclysmic battle. In the end of time, and the subsequent new and perfect creation, both perfect joy and a perfect social order coexist. All these are common religious doctrines and very important doctrines for the religion's view of the real self, transcendence, and ultimate reality.

## DETERMINING TRUTH IN RELIGION

After looking, as we have, at many different styles of religious belief and many manifestations of religion, one may ask—whether in eagerness, indifference, or despair—if it is possible to determine what in all of it is true. Some people, in fact, may reject the word *true* altogether and only ask what in religion has *meaning*—what, in other words, would provide a workable symbol system for the individual concerned. I have had vehement discussions with students about whether truth in religion can be ascertained, or only meaning or value for the individual.

Nevertheless, let us keep the word truth; I cannot quite persuade myself that there could be real meaning or value in a religious experience or symbol one was not convinced was founded on some sort of truth. The means for determining what is true in religion are diverse, however, though not as varied as the beliefs themselves. Yet it is fair to note that different sorts of beliefs carry with them distinctive styles of verification. Belief in a sovereign creator God is likely to include an appeal to reason, as in the cosmological argument previously discussed; belief in salvation and after-death states is likely to include appeals to personal experience and teachings accepted on authority. The following are some major approaches to determining truth in religion.

### Reason

This approach is based on the presuppositions that the mind can know truth through the honest and unbiased use of its capacities to work through logical processes from sure premises to their consequences and that, fundamentally, the universe is orderly and works by cause and effect. If these presuppositions are granted, it seems justifiable to assume that a logical process can parallel the way things are when it starts from accurate data and is procedurally flawless. It would then yield up real truth, even to knowledge of the God who is the source of all other truth.

The most famous example of an approach based on reason is that of Thomas Aquinas, the great philosopher and theologian of the thirteenth century, whose five proofs of the existence of God are the basis of the earlier discussion on this matter (apart from the treatment of the ontological argument, which Aquinas rejected). Other philosophers, such as the Mahayana Buddhist Nagarjuna, of approximately the first century A.D., and David Hume (1711–76) in Britain, have used reasoning processes to show the limitations of reason, of cause-and-effect thinking, and of language itself. They would say that most reasoning, including traditional proofs of God, is really circular and proves no more than what is implicit in the way the original premises are put, which in turn is based on our human modes of perception. (Perhaps it is the mind, not nature itself, in which everything is intricately interrelated, that sets up the neat patterns of cause and effect from which we extrapolate a First Cause or that isolates out of infinite variety phenomena we call evidence of purpose because they happen to parallel what we as humans could understand as purposeful.)

Reason as a means of determining truth in religion has the advantage of seeming to be as independent as possible from emotion or bias. Critics point out that this is not as much the case as practitioners of reason may assume; a facade of reason can mask decisions made on quite different grounds or be based on premises themselves assumed on nonrational bases. Furthermore, reason is said to be cold and even inhuman—a poor basis for determining something as warmly human as religious commitment. Reason is not especially in fashion today as a way of determining truth in religion. Many are suspicious of it and prefer to follow the late twentieth-century emphasis on experience as the royal road to spirituality and personal growth. If you have experienced something, we tend to say, that is better than merely deducing it (or criticizing it) from out of cool reason alone. Perhaps we need to have a chastened rebirth of confidence in reason; while it can easily go awry, it does affirm a precious human capacity, the power of the mind to think.

### Experience

This is the great alternative that stands against reason in the minds of many. Whether in conversion, mysticism, or simply gradual growth through worship and reflection to subjective religious surety, felt experience of religious reality convinces in its own way. It seems beyond doubt or at least adequate for the individual. Its advantages are that it is accessible to all regardless of intelligence or education, it has immediacy, it is something that involves the whole person, and above all it provides religious motivation at the same time that it gives conviction. There are weighty objections, however, that can be made against depending on experience alone as a religious guide. One can never be sure whether some psychological explanation is possible. Furthermore, intense and convincing experience can be found in all religion; in general, one does not find that it points to any particular truth. If one tried to determine what is religious truth from religious experience in general, rather than just his or her own, one would quickly be very confused about everything except that there *are* such experiences. (He or she may even be confused by personal experiences; those of one person are often far from consistent, and in following them exclusively one can be swept far out to sea on tides of emotion and subjective imaginings.) Usually one's religious culture does much to explain the content of religious experience (for the experience itself, say a sense of the numinous or transcendent, is not the same as the interpretation, even that which the experiencer immediately makes to himself—that it is an experience of God, or Christ, or a bodhisattva, or of certain gods). It would perhaps be safest to say that while certainly religious experience is real and significant *as experience*, we need to think deeply about what the experience is saying and from whence it comes; there may be important guides to truth and meaning in it, but they may not always be those that appear on the surface.

### Empiricism

Empiricism is the basing of claims to truth on direct observation of external things, rather than on inward experience or reason. A number of possible empirical tests of religious truth have been advanced by re-

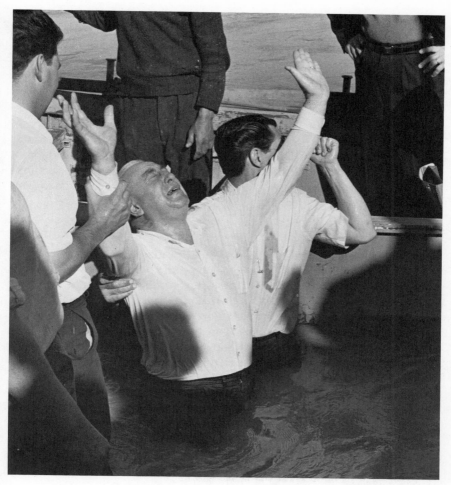

Dorka Raynor/Leo de Wys, Inc.

This picture of American Protestants being baptized in the Jordan River, the stream in the Holy Land in which Jesus was baptized, indicates the intense subjective experience that to many is a reliable guide to religious truth.

ligionists. Eighteenth- and nineteenth-century philosophers such as William Paley drew from alleged evidences of design in nature to support the teleological argument. Others bring in claims of prayers answered, lives changed, and the beneficent effects of religion on human history to support its truth. Still others show that data of the sort produced by psychical research—telepathy, cases suggesting reincarnation or survival of physical death, nonphysical movement of matter—tend to affirm the religious world at least by demonstrating invisible forces and realities. Some go further to say that the existence of miracles, the soul, and life after death can be affirmed in this way, and so validate much of traditional religion empirically. We cannot assess the many empirical arguments for religious truth here. We can point out, however, that in an age when science, in which empirical data and testing are of crucial importance, has such great prestige and use, it is natural that empirical arguments in religion should become increasingly used, even as they have always (in prescientific or nonscientific forms) been central to popular religious advocacy. Whether they have much of a future in philosophical religious thought will depend on whether religion comes to parallel the sciences in method and kind of knowledge sought or whether it is essentially perceived as something very different—perhaps more akin to the poet's way of "knowing"—for which such quasi-scientific proofs are peripheral.

## Authority

For millions the real touchstone of religious determination of truth is an authority—scriptures, tradition, church, pope, guru, and so on. Arguments from authority, of course, are finally dependent on other arguments, those by which the authority is established. These are often arguments from reason, experience, and empiricism, the last often generalizing from ways the authority can be shown to be correct. To say something is true because the Bible or the pope says it is true is meaningful only within a context in which that authority is accepted. Context, however, is a major point in arguments from authority—they not only deliver a content message by affirming the point in question but also deliver a structural message by reinforcing belief in the authority. They also affirm the sociological ground of the religion as a group sharing common structure and values based on the authority, and symbolized by it.

## Sociology

Sociological considerations do not precisely argue for truth but for meaning and value, although they may be virtually a form of the argument from general consent discussed above. For many people sociological criteria are immensely important. The operative determinant for them in identification with religious statements is their role in groups important to them—given groups, such as family or ethnic tradition; or peer groups, activity groups, and other groups they want to feel a part of. Usually when people use such grounds to decide on religious truth, ultimate truth is not an issue; it is either taken for granted or handled relativistically ("This is our way; it's all we know. We follow our way and others can follow theirs") or pragmatically ("This must be true because it works for us"). Sociology does not answer all the questions that a highly philosophical mind might raise, but it indicates one of the main things a religion ought to fulfill—a sense of group coherence.

### Existential Choice

This approach is based on the premise that religious truth *cannot* be proved by means extraneous to the real nature of religion, which is commitment. Means such as reason, empiricism, sociology, and the like are really distractions that only lead one to false sorts of religion since they set up something less than God, or the absolute, as the real object of worship, be it the human mind, scientific method, or society. True religion can only be seized by faith, meaning a choice *not* based on such secondary support. The existential choice approach was classically stated by Soren Kierkegaard, mentioned in chapter 2. He said that the evidence for and against the existence of God in the philosophical arguments are equally balanced; from the vantage of the human mind, as much can be said on one side as the other. Therefore, whether one believes in God or not is pure choice, and that is the way it is meant to be. One must decide and gets what he or she decides for. One can choose no God or even a "God" who is merely a God of reason or of social convention and live a fairly comfortable life devoted to aesthetic gratification or even ethical goals. Deep down, however, one feels in them a kind of emptiness. One can also choose a truly religious life of faith and commitment to the ultimate God, which may be hard and separate one from both the philosophers and society but which is in touch with the highest meaning. It is through choice that one comes to this truth, but it is not choice that makes it true—rather, religious truth is a special kind of truth accessible not to reason or the other means but only truly discoverable in a decision for that greater than oneself.

## ARE RELIGIOUS BELIEFS IRREFUTABLE?

The advantage of the existential choice approach is that it cannot be refuted. If one believes something simply because he or she chooses to believe it, there is really nothing anyone else can say. Some would say, however, that all religious beliefs are really of this character; while supportive arguments from reason, experience, consent, and so forth can be brought in, religionists easily shift from one to the other, and finally it is not possible to prove any beliefs are *untrue* so long as they are held as religion. According to the rules of modern logic, however, a statement must be falsifiable (that is, one must be able to show how it could be proved wrong) or it cannot really be considered verified as a newly deduced truth, either; it is only a tautology (that is, something that says in different words what you started out with). An example is the affirmation, "God is Creator." One can support it through arguments such as the cosmological, but it is hard to think of an equal argument that would prove God is *not* Creator if one is thinking in terms of God and Creator at all. This is because the two terms really imply each other by definition. Nonetheless, as a devotional or even creedal statement, the sentence might have deep religious meaning for those in a circle of believers and even be incapable of *disproof* for them. For every group has ways of handling within its own circle of symbols most of what happens in life. Suffering, joy, doubt, and all sorts of experiences are given different meanings by different religions or even nonreligious ways of handling life.[7] A mystical vision has one meaning to religion—though particulars may vary with religions, as Hindus have visions of Krishna and Roman Catholics of the Blessed Virgin Mary—but by nonreligious people can be dealt with as psychologically explicable projections. As the great philosopher David Hume said, miracles may happen, but there could never be *reasonable* grounds for believing in them since by definition they go against reason. It also seems to be the case that there is no religious phenomena for which reasonable (that is, nonreligious or at least nonsupernatural) explanations that convince many people cannot be adduced. (Of course for some religious philosophers, like Soren Kierkegaard, this is only to be expected since it is precisely what makes choice and faith genuine for those who elect the religious life.)

On the other hand, the trouble with relegating religion to just being the language game of a particular circle is that circles of belief are not airtight. A given circle of belief can explain everything except the existence, or rather the subjective experience, of others with other systems once the others are genuinely acknowledged to be there, and this must increasingly be the case in our pluralistic world. Thus, whatever circle we are in, of one religion or another or of nonreligion, there is increasingly a price to be paid intellectually and spiritually for the privilege of remaining in that circle. We cannot help but be more and more aware of the *concrete* possibility, for *ourselves*, of other modes of life. By the same token, we must be increasingly aware of the *nonabsoluteness* of language games because we are compelled to recognize, in most of our dealings with other people whether they are within our religious circle or not, a common humanity that suggests there are, regardless of religion, common human languages of value, logic, and experience.

The philosophical theologian Charles Hartshorne, then, is able to argue that what a proof of God's existence (and, by implication, a proof of

[7]See Frank B. Dilley, "The Irrefutability of Belief Systems," *Journal of the American Academy of Religion*, XLIII, 2 (June 1975), 214–23.

God's nonexistence, although he and others would argue this is logically impossible) would do is to show the intellectual price that must be paid by rejecting the argument.[8] As suggested in the section on ontological argument, a putative proof of God does not so much prove God as show what one gives up if he or she elects to live in a universe in which God is not tenable. It shows the cost of living in a situation in which logic and language have *no* validity except that given them by the person or circle using them at the moment. What logical proofs of God (as universal being and so symbol of universal meaning or the possibility thereof) contend, then, is that while logic may only appear as *proof* to the user and his or her circle, it also has some universal meaning as it states what one is giving up by being outside of the circle or even by holding that there are no universals and that truth is *only* relative to circles. A person outside a religious circle may not find the meaning that believers do in the cosmological argument, but he or she *still* must live without a sense of a divine first cause in a world in which such arguments do not work and without whatever meaning a first cause gives.

In fact there have been counterarguments to the insistence of some philosophers that language, in the sense of meaning and especially religious meaning, only works within circles who accept the rules of the particular language game being played. The French philosopher Michel Foucault argues that it is precisely language that can unify human life.[9] Language poorly used, reduced to jargon, may give us a sense of things being disparate and disconnected, of meaning and experience being reduced to atomistic subgroups, or reduced to social science or psychological categories that give a sense of experiences being explained away in a manner that devalues them.

Nevertheless, just as it is possible for a master translator to translate great literature from German, Russian, or Chinese into English in a manner that enables the English reader to participate richly and with understanding (even if *something* may be lost) in the experience behind the original, so it should be possible to translate through language, or rather in the mind and spirit of one attuned to the meanings behind language, the experience of each religious "game" into a meta-language (in whatever tongue it is written) revealing a meta-meaning that is universal. This is the interpretative task of the history of religions; it can also be the task of theology—which has the added burden and joy of showing what price must be paid for not accepting such meanings as it can bring forth, and articulate in universals understandable by all men and women.

[8]Charles Hartshorne, *A Natural Theology of Our Time* (LaSalle, Ill.: Open Court Publishing Co., 1967), p. 30.
[9]Michel Foucault, *The Order of Things* (New York: Vintage Books, 1973).

This is an artist's conception of a future space colony located between earth and moon. A spectacular view of the real earth and moon is visible through a panel. Within the cylinder, several hundred thousand people will live amid scenes resembling the land and sky of earth. What new images of humanity would suggest themselves to persons living in this new environment, which will probably be realized within the next few centuries?

# CHAPTER SEVEN

# RELIGION
# AND THE FUTURE

## NEW PARADIGMS OF SELF

This chapter is not an attempt at prediction but an endeavor to bring together the material presented in this book by looking at what is going on in religion and society today and extrapolating a little from it. A few specific areas in which present changes in human life or new ideas are raising issues of immense consequence for the future of religion are discussed because they are of great importance for our future. Fundamentally that is because they present new images of what a human self is.

This book began with the idea that religion creates scenarios for the real self. This means that each religion presents a paradigm, or ideal image, of a real self or of real personhood. Proceeding through the book, the symbols, worship, sociology, and concepts of religion expressing paradigms and acting out the scenarios going with them were discussed. Now some new materials for paradigms of self, materials that raise far-reaching questions about what sort of religious paradigm of self might go with each, or might be negated by each, are examined. In each example there are doubtless implicit symbols, worship, sociology, and religious concepts. The task of discovering and articulating them is left to the readers, especially to those who will live long in the world molded by these new shapes arising over the horizon. Some starting clues are offered by pointing to the new paradigms of personhood cocooned in the present.

Paradigms of personhood, of course, are not presented only by religion but also by other societal worlds—the worlds of sports, politics, commerce, science, youth culture, retirement, and the like. The paradigms of personhood continually change as these paradigms change in interaction one with another. For example, the ideal of the political person has changed as a result of modern science. It is now immensely important that a politician be able to communicate his or her charisma effectively over radio and television and operate in a political arena in which public opinion is shaped by the immediacy and the brevity of the evening news—qualities his or her predecessors in the days of Queen Victoria did not require. Moreover, values emergent out of the 1960s youth culture have suggested that a real person has a "cool" sort of charisma; thus, this is the style of the effective politician, rather than the combination of a "hot" kind of ambition with a facade of white-shirt-and-tie dignity characteristic of an older school.

What are some changes in paradigm of personhood or self going on now, and how will they affect religion? What is happening in society, science, medicine, and literature in interaction with religion that could betoken paradigm shifts? If religion means a scenario for the real self, *anything* that affects *how* people think of their real self will have major consequences for at least the language, style, and structure of religion, and perhaps the content as well. Only a few representative questions along these lines are raised and discussed; readers will probably want to add to the data from their own observation or study and think through their own answers.

## SPACE AND HUMAN DESTINY

What new paradigms for personhood are emerging because of space? This is an obvious example of a situation in which people are doing new things and existing in new places. Does space travel in any way change our basic images of what a person is?

At first it may seem exaggerated to say that the exploration of space creates a new person, or a new paradigm of personhood. It may seem that astronauts are just the same old humans up to new tricks, but in fact what people do and what they think, their environments and their subjectivities, have always gone hand in hand. If the histories of religion and philosophy teach anything, it is that the nature of work, economic activity, and the extent of knowledge about the universe do change religion and philosophy in the long run. So it was with movement from a hunting to an agricultural society, and from village to city; from local barter to exploration of the earth, and from the terrestrial horizon to modern telescopic and microscopic knowledge of the large and small.

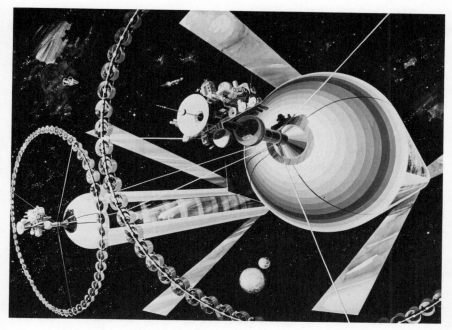

Exterior view of the space colony on page 170.

Over the next few centuries, the fact of mankind's environment being several worlds tossed into the depths of space—indeed, the universe itself—rather than one planet, may get through. We may be, in space, creatures of a more totally self-made, artificial environment than necessary on the bosom of earth; we may spend entire lifetimes on artificial worlds or as colonies on the faces of inhospitable planets. Yet we will also be unshackled in new ways, masters of our own destiny before a virtual infinity of space and time. We might even meet other intelligent beings, with unimaginable results. However, the very fact of the exploration of space—what it means that we are able to do this—will affect the spiritual life of the sending culture more than anything that is discovered out there. For the religious values of an expanding culture with a sense of an open-ended future is quite different from that of one hemmed-in and static. The concept of what it means, or can mean, to be a human self is quite different in the two.[1]

[1]A related area of scientific knowledge that is presently expanding into mind-boggling new ideas and that may well have profound interaction with the religion of the future is cosmology, or the science of the beginning and end of the universe. The matter is too complex for discussion here, but just to give an impression of the kind of ideas now being bandied about by thinkers on the cutting edge of astronomy,

## THE MEDICAL REVOLUTION

Another area in which science is creating new paradigms of human personhood is medicine. Many old and new issues involving ethics and, ultimately, philosophical or spiritual ideas about what it means to be a human person cluster about the field of medicine today. Even old issues that were known and discussed as far back as ancient Greece, such as artificial birth control, abortion, voluntary euthanasia or the right to die, and experimentation on humans, are revamped today because of immense advances in medical research that have vastly expanded possibilities, as well as intensified the moral problems.

There are also new issues growing out of explosive new possibilities for biological engineering — shaping genetic transmission and physiological nature in ways that would have seemed like science fiction only a few years ago, and that may still seem fantastic to those who have not kept up with the new research. Today such things as the following are definitely on the horizon: the alteration of cells, the transfer of genes and so of heredity from one person to another, making genetic copies enabling the genes of one person to be indefinitely multiplied and implanted in many other organisms, cloning or nonsexual reproduction from a tissue specimen, the predetermination of an infant's sex, and (much farther off) the artificial creation of organic life and maybe even of humans.

This sort of biological engineering, which will seem to many like "playing God," causes questions to rush through the mind. What changes are desirable? What values must come into play? Who decides?

---

theoretical physics, and mathematics, here are a few samples: the space-time continuum of our own universe is only one expression of a vastly larger entity, a "hyper-space," in which our physical laws may not apply and in which an indefinite number of other universes, alternative realities, may coexist; the "black holes" and "white holes" in our own space, now virtually established by astronomy, where ordinary physical laws are negated by superintense gravity, may provide access to "wormholes" through space and time by means of which one could time-travel or travel to alternative universes coexisting with ours; the primordial particles that make up ordinary matter-energy may be miniature black holes and white holes; the constituent of existence that expresses itself in us as consciousness may be especially aligned to this capacity of matter-energy to transcend space and time and particular planes of universes in the larger hyper-space field. In other words, the laws of physics may be partly determined by the state of consciousness of the percipient-participator (an idea implicit in quantum theory), and simple ideas of time and distance are illusory. Still over the horizon, but one feels implied by the new cosmology, is an idea of consciousness as even more fundamentally interpretative of space, time, energy, and being itself than anything else. See, for example, John A. Wheeler, *The Physicist's Conception of Nature* (Amsterdam: Reidel Publications, 1974). For a simple, though sometimes tendentious, presentation of these new ideas accompanied by graphic illustrations, see Bob Toben, with Jack Sarfatti and Fred Wolf, *Space-Time and Beyond* (New York: E.P. Dutton & Co., Inc., 1975).

Can scientists be trusted with such power, or can politicians or anyone else who is *not* a scientist?

More basic is the issue of what image of a human person, of what it means to be a self, would be operative as one decides such momentous matters. To be a person in the fullest psychological and spiritual sense— in traditional terms, to have a soul and be a child of God—is it necessary for one to have been a product of the genetic lottery in the traditional way? Would a genetic copy, a clone, or a "test tube baby" be a person with a soul?

Actually, there has been genetic engineering by other means for a long time, often under the strictest religious sanctions. The caste system in India in effect maintained gene pools and so controlled heredity under Hindu religious sanctions. The social class systems of Europe and America by which nobility or comparable elites were expected to mate and marry only within their class received implicit or explicit sanction by Christian churches. Even the institution of marriage itself is a socially and religiously sanctioned practice that in various complex ways controls human genetics with results far different from other conceivable arrangements for reproduction. The fact is, however, that class, caste, and marriage make the evolution of human biology a slow, half-conscious process that is the byproduct of social and spiritual agendas, whereas the new possibilities force immediate, conscious decisions upon us that shake our concepts of the relation of humanity and biology.

All the new prospects are not genetic. There are also emerging new ways of engineering human life after birth. The coming possibility of extensive organ transplants raises the issue of just what *is* a physiologically separate human. Suppose one could transplant or make artificially all organs, even the brain. We would have problems such as the ethicality of transplanting the brain of a dying genius into the body of a physically healthy but feeble-minded youth. Even now decisions of this sort must be made in regard to kidney transplants.

Transplanting even brains makes one begin to wonder where one life ends and another begins. In a world of procedures such as this, it might seem that human beings are not separate entities given a span of life by chance or God on this world but are configurations of an ongoing human biosphere that can be rearranged continually. (Of course, this is already more true than we often acknowledge on the psychological level; our minds and consiousnesses are the result of continual exchange— transplants, if one wish—of ideas and moods between one another.)

So if bodies can be mixed up, do separate bodies really make separate persons? Or *is* there such a thing as a separate person? Is the new biology saying, as the new physics also seems to be indicating, that the universe is a single energy field taking many forms and that the mystics who have said that selfhood is an illusion were right all along? Or are these sciences looking at it from one angle only?

What would the world of the new biology be like? Would this new earth of immensely enhanced physiological interchange, in which through genetic manipulation every child could be born a genius greater than Leonardo da Vinci or Albert Einstein, and perhaps even death could be made obsolete, be a utopia of wise and godlike immortals? Or would it reduce humanity to a beehive? Bees through instinct also perform remarkable feats of biological engineering. Even worse, would it provide the means for some set of totalitarians to take control of the human race and, quite literally, to shape it irreversibly to serve their ends?

One is not reassured concerning this last possiblity by still another prospect now coming into realization, the control of the pleasure and pain and learning centers in the brain by wired stimulators. It appears possible through mild electric charges at the right places in the brain to facilitate learning, modify memory, enhance intelligence, and curb aggressiveness, or effect the reverse of any of these. Again, such manipulation seems to offer vast opportunities for improving the human condition—or for making possible totalitarian control beyond the dreams of

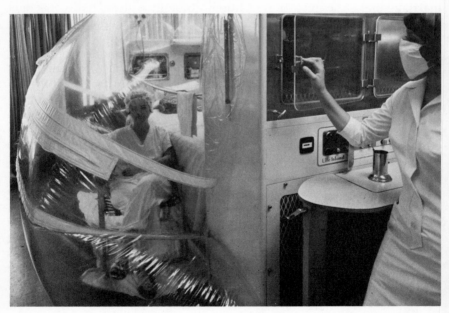

One dramatic new development in medicine is the creation of a nearly germ-free "life island" for persons whose resistance to microbes has been severely affected by immunotherapy.

a Hitler or a Stalin, possibly bringing the latter in the guise of the former. Yet, as brain research touches the physics and chemistry of consciousness itself, its advocates rightly remind us that they only offer opportunities for free control of what has so often been only illusory freedoms, so subject has mind itself been to vicissitudes of diet, disease, poor education, and repressive environment.

One thing seems certain; the future of religion will be very greatly affected indeed by these new images of personhood. And if religion does not come to terms with these issues, it will increasingly seem irrelevant.

It is just as important to realize that some decisions like those indicated are being made now. Physicians and society must continually make life and death decisions and decisions between one life and another. Dramatic instances occur when only so many transplants, or artificial kidney machines, are available, and their allocation must be determined by a hospital "God committee." Questions such as abortion and human experimentation provide current foci for the kind of issues raised here. Society also decides the biological life and death of individuals when it decides how to allocate resources for preventive medicine, what medical facilities it provides or fails to provide for the underprivileged, and for what issues it will dispose of human life in war.

## THE ROLE OF WOMEN IN RELIGION

There is a science fiction novel by Ursula LeGuin, daughter of the distinguished anthropologist A. L. Kroeber, called *The Left Hand of Darkness*. It presents a world in which all the people are both male and female. They go through monthly cycles in which they are first one sex, then the other, and the mentality, institutions, and customs of that society are permeated with the ramifications of this unearthly biology.

In our society, however, no fact is more basic than the division of humanity into people who are permanently female and people who are permanently male. This, together with the need to nurture children, affects everything from family structure to world politics and is profoundly reflected in the symbols and institutions of religion, from the Madonna or mother and child as a transcendent symbol to the almost exclusively male control of most religious institutions. While occasionally religion may rise to the purport of Paul's dictum that "in Christ there is neither male nor female," it is also very conscious, even obsessively conscious, of the fact that humanity was created male and female and that there must be great meaning behind this. Religious myths, symbols, and roles (and society as sanctioned by religion) are shot through with images implying set male and female patterns of life. It is fair to say that most traditional religion has been patriarchal in that it

A woman Methodist minister, one of the relatively few women who have been ordained by a major American denomination.

has made men the sources of authority and correct teaching in both church and family.

Today, the idea of distinctive male-female roles, and the validity of religious symbols and lines of authority based on distinctive sexual biology, are being challenged as never before. Women in particular, aware that traditional symbols and structures in religion and society have usually served to put them in a secondary role, have pointedly queried whether women should be ordained ministers and priests or whether God should exclusively be called Father. These challenges have had a profoundly disruptive effect because they raise issues and feelings that go very deep. For some religion should sanction the hierarchy of heaven and earth, with the father head of the family on earth as God is in heaven. For others God is beyond gender, can transform all social structures, and liberates each person to be what she or he is as an individual self rather than just to follow a predetermined sexual or social role.

If the latter attitude prevails, religion in the future will be affected by paradigms of personhood much less categorized by sexual roles than in the past. A person will be one of either sex who can do and be virtually anything—and this capacity will need to be reflected in roles in religious institutions as well as in religious language and symbols. One feels that the greatest challenge Christianity and Judaism, together with other religions, will have to face in the next few centuries will not come from science, or political revolution in the usual sense, or new vogues in philosophy or theology, but from the far-reaching implications of these changes in sexual images and roles. Some deeply touch the structure and the very language of these faiths, from God as Father on down. One could well ask how much change on such a deep level Judaism and Christianity could take without really becoming different religions. For some, such a transformation would be welcome, for others tragic.

Not all who urge equality of women in religion, of course, insist that male-female roles should be flatly identical, as though there were no differences between the sexes except some physiological details. Instead, they feel that both have distinct and equally valuable contributions to make to worship and theology—which in itself does mark a radical enough change, since heretofore perhaps 90 percent of theology has been written and worship conducted by males and undoubtedly reflected mostly male experience. No doubt this is indicated in the predilection of much orthodox, masculine religion for divine sovereignty and law and in the teachings of feminine spiritual leaders, such as Mary Baker Eddy and Helena Blavatsky, for ultimate unity and spiritual evolution on the analogy of, perhaps, the womb and nurture. In the same light, the image of a woman behind the altar, bringing forth bread and wine, might be congenial. I once attended an ordination ceremony in a tiny, modern Gnostic church in which the practice was for a husband and wife to be ordained as priests together and thereafter to celebrate the Gnostic mass jointly and equally, each performing parts of the service that especially emphasized the sacred meaning of his or her sex.

## RELIGION AND PSYCHIC RESEARCH

One of the most fascinating and controversial areas of modern discussion is psychic research, a term that covers investigation into a variety of phenomena. What they have in common is that they all suggest human minds operating outside the limits normally imposed by the senses and the physical body. These phenomena include telepathy, precognition (ability to see future events), retrocognition (seeing past events as though present), psychokinesis (control of physical objects by the power of thought alone), mediumship (transmission of messages from the spirits of deceased persons) and other evidence of survival after death.

It should be emphasized that psychic phenomena are not religion. In themselves they do not imply transcendence or ultimate transformation and have none of the three forms of religious expression—though they may imply the existence of an invisible world and non-material realities. Many leading people in psychic research, however, insist that the field has nothing to do with religion.

Many religious people, conversely, would vehemently insist that their faith is based on grounds quite independent of the results of current psychic research and in fact seem to find it highly suspect and disturbing. They would prefer miracles be content to stay just in their scriptures or at best within the circle of true believers. This attitude is understandable from the point of view that religion is an integrated symbol system founded on concepts, practices, and sociology, not just a haphazard affirmation of marvels and spirits.

Nonetheless, psychic research has much common ground with the concerns of religion, and some results in psychic research could well produce changes in paradigms of personhood that in turn modify religious attitudes and symbols. For these empirical results could suggest that consciousness can be somewhat independent of the transient physical body and even of space and time. However religion would deal with such a finding, it would, if widely received as scientifically or empirically known, massively affect the paradigms of personhood operating in the religion's culture in areas close to the concerns of religion. Religion would have to deal with this fact.

While much of the data of psychic research appear convincing, the field is still very controversial. Some of its results are based on experimental work, some on spontaneous cases. An example of the latter would be a dream in which someone thought living is dead, that someone having died that same night. I had a feeling one night, while drifting off to sleep, that my car would be stolen; on awaking, I found it was still there but had been broken into.

However, it is hard to verify that there is absolutely no ordinary explanation of such cases, given the human propensity for self-deception. In any event, those disinclined to accept psychic phenomena are likely to apply David Hume's conclusion about miracles, already cited, that while they may happen it would never be reasonable to believe that they happen. Even laboratory work with ESP, while often impressive, has been faulted for poor statistical control. One has a feeling, however, that acceptance or rejection of psychic phenomena has largely to do with one's prior paradigms establishing what one believes is possible, since classes of observations that become controversial in psychic research frequently would be doubted by few if they were of more ordinary matters.

Here the real complexity and importance of the psychic for modern thought and religion come in. The psychic forces us to face how powerful the will to believe (or to disbelieve) is—that is, how our conceptual framework and paradigmatic images shape what we believe is possible and so expect or want to see. A view of personhood emergent out of some things suggested by psychic research would challenge, in about equal degree, conventional science and religion today.

## THE PERSISTENCE OF RELIGION

Numerous ways in which religion, the drive to be a real self in the context of infinite reality, has manifested itself have been examined in this book. The roots of this process, or of some of the phenomena connected with it, have been observed deep in the animal world and in our successive self-discoveries of our own nature. Its association with certain states of consciousness, its representation in symbols, rites, social groups, and intellectual concepts, have been noted.

It is evident that religion has always been changing in outward manifestation. Its institutional structures, symbols, services, and words are never the same from one age to another, whether or not one feels that the essence of religion or of a particular religion remains constant beneath the changes. The four currently changing aspects of human life presented in this chapter represent, among others, factors that undoubtedly will affect future changes in religion as it continues in the developmental course it has long followed.

However much religion varies and changes, the prophecies of those who say it will finally run through all its possible changes and become extinct never seem to be fulfilled. Religion, or its close parallels in ideological movements like that in China today, can take new updated guises—sometimes even without the name *religion*—whenever it seems in really serious danger of becoming obsolete. It seems finally to have a persistence like that of biology itself. Just as life wants to find ways to defeat death, at least until it has reproduced itself on the physical plane, so the spirit wants to defeat its own extinction until it has found a larger context or purpose in which it lives beyond shifting appearance. This is the realm of the real self, or of religious constructions of reality, and it does not seem the drive to actualize its reality will lose power soon.

# BIBLIOGRAPHY

The following lists of books present a few suggestions for further reading in several of the areas touched on in this introduction to religious studies. This bibliography should not be thought of as more than a sampling. I am well aware that many, many, many pages could be filled with worthwhile titles in any one of these areas. In assembling this bibliography, the needs of undergraduates and other interested but beginning students have been kept uppermost in mind. Thus, I have tried to include not only such books as would be considered best or most significant by specialists but also books that do an especially good job of whetting a budding interest in an area, or providing an introductory aperture to it or a useful general overview of the history and current state of that area. Also, some books particularly important for the angle of presentation selected in the text of this book have been mentioned. Most of the books given in footnotes have not been repeated here, except for the most important; they are, however, also recommended. Many of these books themselves contain extensive bibliographies in their own fields, to which the reader is referred.

CHAPTER ONE

BELLAH, ROBERT, *Beyond Belief: Essays on Religion in a Post-Traditional World.* New York: Harper & Row, Publishers, Inc., 1970.
A collection of essays by a first-rate modern sociologist of religion;

it contains perceptive insights into the meaning of transcendence, religious experience, and civil religion today.

BERGER, PETER L., *The Sacred Canopy*. Garden City, N.Y.: Doubleday Company, Inc., 1969.

A standard presentation of the social construction-of-reality interpretation of religion's role in human life, with a deep reverence for the validity of religious reality.

BERGSON, HENRI, *The Two Sources of Morality and Religion*. New York: Henry Holt and Co., 1935.

A classic treatment of the ambivalent roots of religion as enforcer of the normative values of society and as producer of the new in prophetic utterance.

ELIADE, MIRCEA, *The Sacred and the Profane*. New York: Harcourt Brace Jovanovich, Inc., 1959.

A modern presentation of religion as centering around the experience of sacred time and sacred space.

LANGER, SUSANNE, *Philosophy in a New Key*. Cambridge, Mass.: Harvard University Press, 1957.

An interpretation of religion, art, and language centering on the importance of symbolism.

STRENG, FREDERICK J., *Understanding Religious Life*, 2nd ed. Encino, Calif.: Dickenson Publishing Co., Inc., 1976.

An excellent introduction to religious studies, based on an interpretation of religion as means toward ultimate transformation.

TILLICH, PAUL, *What is Religion?* New York: Harper & Row, Publishers, Inc., 1969.

A great theologian's interpretation of religion as "directedness toward the Unconditional."

VAN DER LEEUW, GERARDUS, *Religion in Essence and Manifestation: A Study in Phenomenology*. New York: Harper & Row, Publishers, Inc., 1963 (first published 1933).

An important presentation of types of religious expression and personality, together with the phenomenological approach that endeavors to see things just as they appear.

WACH, JOACHIM, *Sociology of Religion*. Chicago, Ill.: University of Chicago Press, 1944.

A view of religion in society emphasizing the three forms of religious expression: theoretical, practical, and sociological.

WHITEHEAD, ALFRED NORTH, *Religion in the Making*. New York: The Macmillan Company, 1926.

A prominent philosopher's view of religion as "the art and theory of the internal life of man, so far as it depends on the man himself and on what is permanent in the nature of things."

## CHAPTER TWO

DE VRIES, JAN, *The Study of Religion: A Historical Approach*. New York: Harcourt Brace Jovanovich, 1967.
  A history of the academic study of the history of religions.

DURKHEIM, EMILE, *The Elementary Forms of the Religious Life*. New York: Collier Books, 1961 (first published in French, 1915).
  A classic view of primitive religion as an expression of the "mystique" of a group.

EVANS-PRITCHARD, E. E., *Theories of Primitive Religion*. Oxford: The Clarendon Press, 1965.
  A useful overview of anthropological theories of primitive religion.

JASPERS, KARL, *The Origin and Goal of History*. London: Routledge & Kegan Paul, 1953 (first published in German, 1949).
  A study presenting the concept of the axial age of transition from prehistoric to historic modes of human consciousness marked by the great religious founders.

LESSA, W. A., AND E. Z. VOGT, EDS., *Reader in Comparative Religion: An Anthropological Approach*. New York: Harper & Row, Publishers, Inc., 1965.
  A valuable resource, especially for the material on religious origins, concepts, and roles in societies.

LING, TREVOR, *A History of Religion East and West*. New York: Harper & Row, Publishers, Inc., 1968.
  A history particularly valuable for its idea of the comparative treatment of developments in the same historical period in Eastern and Western cultures.

MACQUARRIE, JOHN, *Twentieth Century Religious Thought*. New York: Harper & Row, Publishers, Inc., 1963.
  A very competent overview, purveying nineteenth- as well as twentieth-century theology and philosophy of religion.

NORBECK, EDWARD, *Religion in Primitive Society*. New York: Harper & Row, Publishers, Inc., 1961.
  A good introduction that includes discussion of the origin of religion in anthropological thought as well as emphasizes religious concepts and religion's role in societies.

TYLOR, EDWARD B., *Primitive Culture*, 2 vols. London: J. Murray, 1873 (several reprints).
> The second volume of this pioneer anthropological classic deals with religion and presents the theory of religion's origin in animism, or belief in souls in persons and objects.

WILSON, EDWARD O., *Sociobiology: The New Synthesis*. Cambridge, Mass.: Harvard University Press, 1975.
> A controversial but important new book on the biological basis of human culture and, by implication, religion. It argues that traits such as altruism and social organization have prehuman origin based on their survival value for the species.

### CHAPTER THREE

ALLPORT, GORDON, *The Individual and His Religion* New York: The Macmillan Company, 1950.
> A standard text that is especially important for its treatment of stages of religious development.

BECKER, ERNEST, *Escape from Evil*. New York: The Free Press, 1975.
> A challenging book that argues that desire for immortality (though not mere preservation of physical life) is the fundamental human psychological drive; evil is that which threatens immortality. Culture and religion express this drive in manifold complex ways.

JAMES, WILLIAM, *Varieties of Religious Experience*. New York and London: Longmans, Green and Co., 1902 (reprinted several times).
> A classic on the psychological interpretation of religion that is full of case studies in religious experience.

JOHNSON, P. E., *The Psychology of Religion*. Nashville, Tenn.: Abingdon-Cokesbury, 1945.
> An easy-to-read introduction that is sympathetic to religion.

LEE, R. S., *Freud and Christianity*. New York: A. A. Wyn, 1949.
> A simple and vivid study that provides an excellent introduction to the issues.

LEWIS, I. M., *Ecstatic Religion*. Harmondsworth, England: Penguin Books, 1971.
> A valuable study of shamanism and ecstasy in religion, especially in their role among oppressed groups.

MASLOW, ABRAHAM S., *Religions, Values, and Peak Experiences*. Columbus, Ohio: Ohio State University Press, 1964.
> An influential statement of the view that psychology should start, in its view of human potentials, with the peak experiences—which

have much in common with classic mystical and religious experiences.

MOORE, JOHN M., *Theories of Religious Experiences*. New York: Round Table Press, 1938.
A useful discussion, especially of the views of James, Otto, and Bergson.

RÓHEIM, GÉZA, *The Eternal Ones of the Dream: A Psychoanalytic Interpretation of Australian Myth and Ritual*. New York: New York International Universities Press, 1945.
A representative orthodox Freudian approach to some religious phenomena that is now somewhat dated but valuable as an example of the school.

TART, CHARLES, *States of Consciousness*. New York: E. P. Dutton & Company, Inc., 1975.
A basic book in transpersonal psychology and its state specific sciences for various states of consciousness, including those of mystical and religious experience.

WHITE, VICTOR, *God and the Unconsciousness*. London: Harvill Press, 1953.
An important discussion of religion in the light of Jungian analytic psychology.

## CHAPTER FOUR

CASSIRER, ERNST, *The Philosophy of Symbolic Forms*, 3 vols. New Haven, Conn.: Yale University Press, 1953–57 (first published in German, 1923–29).
A basic philosophical statement of the importance of symbol in communication and society.

DUNCAN, HUGH D., *Symbols and Social Theory*. New York: Oxford University Press, Inc., 1969.
A presentation of the major theories of symbol in society, from Weber and Durkheim to Sorokin, discussing such topics as the symbolic meaning of ceremonial and social hierarchies.

ELIADE, MIRCEA, *Images and Symbols*. London: Harvil Press, 1961.
An interpretation of the subject by a distinguished historian of religion.

————, *Rites and Symbols of Initiation: The Mysteries of Birth and Rebirth*. New York: Harper & Row, Publishers, Inc., 1975.
The interaction of ritual and symbol in perhaps the most important of all religious contexts; a wealth of vivid illustrative material.

HUBERT, HENRI, AND MARCEL MAUSS, *Sacrifice: Its Nature and Function.* Chicago, Ill.: University of Chicago Press, 1964 (first published in French, 1899).
A classic study of one of the most important types of religious rite.

JUNG, CARL, ET AL., *Man and his Symbols.* Garden City, N. Y.: Doubleday & Company, Inc., 1964.
A lavishly illustrated introduction to the subject from the Jungian perspective.

LEHNER, ERNST, *Symbols, Signs, and Signets.* New York: Dover Press, 1950.
Not a scholarly book, but a large illustrated anthology of symbols in religion and other fields; provides a good visual supplement to a study of the topic.

LÉVI-STRAUSS, CLAUDE, *Structural Anthropology.* Garden City, N. Y.: Doubleday Anchor Books, 1967.
An essential introduction to the structuralist approach to myth, culture, and religion, showing how they are all made up of component parts in significant and balanced relationships to serve as "languages."

MIDDLETON, JOHN, ED., *Gods and Rituals.* Austin, Tex.: University of Texas Press, 1976.
A valuable collection of anthropological papers.

ROSS, RALPH, *Symbols and Civilization: Science, Morals, Religion, Art.* New York: Harcourt Brace Jovanovich, Inc., 1962.
Emphasis on scientific concepts and language as symbols in interaction with society; valuable for this perspective rather than for the material on religion.

TURNER, VICTOR, *The Ritual Process.* Chicago, Ill.,: Aldine Publishing Co., 1969.
A stimulating interpretation of ritual and religious experience based on the idea of *liminality,* or going outside of the limits of structure.

## CHAPTER FIVE

ELLWOOD, ROBERT S., JR., *Religious and Spiritual Groups in Modern America.* Englewood Cliffs, N.J.: Prentice-Hall, Inc., 1973.
Presents a number of contemporary groups of the cult or emergent-expansive type, with emphasis on the nature of experience within them.

FESTINGER, LEON, HENRY W. RIECKEN, AND STANLEY SCHACTER, *When Prophecy Fails.* Minneapolis, Minn.: University of Minnesota Press, 1956.
A fascinating study of social process in a UFO group.

GREELEY, ANDREW, *The Denominational Society*. Glenview, Ill.: Scott, Fores-
man and Company, 1973.
An introductory book on sociology of religion in America.

JOHNSTONE, RONALD L., *Religion and Society in Interaction*. Englewood
Cliffs, N.J.: Prentice-Hall, Inc., 1975.
A good introductory textbook on the sociology of religion.

NIEBUHR, H. RICHARD, *The Social Sources of Denominationalism*. Cleveland,
Ohio: Meridian Books, 1963.
A classic study of the interaction of socioeconomic class and de-
nominational affiliation in America.

ROBERTSON, ROLAND, *Sociological Interpretation of Religion*. New York:
Schocken Books, Inc., 1970.
Emphasizes the development of the sociology of religion and the
major issues in the field.

STARK, WERNER, *The Sociology of Religion*, 4 vols. London: Routledge &
Kegan Paul, 1966.
The volumes in this monumental survey are devoted to established,
sectarian, and universal religions and to the types of religious
personality.

WACH, JOACHIM, *Sociology of Religion*. Chicago, Ill.: University of Chicago
Press, 1944.
A survey of religious forms of expression and of types of groups.

WILSON, BRYAN, ED., *Patterns of Sectarianism*. London: Heinemann, 1967.
An important presentation of material on sectarian movements of
various types, indicating that they are not all the same in derivation
or style.

YINGER, MILTON, *The Scientific Study of Religion*. New York: The Macmillan
Company, 1970.
A comprehensive statement of classic categories—church, sect, and
so on—in the sociology of religion.

CHAPTER SIX

BRANDON, S. G. F., *The Judgment of the Dead: The Idea of Life After Death in
the Major Religions*. New York: Charles Scribner's Sons, 1967.
A good example of the study of a major conceptual matter in cross-
religious context.

CARNELL, EDWARD JOHN, *The Case for Orthodox Theology*. Philadelphia, Pa.:
The Westminster Press, 1959.
An example of conservative evangelical religious thought; this author means by *orthodox theology* that which limits the grounds of
religious authority to the Bible.

DEWART, LESLIE, *The Foundations of Belief.* New York: Herder and Herder, Inc., 1969.
A philosophy of religion by a modern Roman Catholic. The basic idea is that essence is the relation of being to consciousness; God as pure essence or reality as such is the reality in relation to which any other reality is real.

HARSHORNE, CHARLES, *Anselm's Discovery: A Re-Examination of the Ontological Proof for God's Existence.* LaSalle, Ill.: Open Court Publishing Co., 1965.
A modern discussion by a distinguished philosopher of both the ontological argument and its alleged refutations.

HICK, JOHN, *Death and Eternal Life.* New York: Harper & Row, Publishers, Inc., 1977.
A well-received, groundbreaking Christian discussion of life after death that draws on data from world religions and psychical research.

————, *Philosophy of Religion.* Englewood Cliffs, N.J.: Prentice-Hall, Inc., 1963.
A highly competent introduction to the field.

HUXLEY, ALDOUS, *The Perennial Philosophy.* New York: Harpers, 1944.
A powerful statement of the view that God as impersonal consciousness realized in mystical experience is the foundation of all existence.

RICOEUR, PAUL, *The Symbolism of Evil.* Boston, Mass.: Beacon Press, 1969.
A difficult but rewarding study of the meaning of evil in various cultures and religions as understood through its symbols.

ROSS, FLOYD, AND TYNETTE HILLS, *Questions that Matter Most Answered by the World's Religions.* Boston, Mass.: Beacon Press, 1954.
A simple and direct statement of what the great religions teach about the meaning and goal of human life; good as an introduction to a study of comparative religious concepts.

MACKINTOSH, HUGH ROSS, *Types of Modern Theology: Schleiermacher To Barth.* London: Nisbet and Co., 1947.
An excellent introduction to the most-talked-about modern Protestant theologians.

## CHAPTER SEVEN

CLARKE, ARTHUR C., *Profiles of the Future: An Inquiry into the Limits of the Possible.* New York: Harper & Row, Publishers, Inc., 1973.
A well-known science fiction writer's view of the future and the changes in human experience that may be wrought by space exploration and new technologies.

DALY, MARY, *Beyond God the Father*. Boston, Mass.: Beacon Press, 1973.
A trenchant discussion of the need for changes in religious conceptualization to correspond to current images of male and female.

FLETCHER, JOSEPH, *Morals and Medicine*. Boston, Mass.: Beacon Press, 1960.
A representative and important book discussing current issues in medical ethics.

GREELEY, ANDREW, *Religion in the Year 2000*. Mission, Kans.: Sheed, Andrews, and McMeel, 1969.
A fascinating look at possible religious futures, emphasizing the persistence of some aspects of traditional religion.

HUBBARD, EARL, *The Search is On: A View of Man's Future from the New Perspective of Space*. Los Angeles, Calif.: Pace Publications, 1969.
A statement of the view that humans must now find a future beyond earth, or they will stagnate.

JEWETT, PAUL K., *Man as Male and Female*. Grand Rapids, Mich.: Wm. B. Eerdmans Publishing Co., 1975.
A Christian discussion of sexual equality before God from an evangelical perspective.

MITCHELL, EDGAR, ED., *Psychic Exploration*. New York: G. P. Putnam's Sons, 1974.
A large anthology that is a good introduction to the entire field of psychic research.

MOODY, RAYMOND A., *Life After Death*. Atlanta, Ga.: Mockingbird Books, 1975.
An intriguing and much-discussed collection of after-death experiences of people who were resuscitated after being clinically dead; significant as possible empirical evidence relevant to the after-death state.

TOFFLER, ALVIN, *Future Shock*. New York: Random House, Inc., 1970.
Important for any understanding of the present and future; emphasizes the significance of rapid change for modern life; some discussion of the implications of change for the religious world.

WERTZ, RICHARD W., ED., *Readings on Ethical and Social Issues in Biomedicine*. Englewood Cliffs, N.J.: Prentice-Hall, Inc., 1975.
A comprehensive and useful introduction.

# INDEX

193

Identity, religious, 12–13
Igorot people (Philippines),
    *18*
India, religion in, 42,
    127. *See also*
    Buddhism;
    Confucianism
    and caste system, 175
    cosmogonic myth in, 103
    creation in, 158
    great and little traditions
        in, 124–25
    hero/savior myth in, 103
    origins of, 44–45
Indians, American,
    64–65, 99
Individuation (Jung), 79
Infancy, religious
    development in, 83
Initiation, 37–38
    stages of, 73–74, 104
International and
    intercultural religion,
    128–29
Ise Shrine and Harvest
    Festival (Japan), 2,
    4, 7, 11, 15, 89, 95, 126
Isis, 43
Islam, 49, *114*, 128
    chanting and rhythmic
        recitation in worship,
        101
    creation in, 158
    nonconceptual verbal
        symbols in, 102
    origins of, 46
    Sufi mysticism, 21
    symbols in, 100

James, William, 52, 58–59
Japan, religion in. *See also*
    Buddhism; Ise Shrine
    and Harvest Festival;
    Shinto; Tenrikyo
    emergent religion, 133
    great and little traditions
        in, 125–26
    Kamakura Buddhism, 48
    origins of, 45
    symbols in, 100
Jaspers, Karl, 47
Jehovah's Witnesses, 135
Jesus Christ, 46, 107, 138
    cross as symbol, 8, 99
    as hero/savior, 103, 160
    as symbol, 89
Judaism
    under communist rule, 96
    cosmogonic myth in, 103
    creation in, 158
    male-female roles in, 178
    origins of, 45–46
    symbols in, *97*, 98
Jung, Carl, 52
    psychological
        interpretation of
        religion, 79
    on religious myth and
        doctrine, 148

and religious symbols, 99

Kaaba Shrine, 113
Kamakura Buddhism (Japan),
    48
Kannon, 100
Kant, Immanuel, 51, 156
Kierkegaard, Soren, 52, 167
King, Martin Luther, Jr., 103
Kingship, sacred, 42–43
Koran, 46
Krippner, Stanley, 55, 56
Krishna, 98
Krishna Consciousness
    Movement, 48
Kroeber, A. L., 177

Language
    sacred, as nonconceptual
        verbal symbol, 102
    as sign and symbol, 90,
        105
    structural role of, 138
Lao-tzu, 45, 160
Last Supper, symbolic value
    of, 107
Latin, 102
LeGuin, Ursula, 177
Lévi-Strauss, Claude, 110
    on myth, 104–5, 110, 148
Life after death, 76, 179
Literate elite, as "great
    tradition," 121
Literature, religious
    normative, 142–43
Lorenz, Konrad, 29, 115
Luckmann, Thomas, 6
Luther, Martin, 49, 52, 136
Lutheranism, 129, 136

Maat (Egyptian concept), 42
Manu, Laws of, 121
Mardi Gras, sacred content
    of, 15
Marx, Karl, 50–51
Maslow, Abraham, 72–73, 80
Mecca, 100, 107, 113
Medical revolution, religious
    implications of,
    173–77
Medina, 100
Meditation, 75
Mediumship, 180
Meher Baba, 69
Menorah, symbolic value of,
    97, 98
Methodism, 122, 124, 136,
    180
Miller, Donald E., 144–45
Miki Nakayama, 132, 133
Modern interpretations of
    religion, 49–53
Monks, structural role of,
    137–38
Monotheism, origins of,
    45–46
Moody, Dwight L., 75
Moon, symbolic value of, 100
Mount Arafat, 113

Muhammad, 46, 100, 139,
    160
Music, 101–2
Mysticism, 21
Mystics, structural role of,
    140
Myth
    meaning of, 148
    as symbol, 103–5
    cosmogonic myth, 103
    hero/savior myth, 103–4
    structure of myth, 104–5

Nagarjuna, 163
Nara (Japan), 125
Naranjo, Claudio, 75, 80
National religion, 129
Navaho Indians, 99
Neoplatonism, 48
Newman, John Henry, 65,
    66–67
Nichiren Buddhism, 102
Niebuhr, H. Richard, 153
Nirvana, 76, 153
Nonconceptual verbal
    symbols, 102
Nonverbal symbols, 101–2
Normative role of religion,
    142–43
Nuns, structural role of,
    137–38

Offerings, 111
Old age, religious
    development in, 84–85
Ontological proof of God,
    155–57
Organ transplants, 175
Ornstein, Robert, 75
Otto, Rudolf, 6–7, 52

Paley, William, 165
Participation in worship,
    112–13
Patterns, religious, symbols
    and, 93–96
Paul, 177
    conversion of, 65
Pentecostalists, 62
Philosophers, structural role
    of, 138
Piaget, Jean, 80-82
Pivotal person, 46–47
Play, animal and human,
    related, 31–32
Polytheism, 43, 154
Popularizers, structural role
    of, 140–41
Prajapati, 158
Precognition, 180
Presbyterianism, 122, 124
Priests, structural role of, 137
Prophets, 119–20
Protestantism, 49, 83. *See
    also individual
    denominations by name*
Psychic research, religious
    implications of, 180–81